water moves

hans fahrmeyer

HAMBURG GROUP

First published in the United States of America in 2016
by HAMBURG GROUP, INC New York, NY

Design by Werner Redman

Forward by Richard D.Piper

If photos are messages, then Hans Fahrmeyer is one of the most prolific messengers of today and of classic times. From his apprentice days of learning his photography craft in the lost art of darkroom developing, you know this man wrestle more out of an image than most emerging and long time photographers. It's his use of lens, light, experience and passion which massages his images to an unexpected portrayal.

But Mr. Fahrmeyer is also part sociologist , psychologist, comedian and life coach. Watching him in the studio or on location, he can either be the fly on the wall when he has to be, or the sorcerer, pulling out the best of the talent in front of his lens.

His latest book, Water Moves, is an illuminating dance of beautiful male images married with mirrors, water, sensuality and balance. There's a blend of powerful images with technical insight. The images become forceful yet arresting. He has produced a collection that mixes the casualness of the snapshot with the artistry of classical photographer. His subjects capture the eye for their immediacy, beauty, and movement.

His three previous books (Colors of Men, Between Men and Women, and Between Men) reflect his stylization. But the new images in Water Moves are even more lively and stronger then the earlier ones. The photos are a timeless provocation as Hans demonstrates the gravity of his models into an art form. Fahrmeyer's use of beautiful muscled men weaves with the reflective properties of water to create memorable masterpieces.

Water Moves makes one yearn for an encore. In cinema, we know by the last scene, there's a sequel planned. By the time you get to the last page, you're hoping for the release of more from Hans Fahrmeyer. Well done.

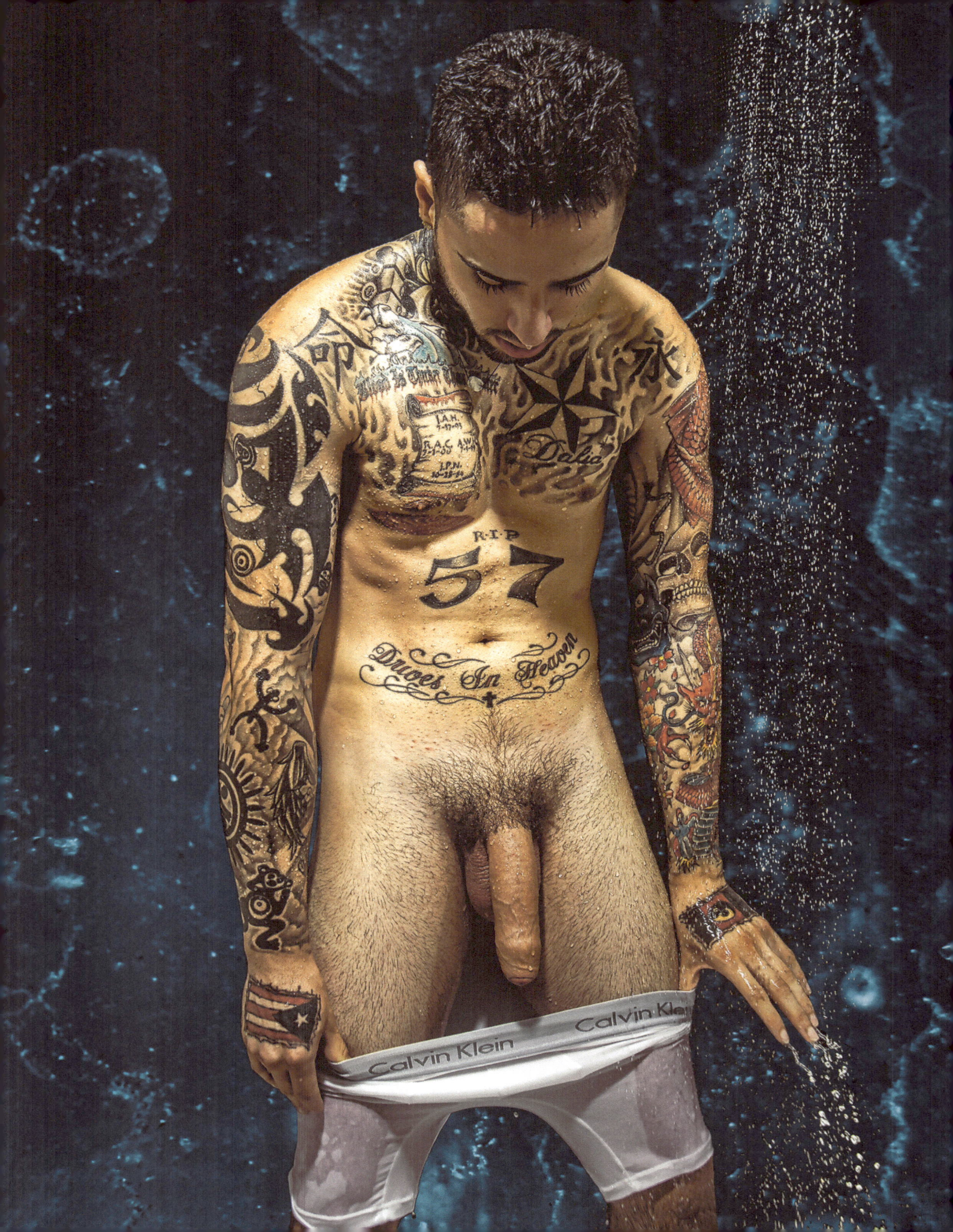

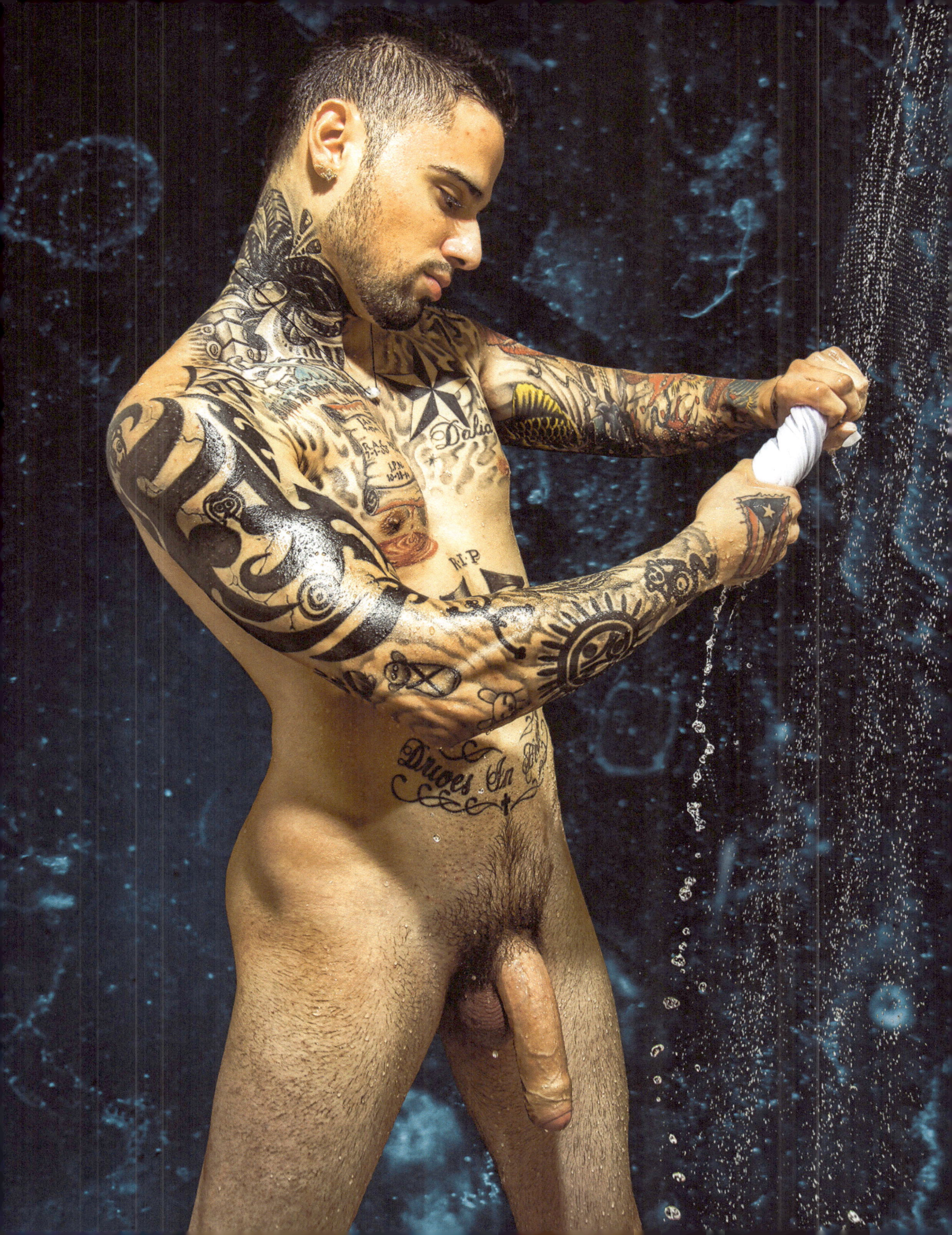

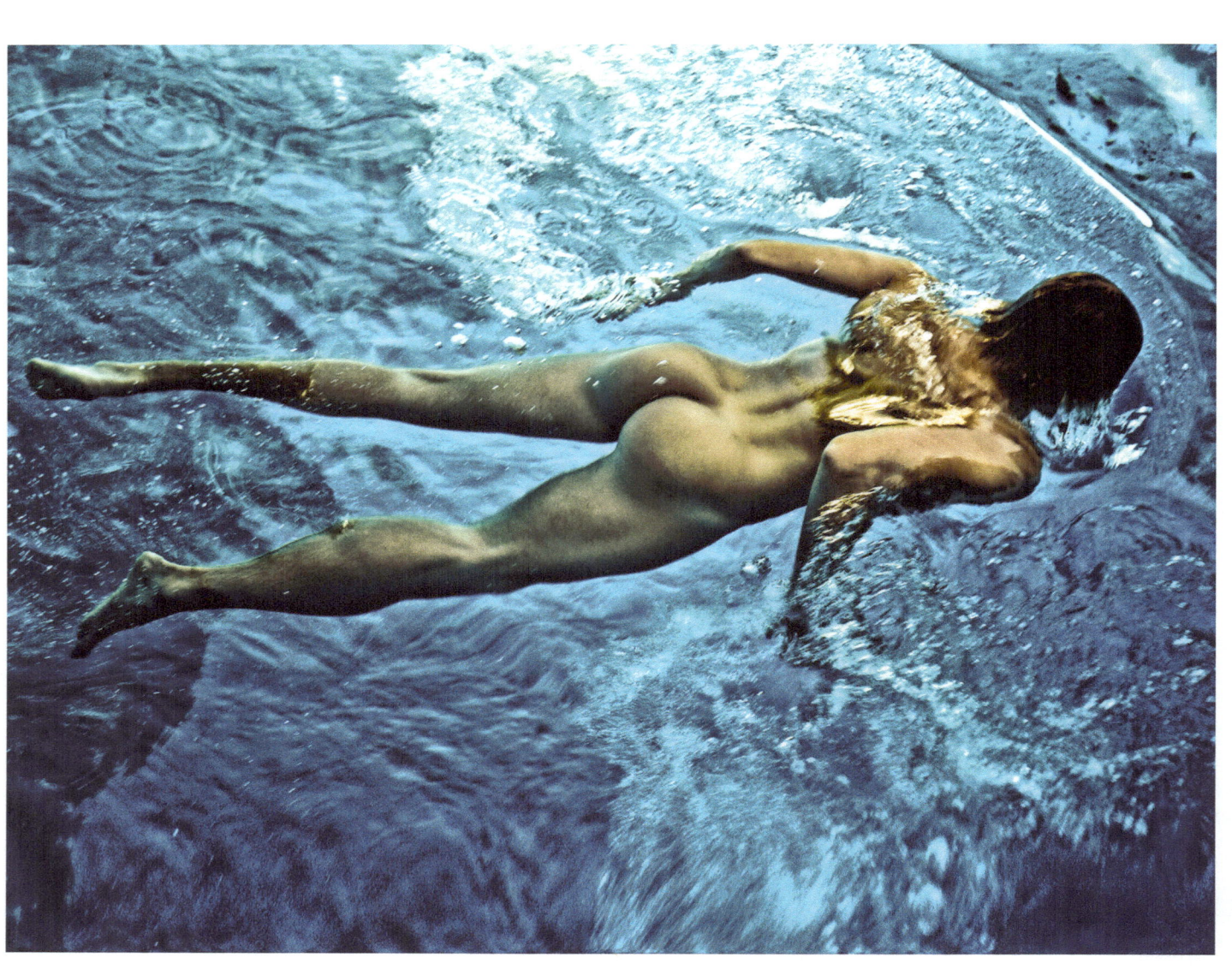

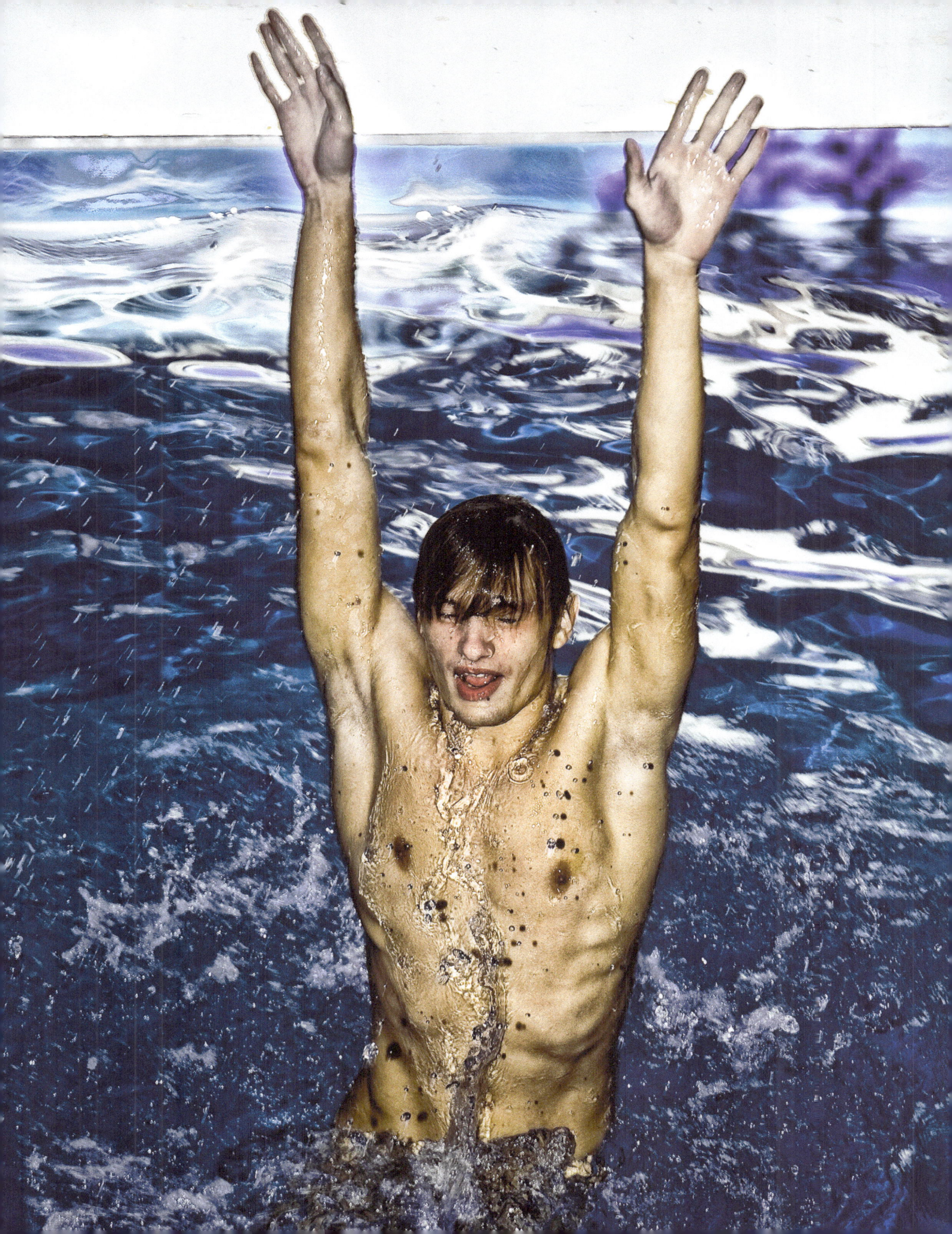

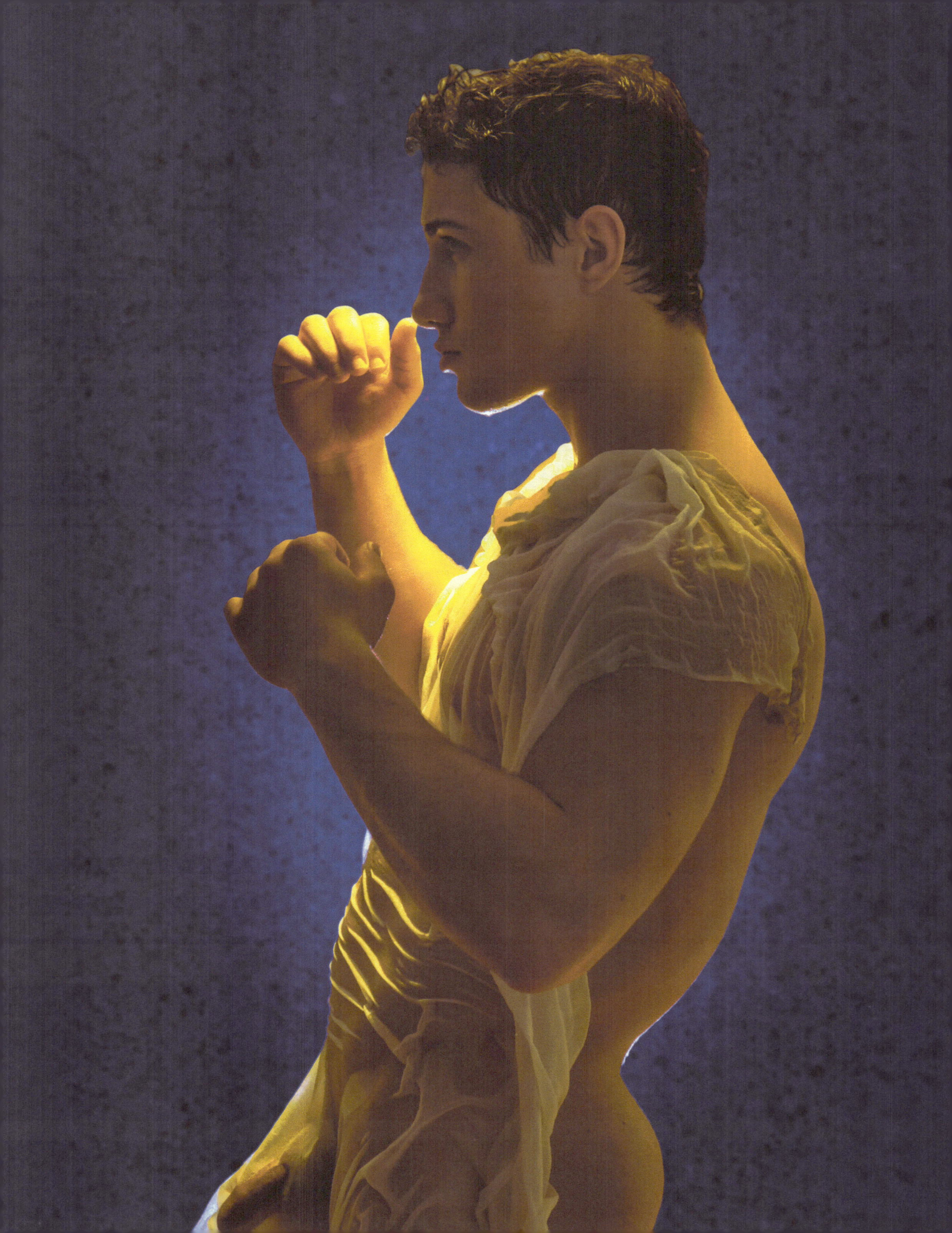

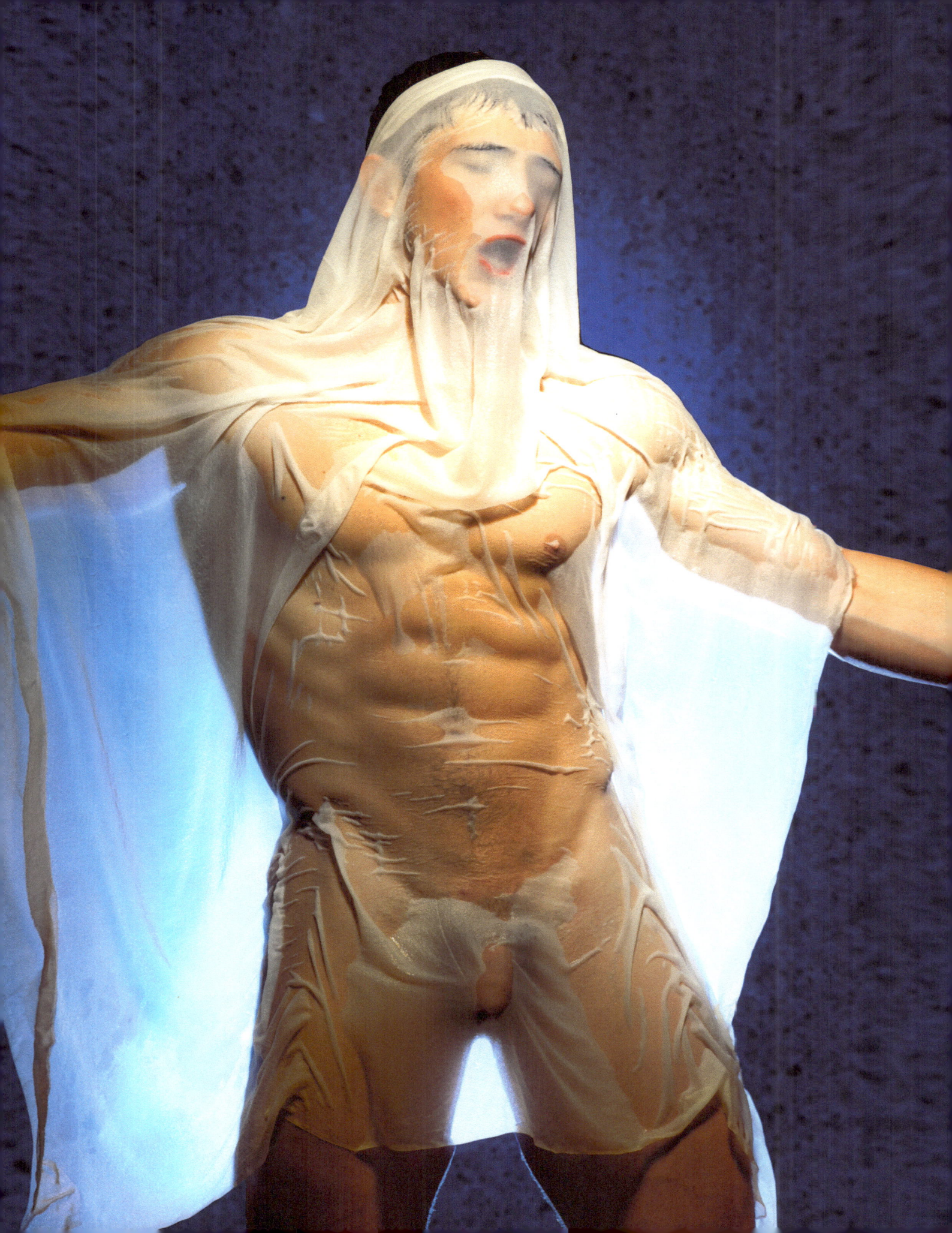

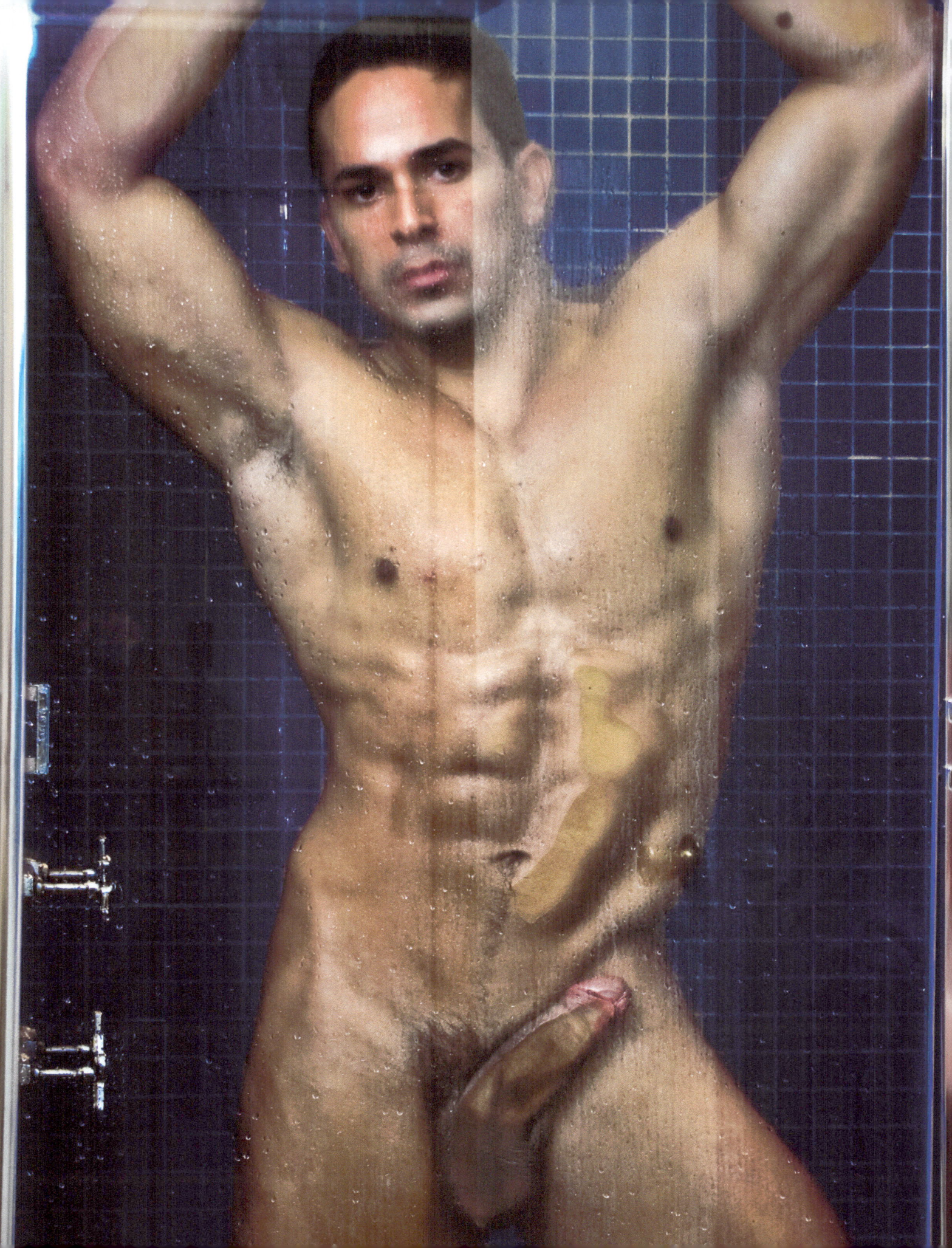

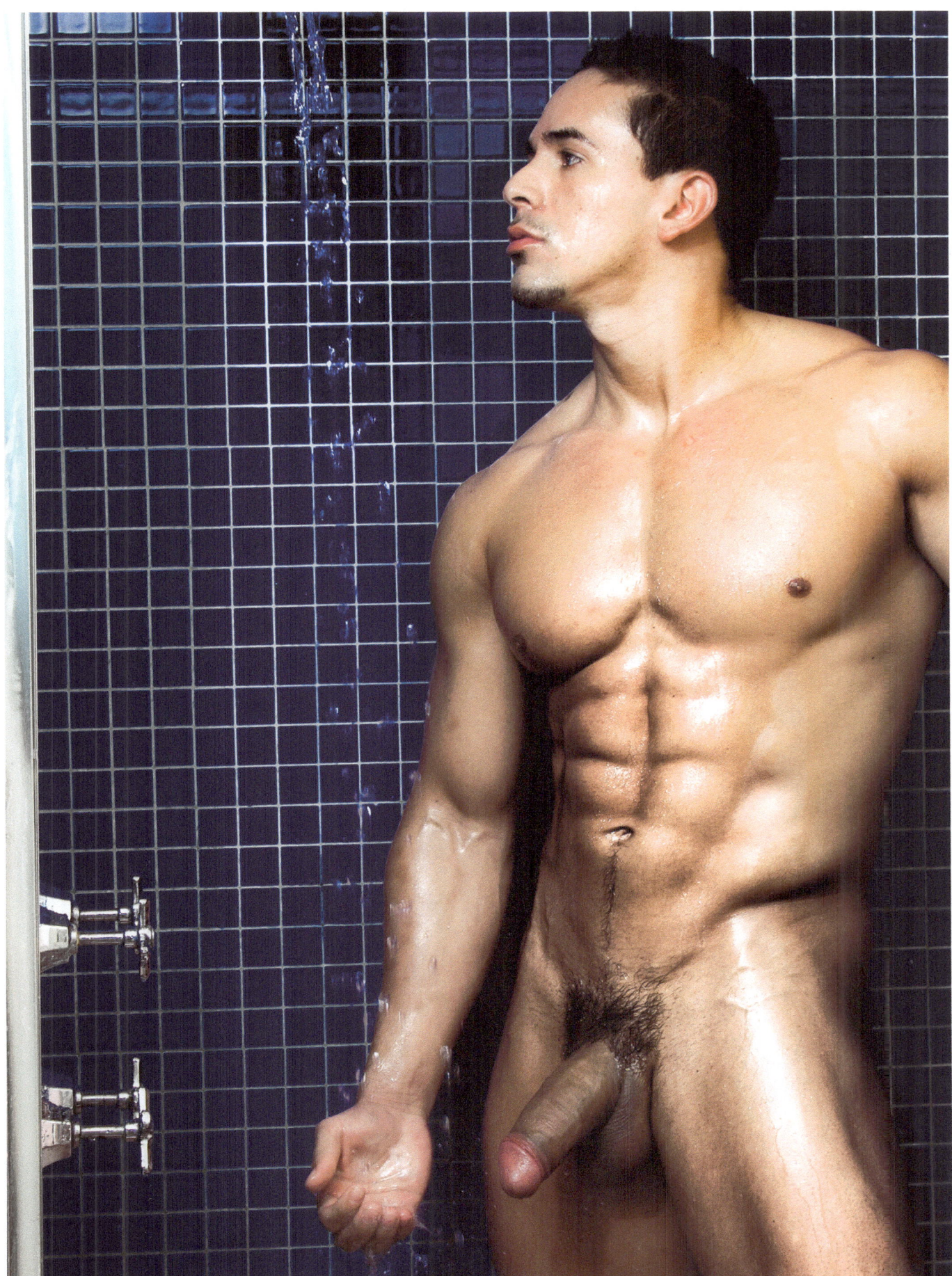

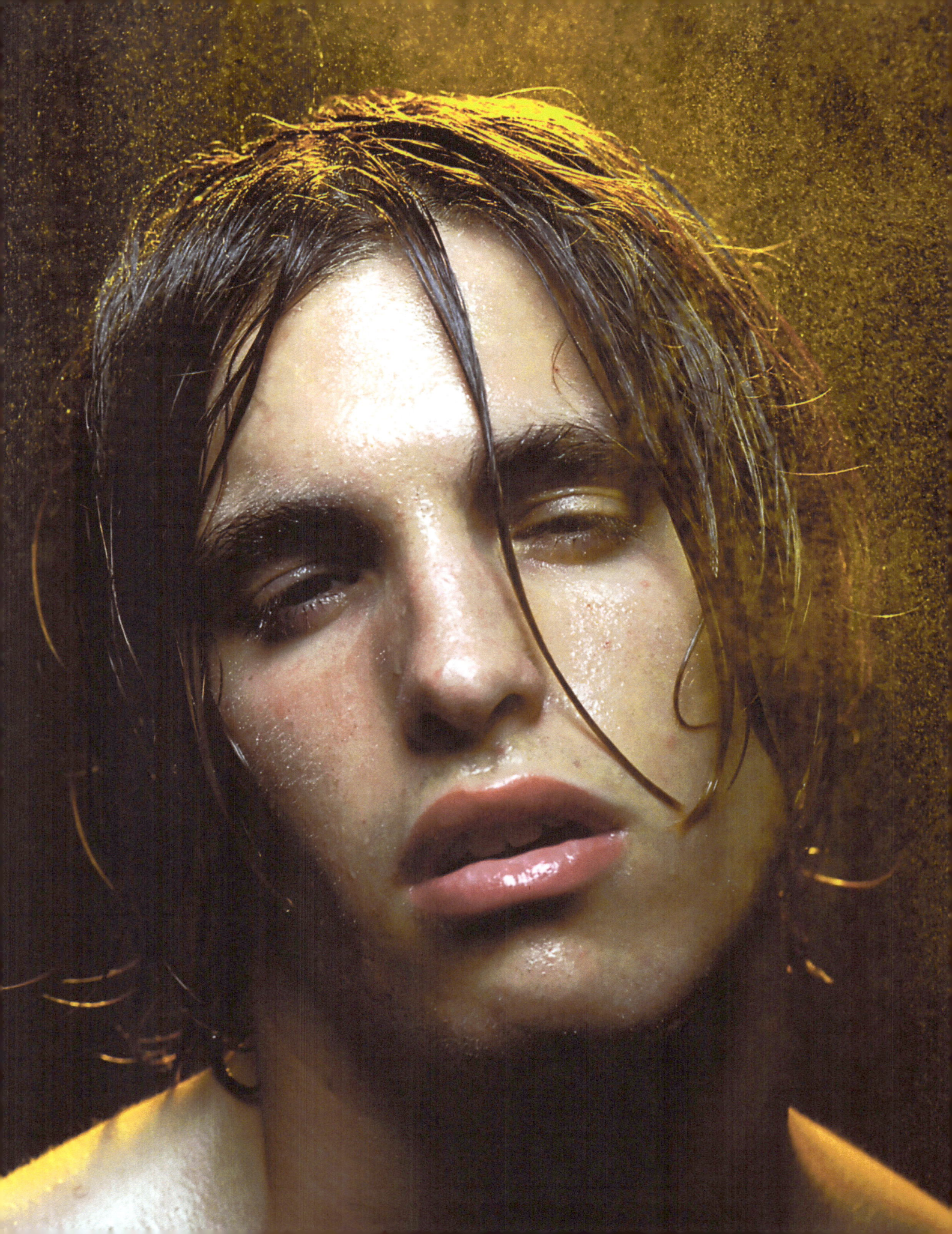

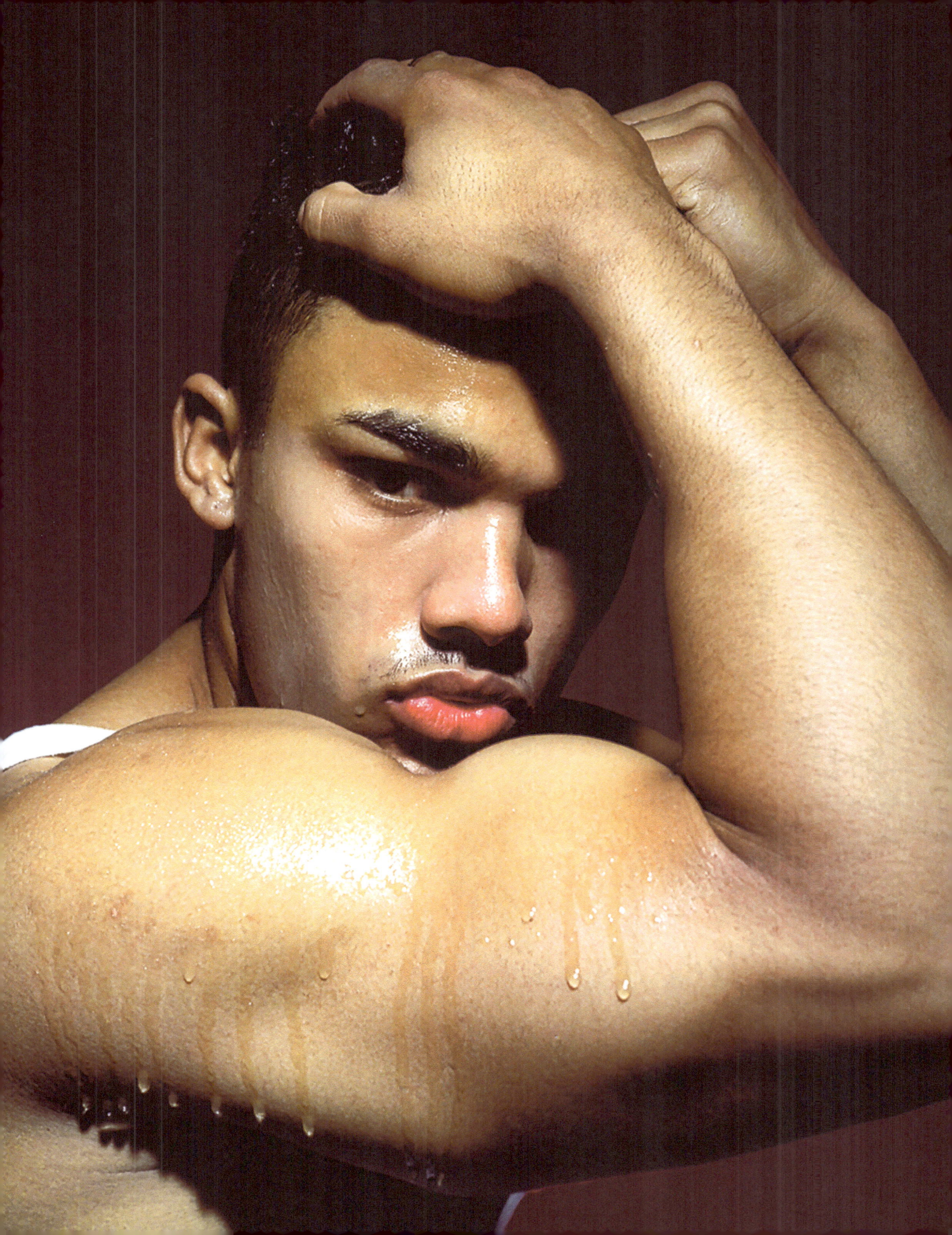

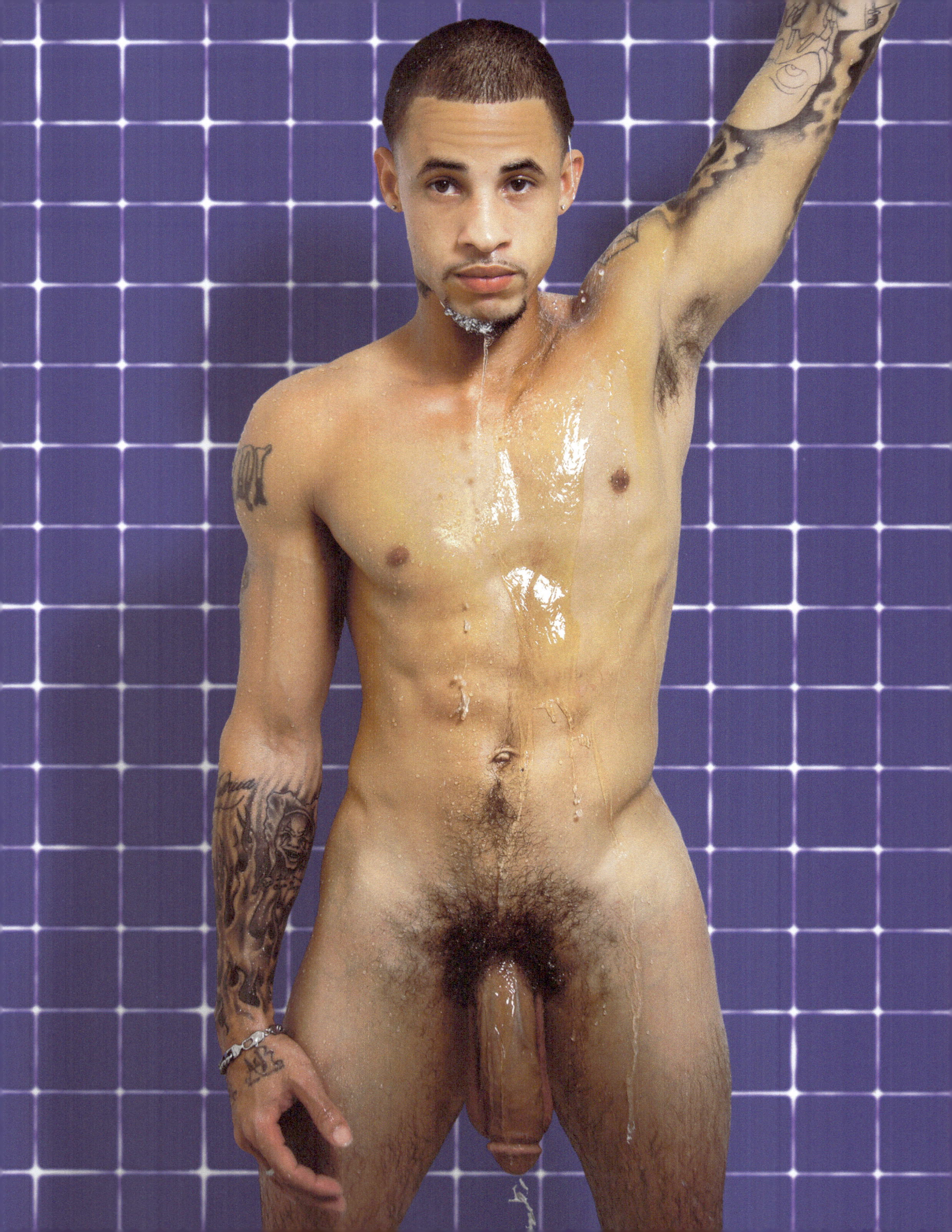

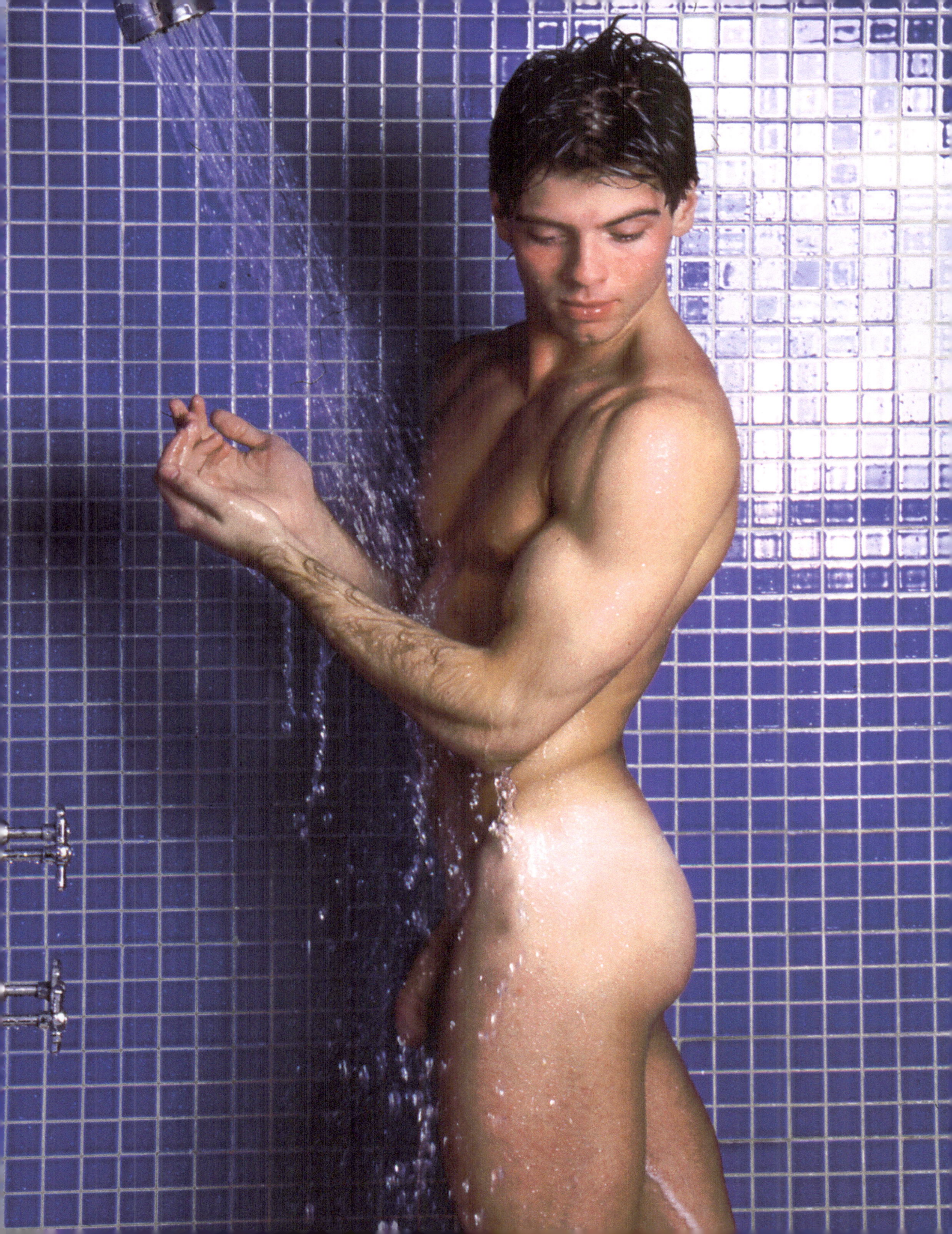

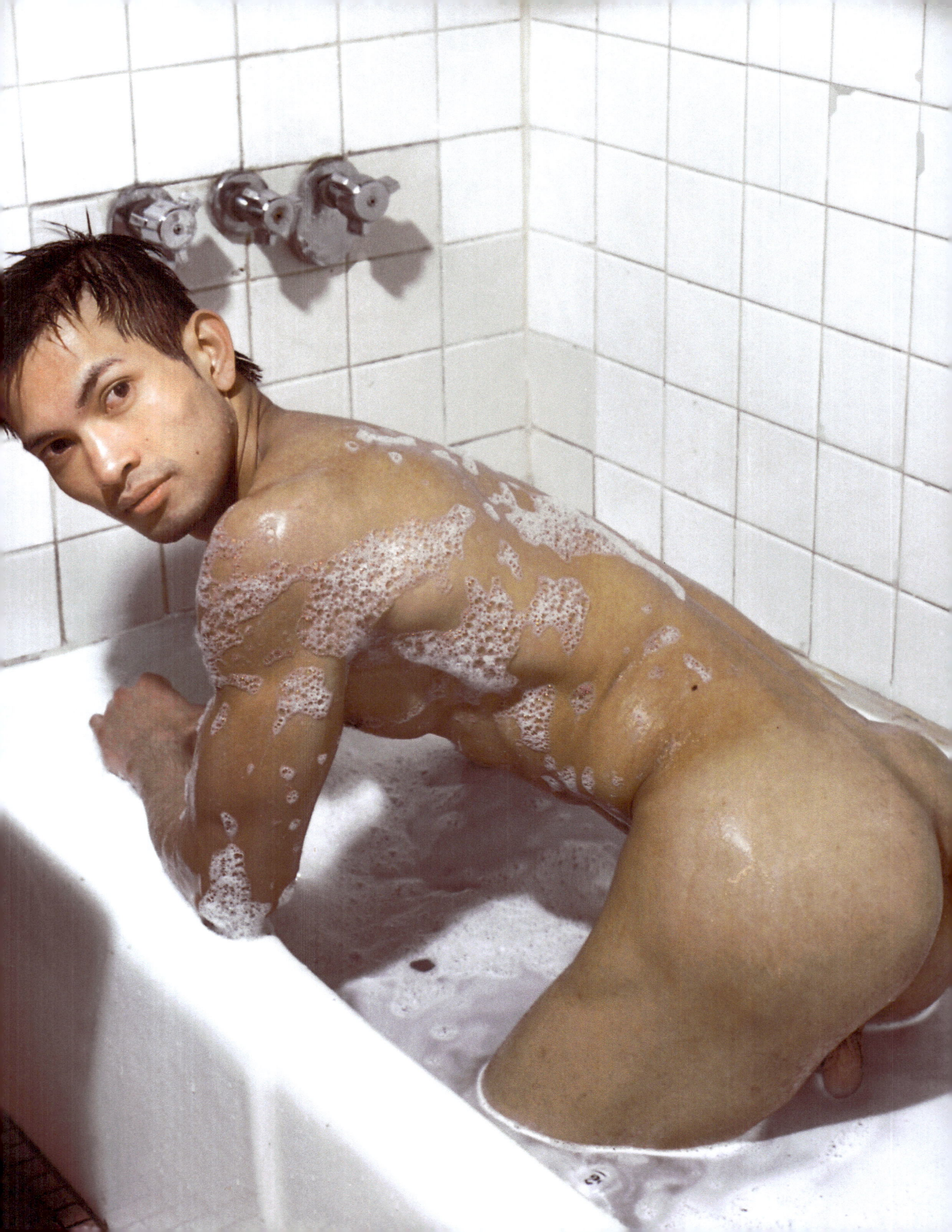

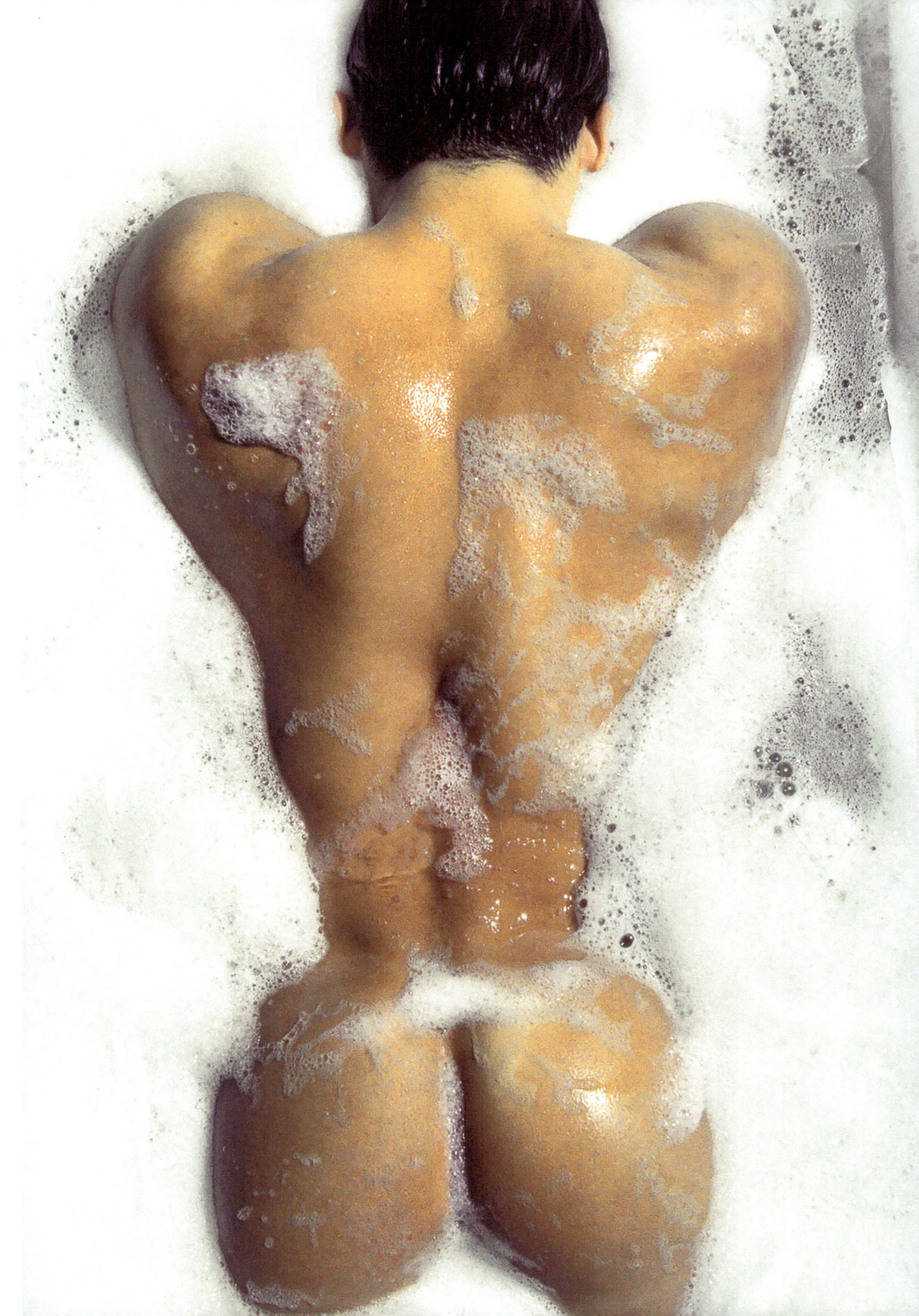

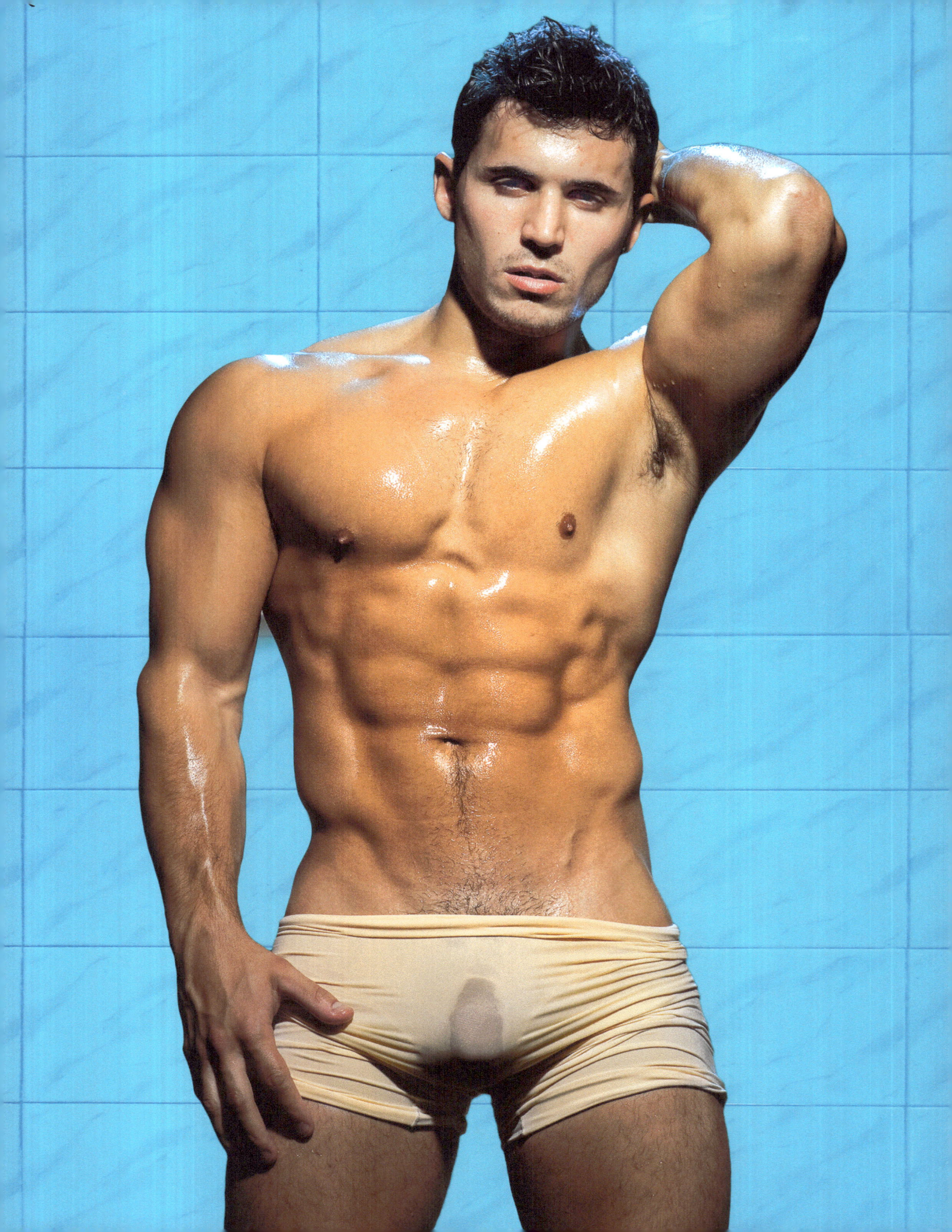

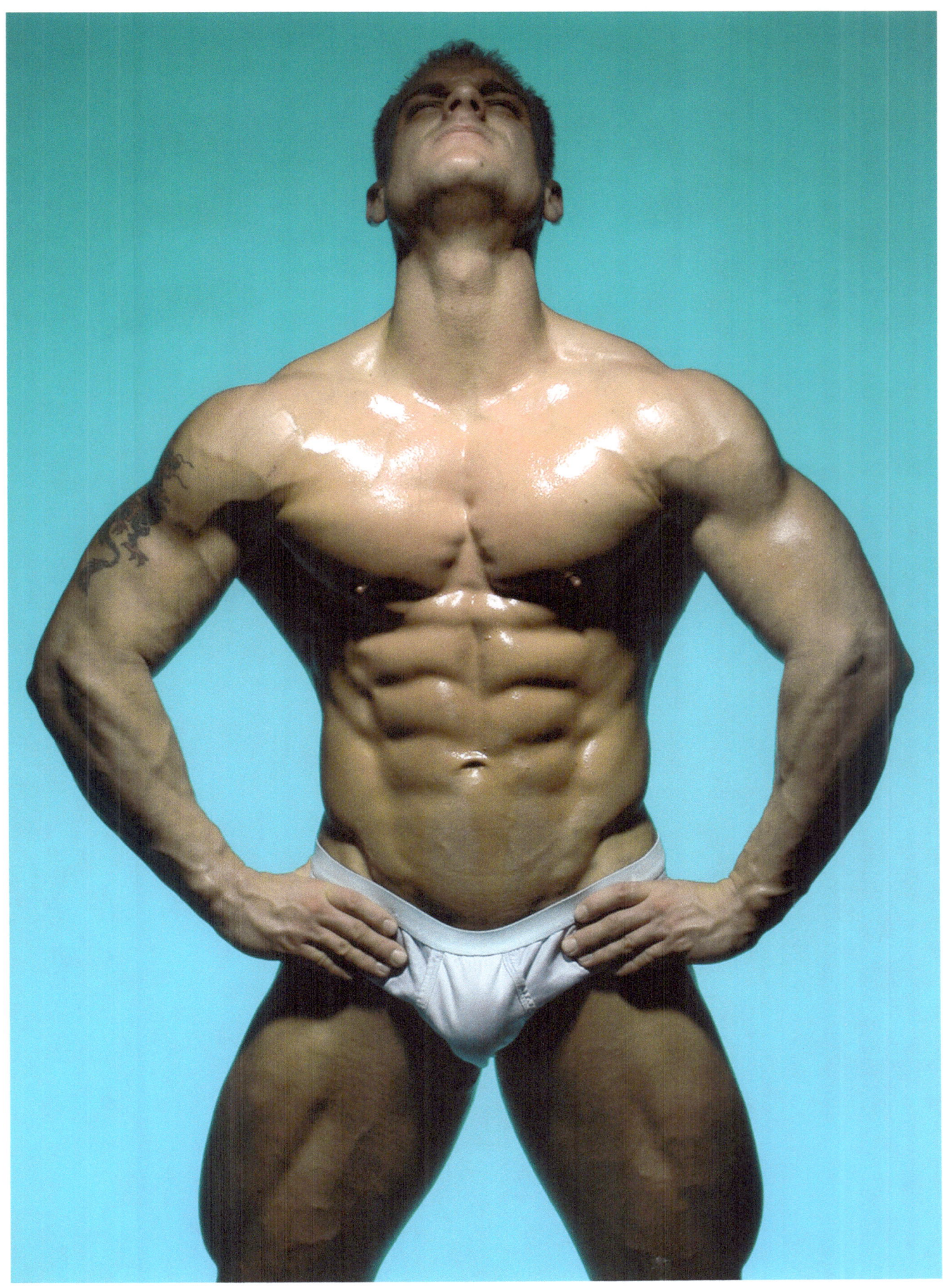

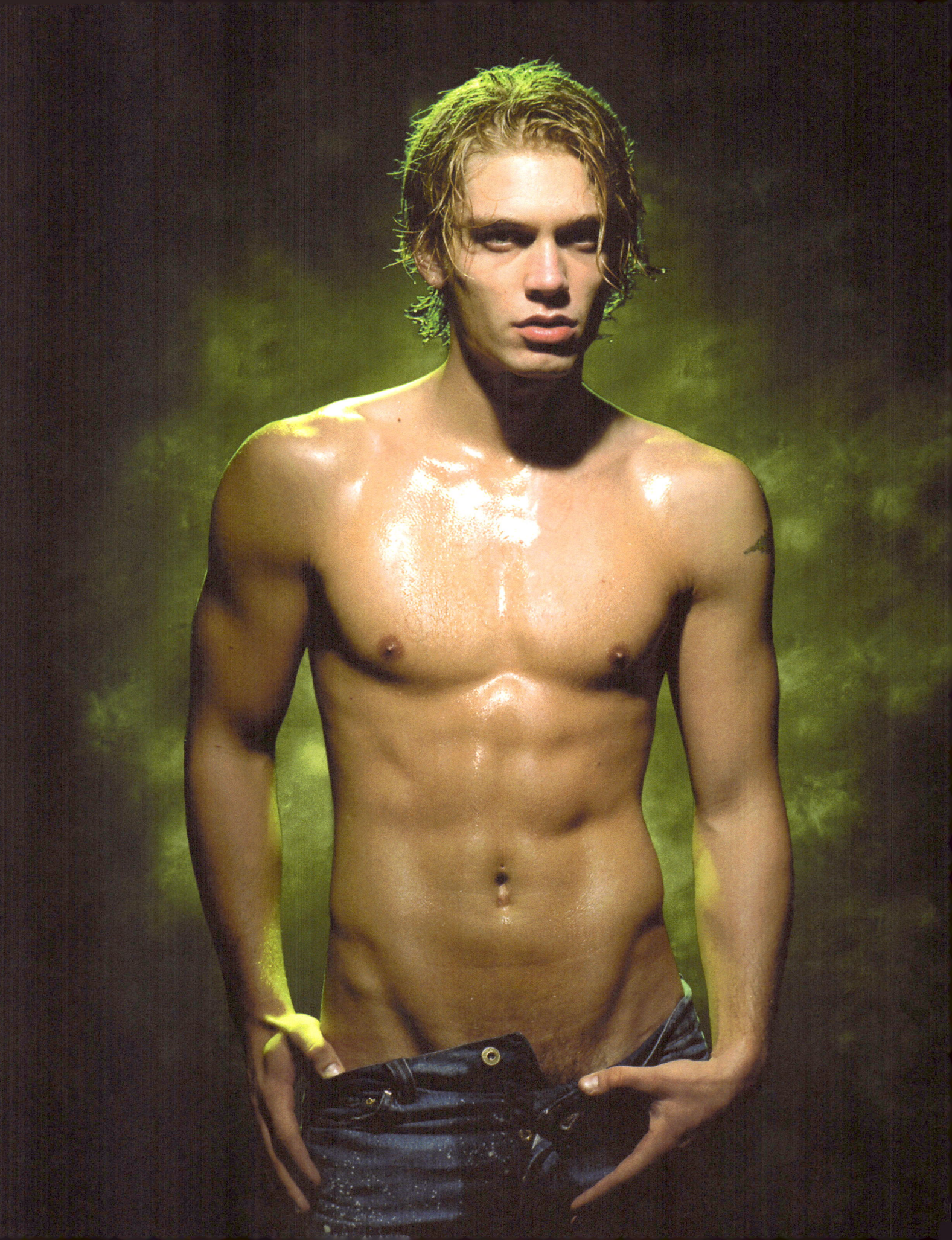

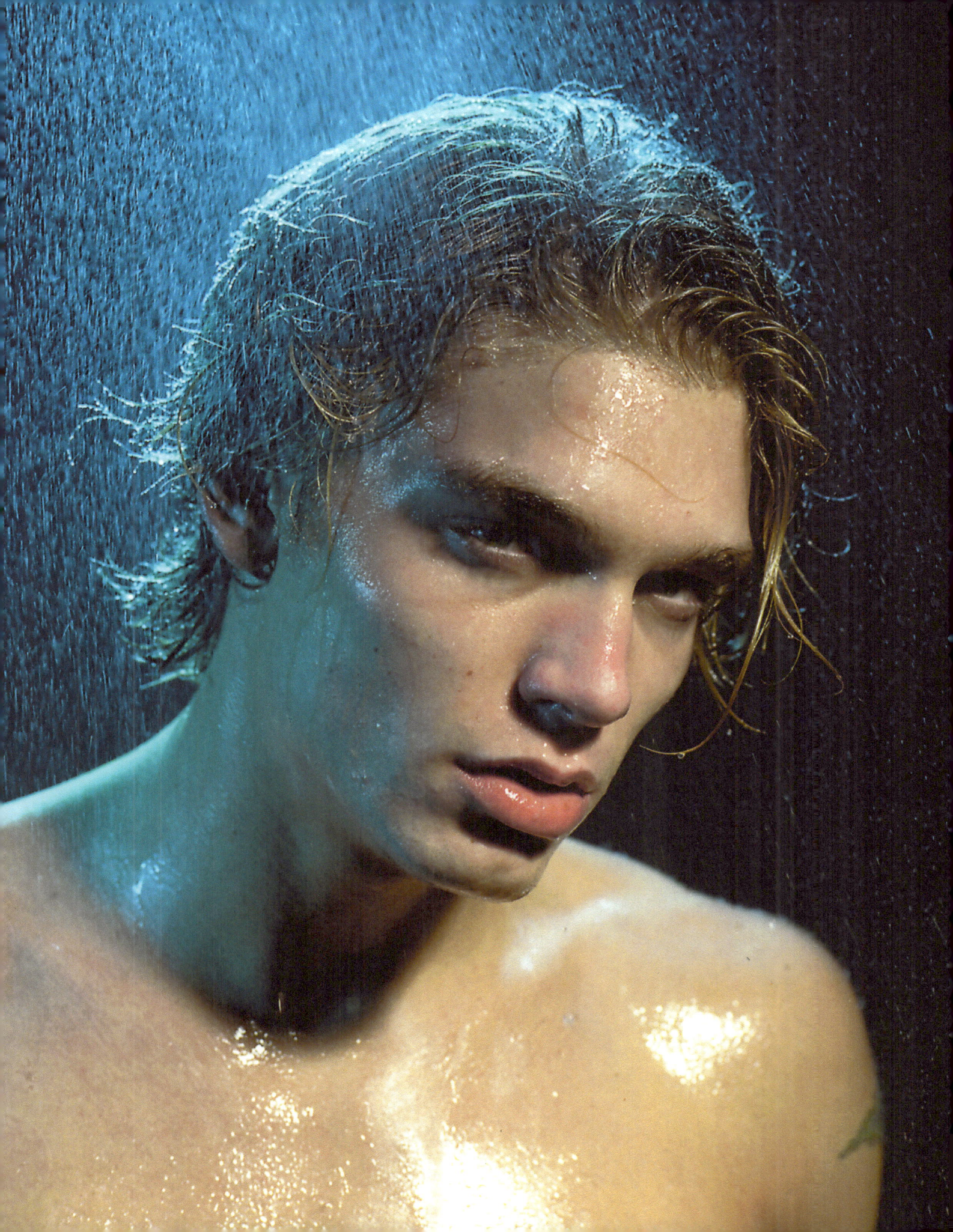

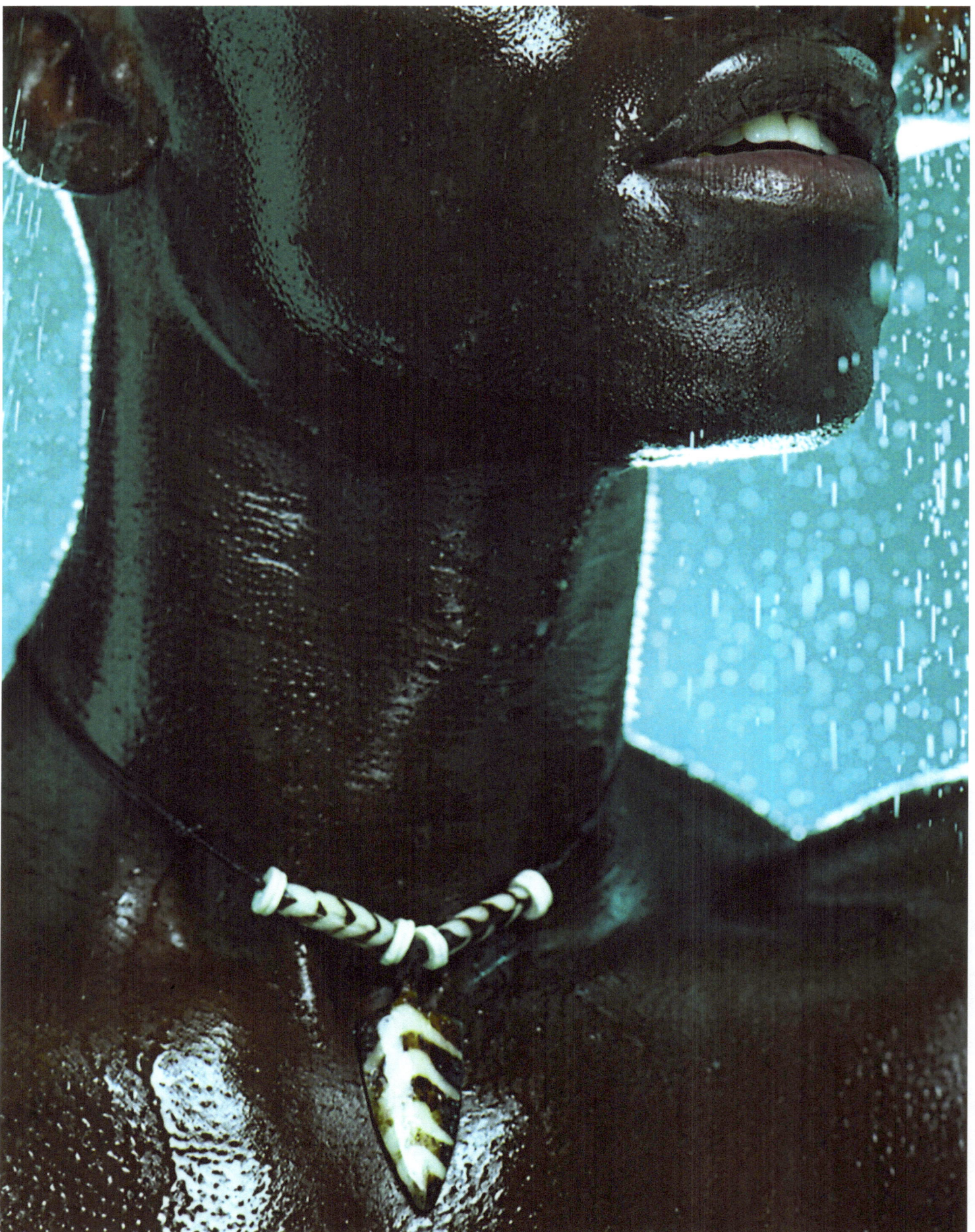

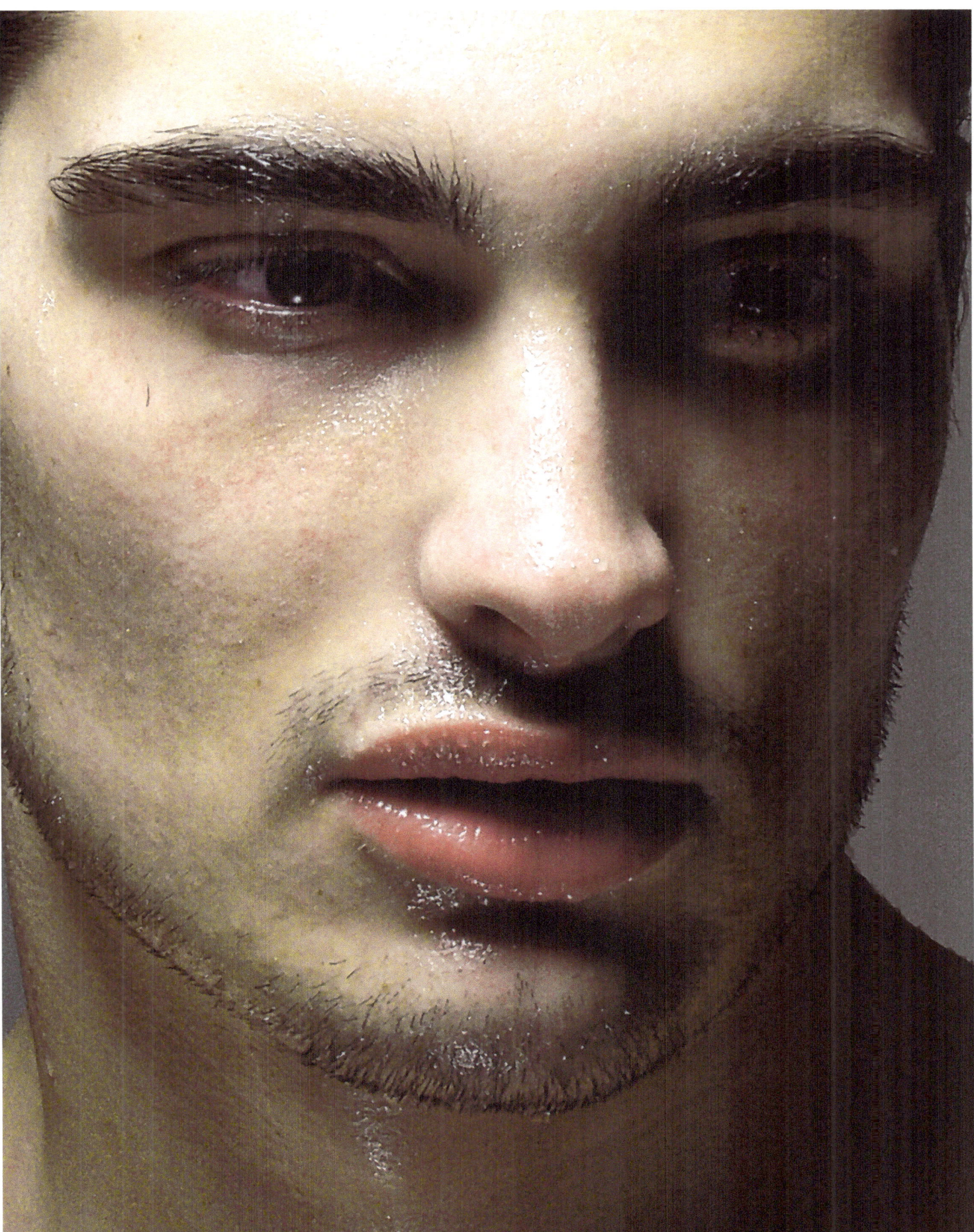

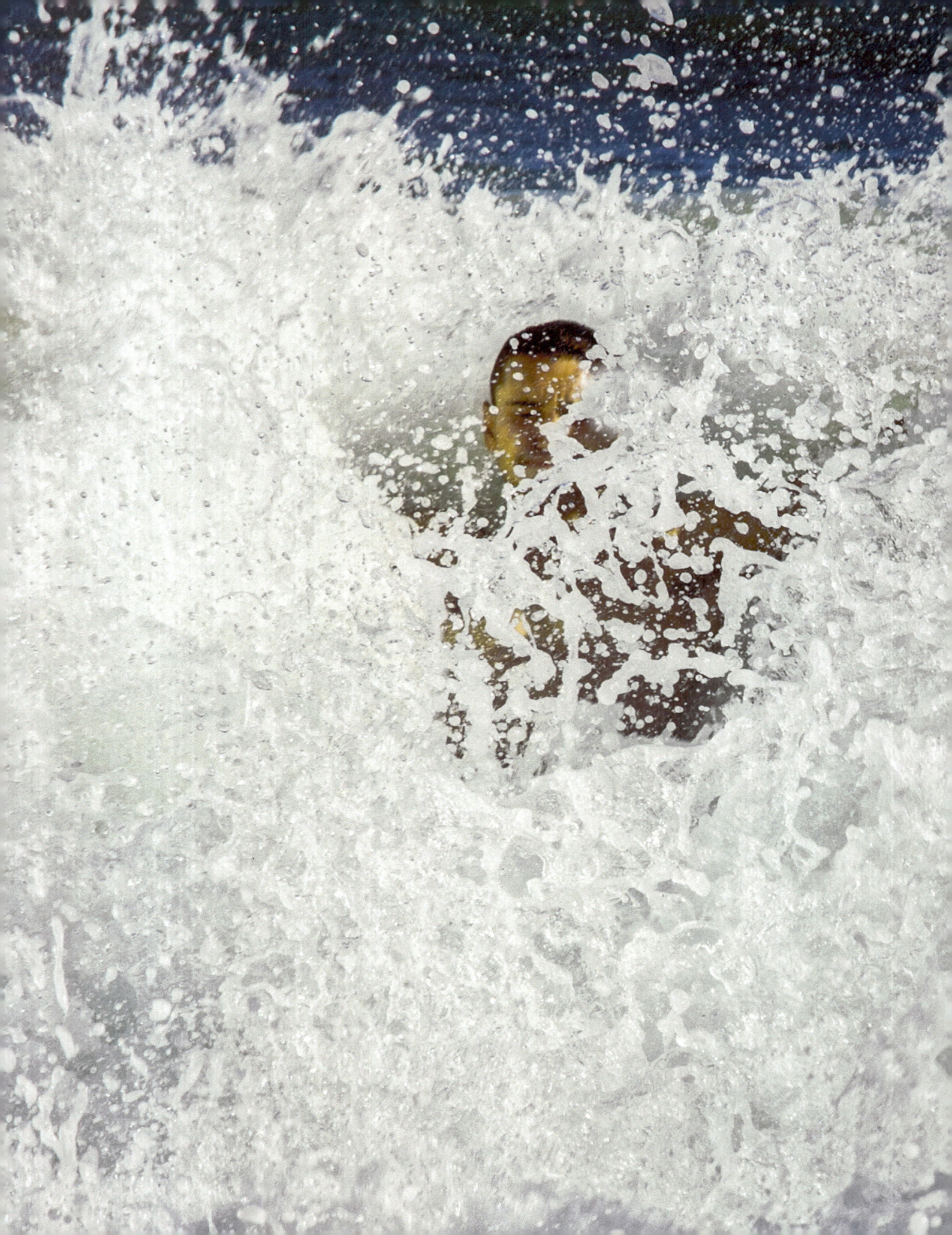

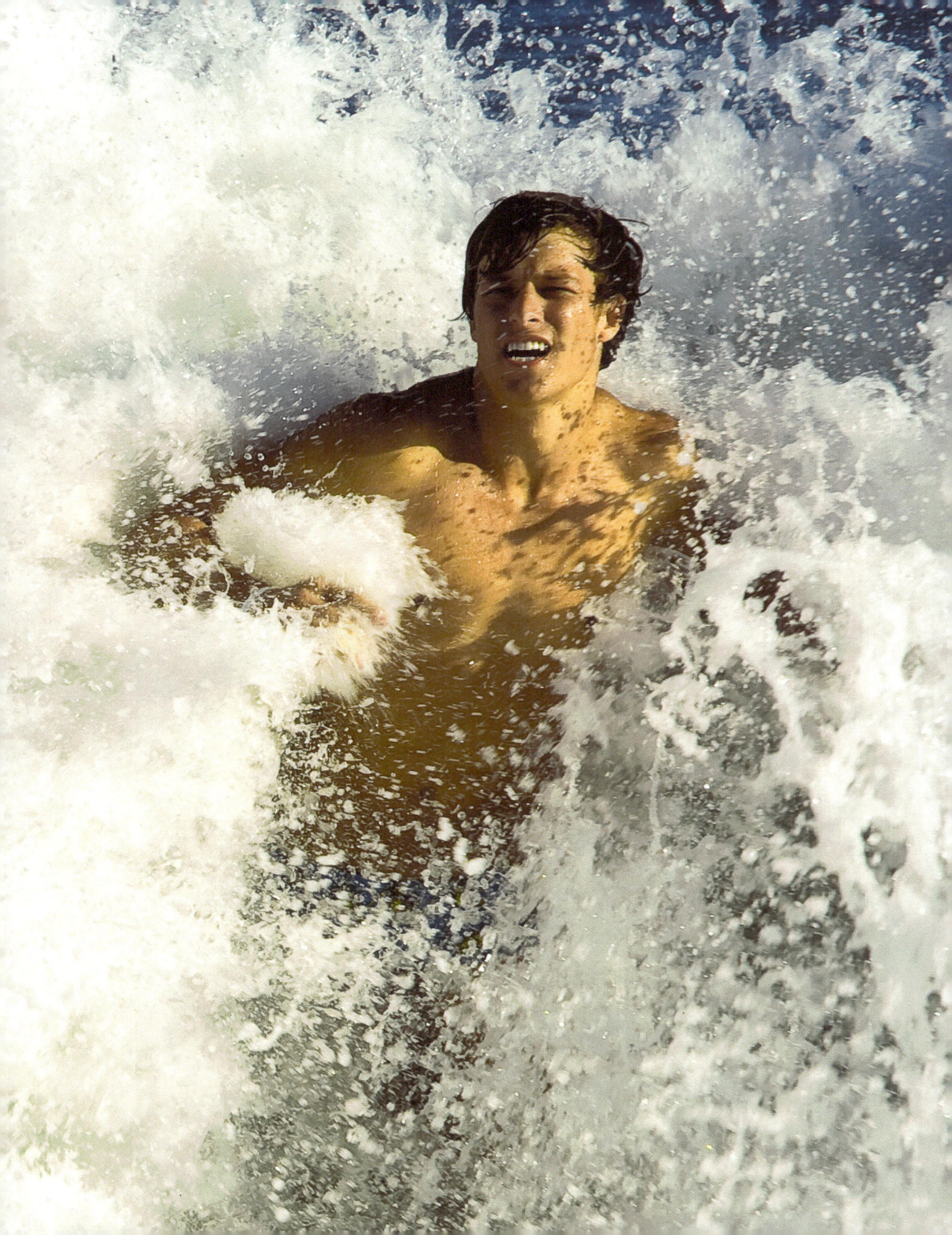

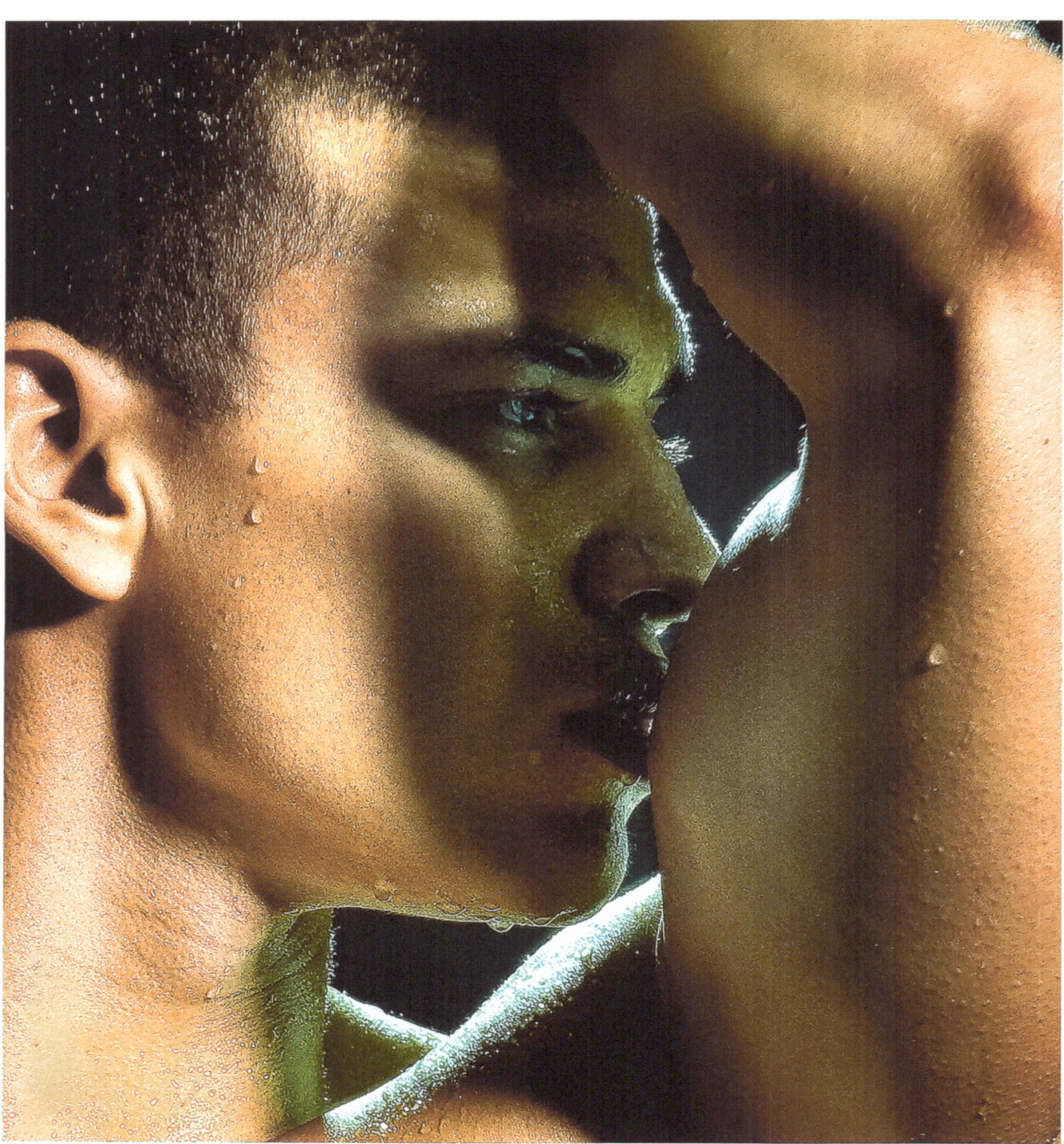

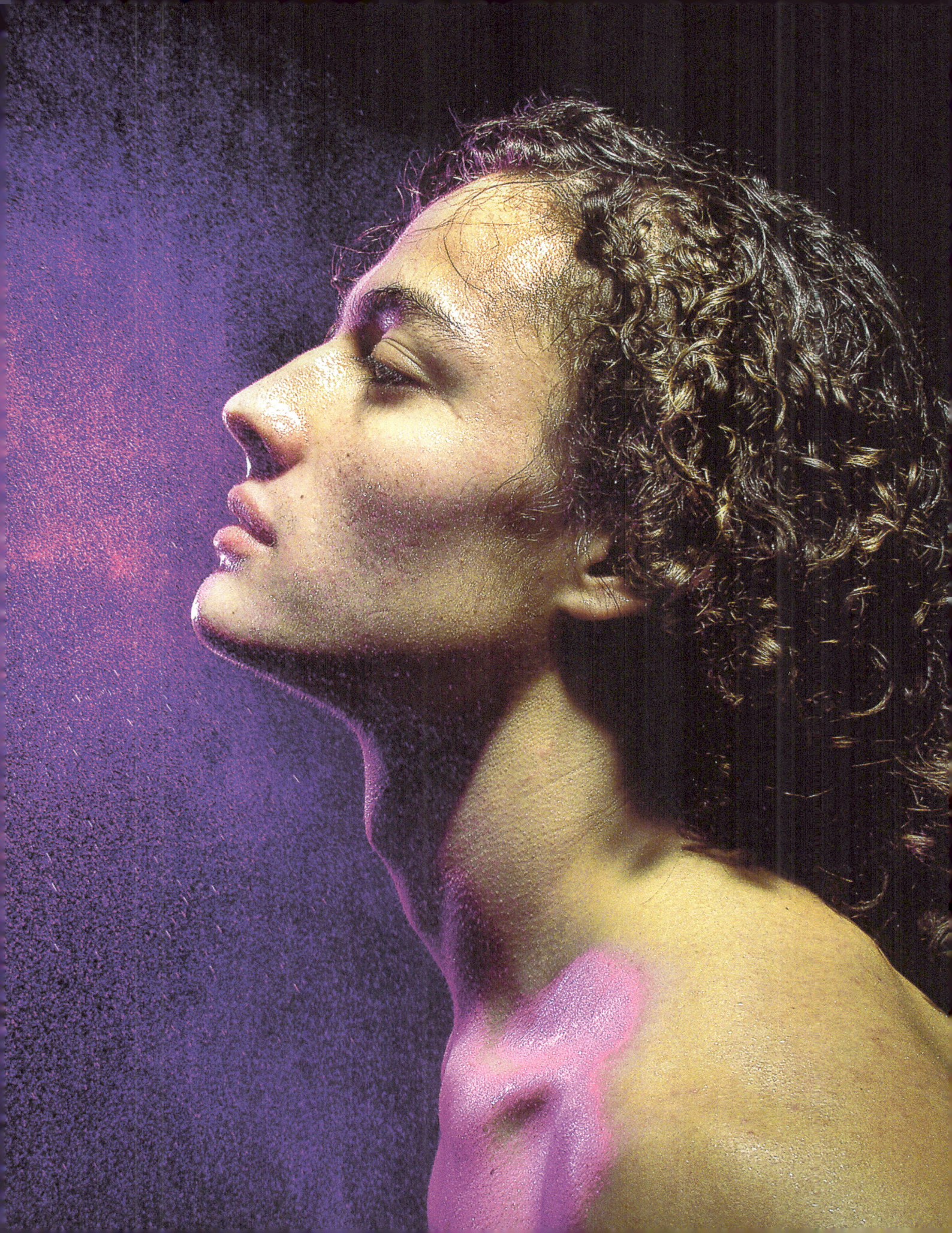

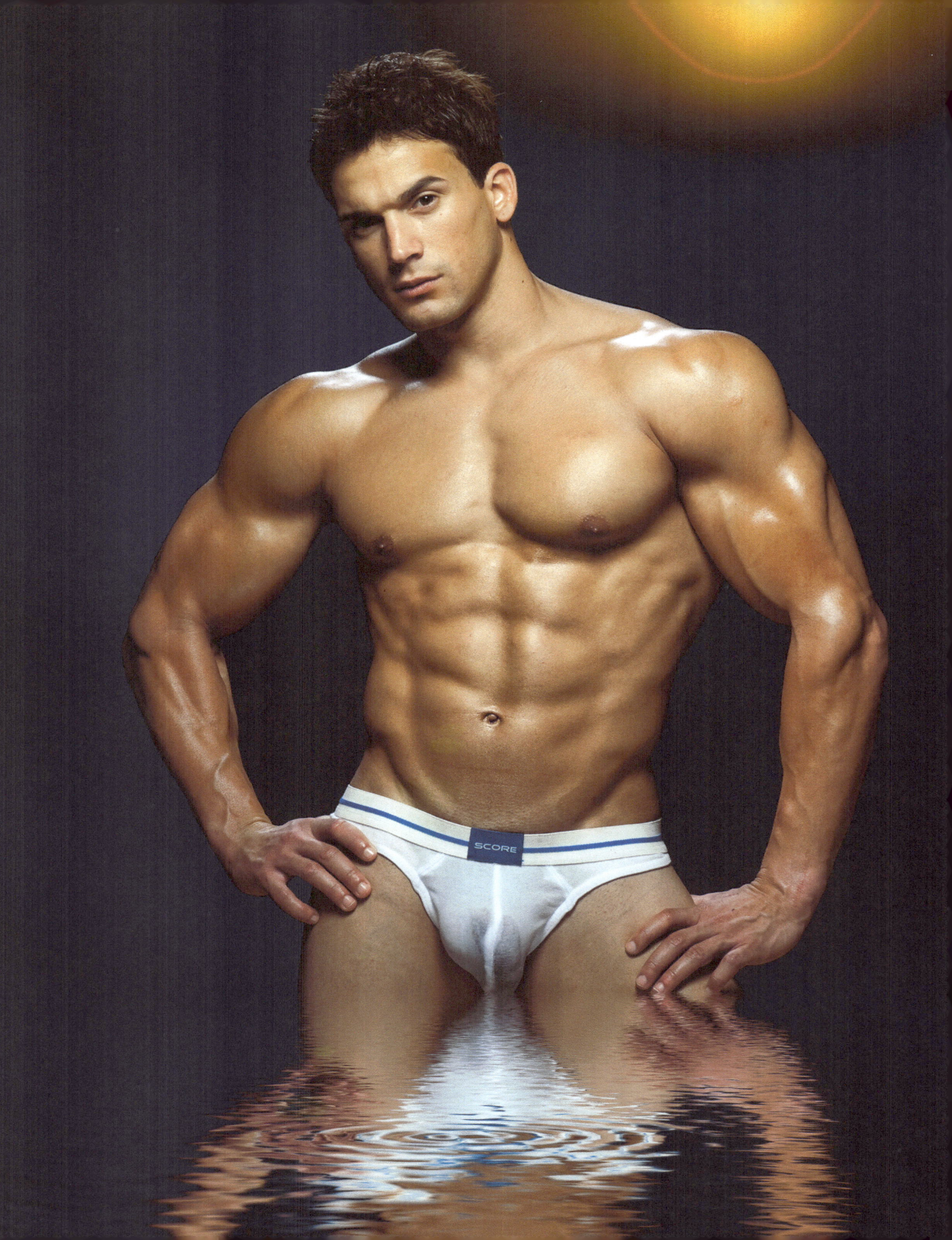

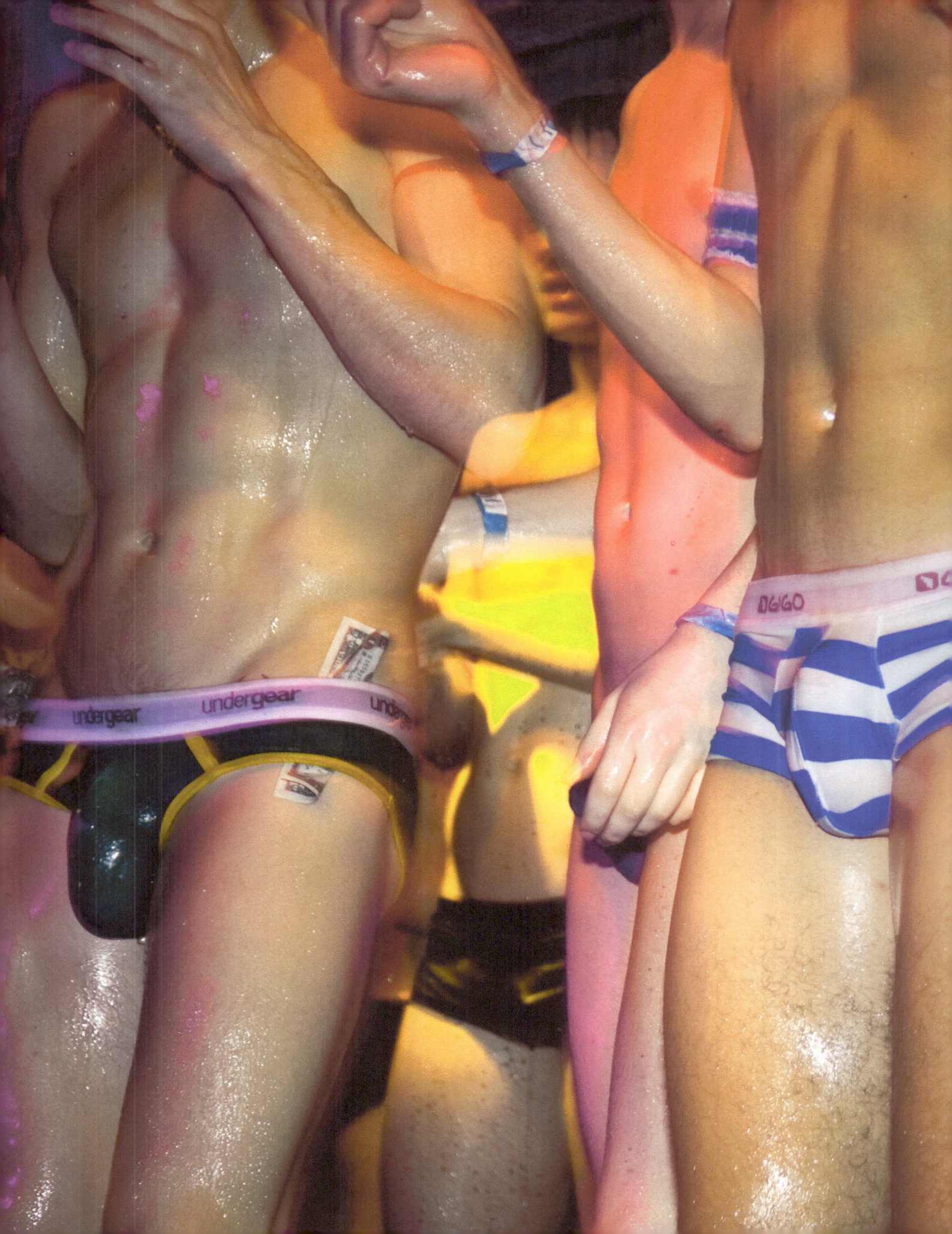

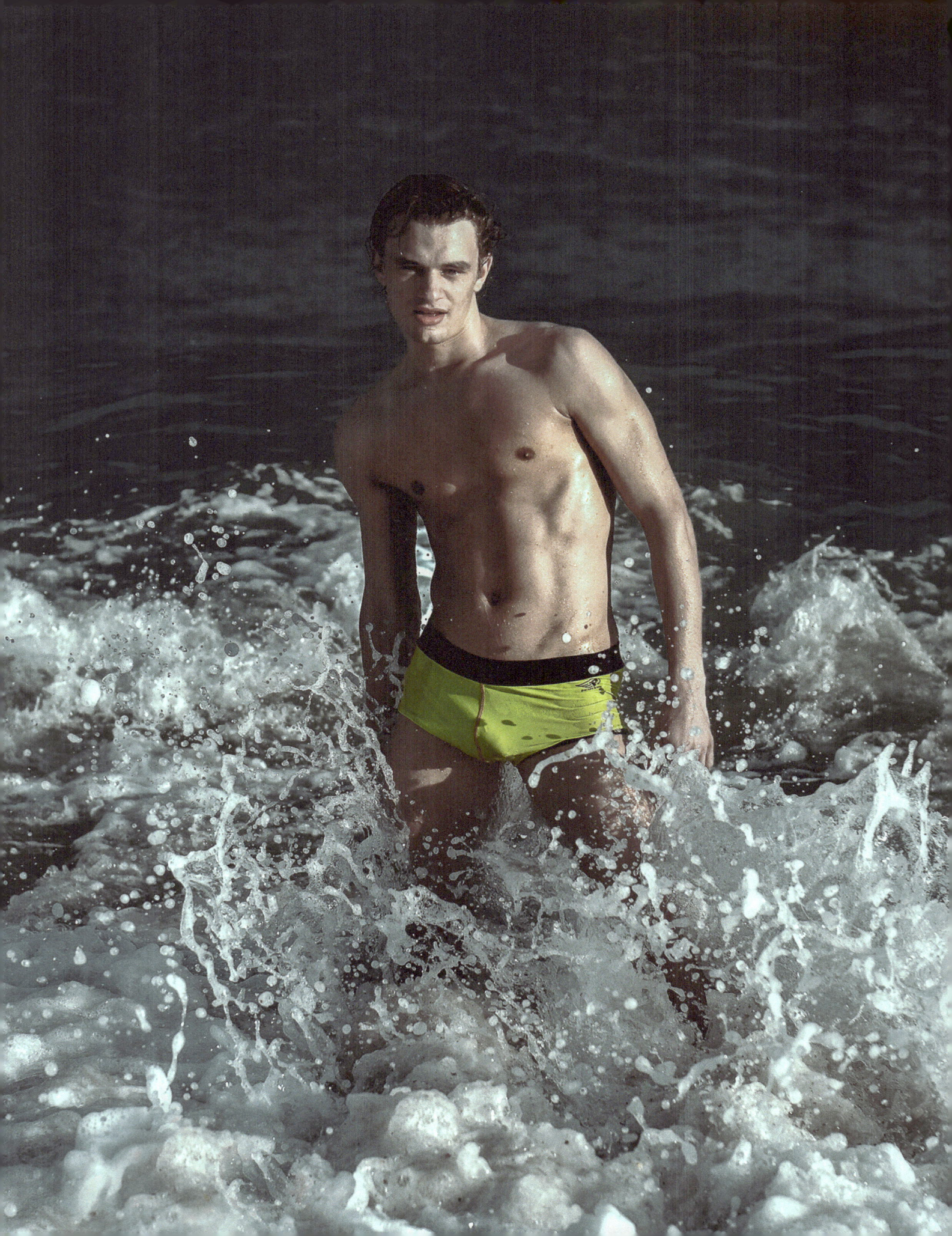

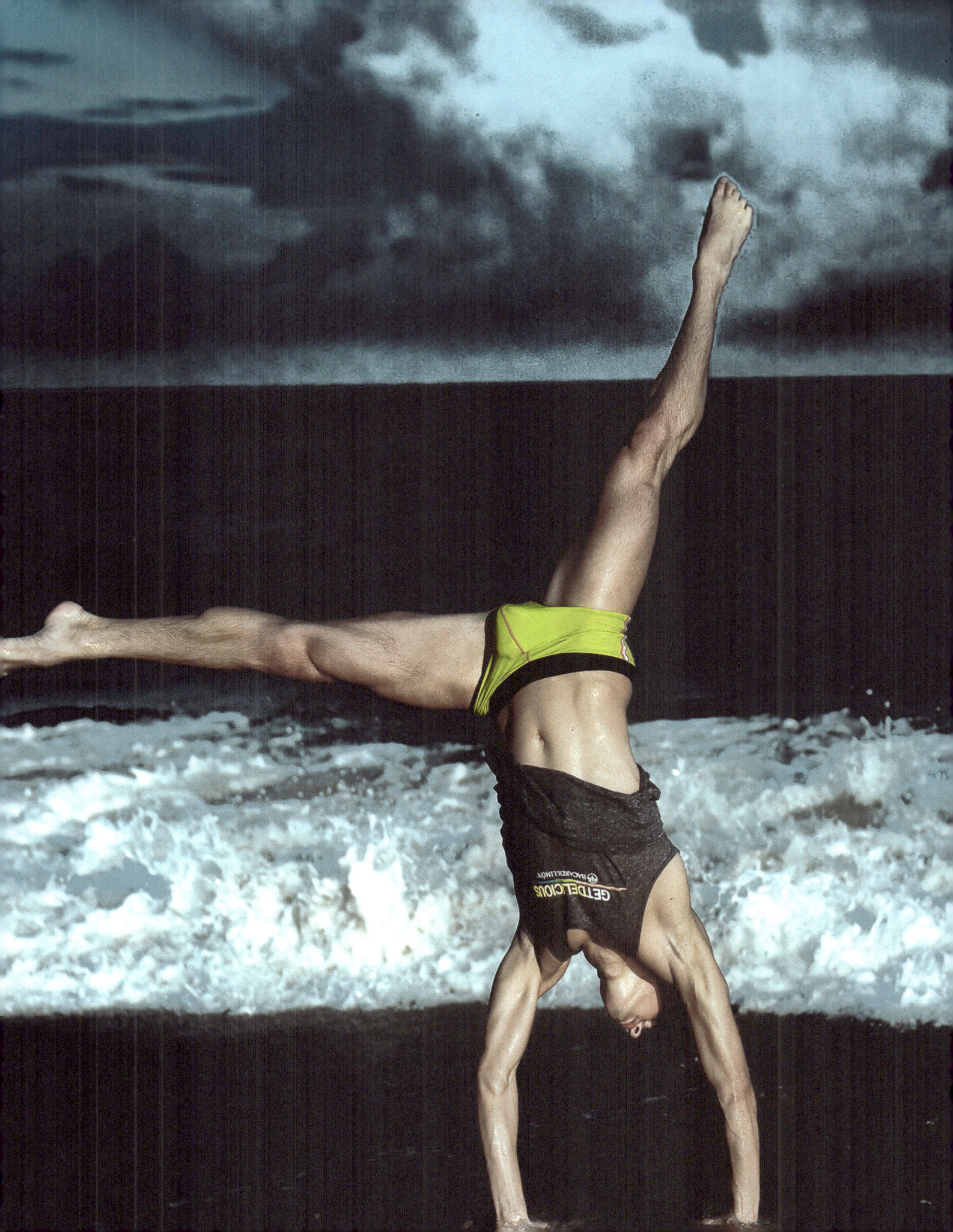

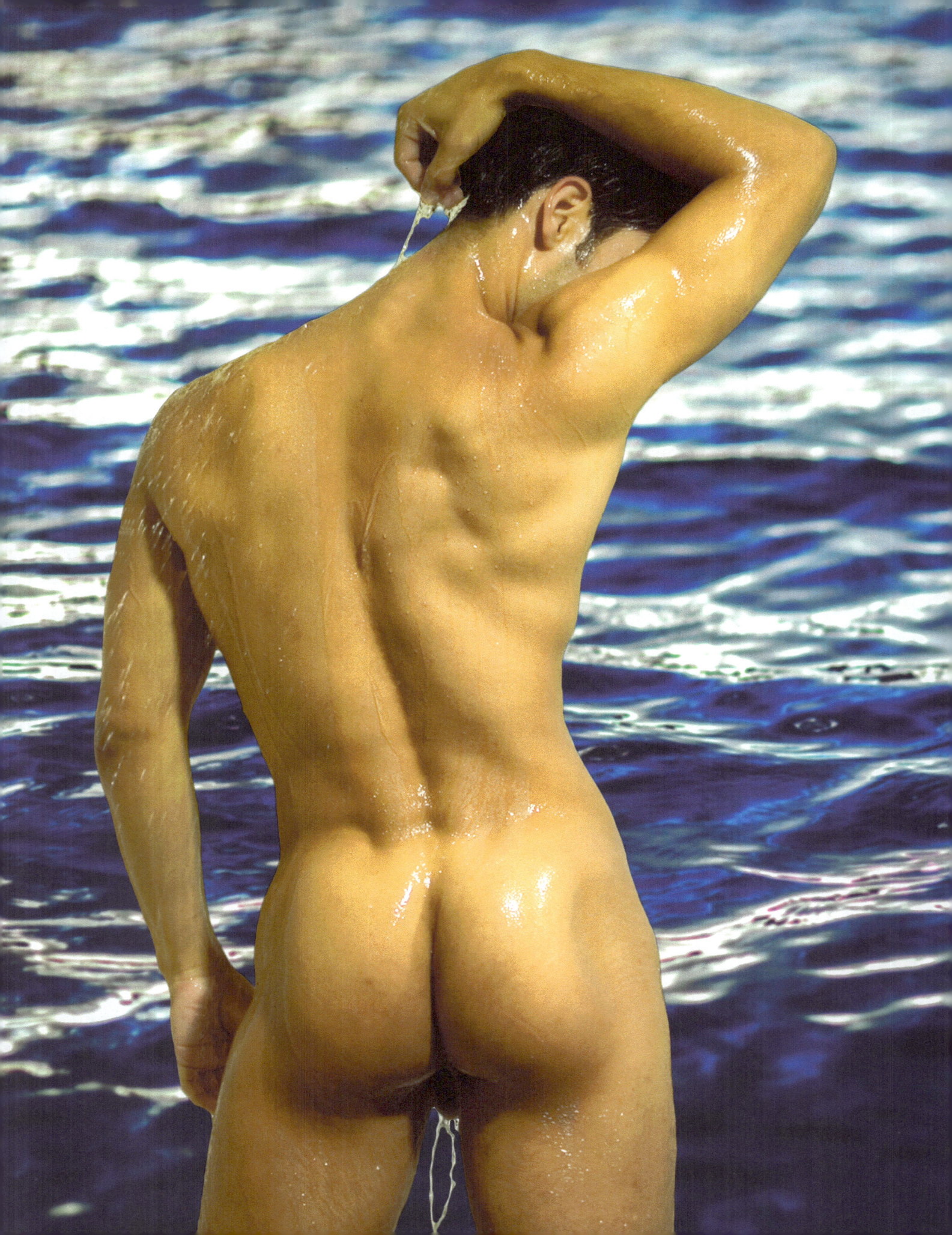

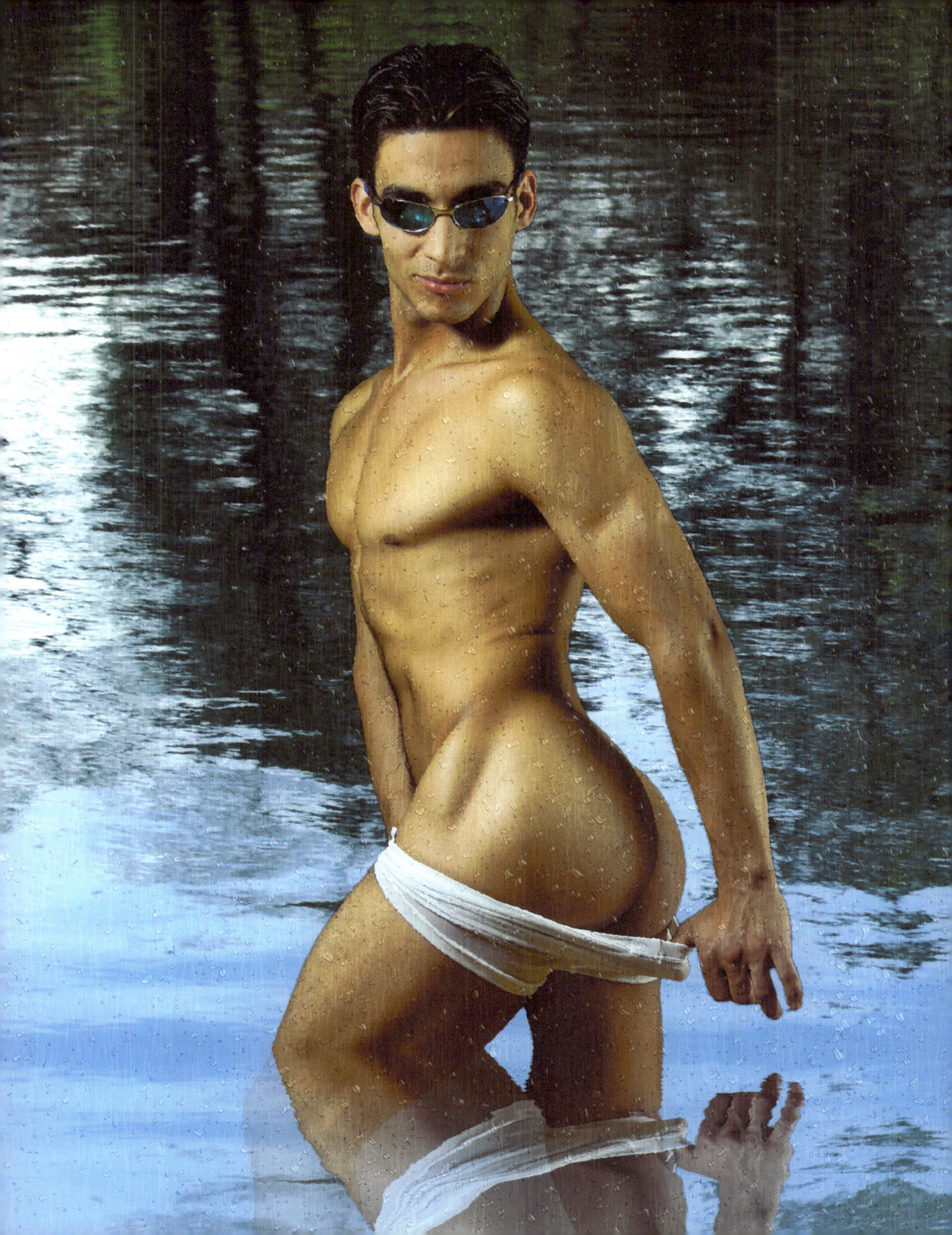

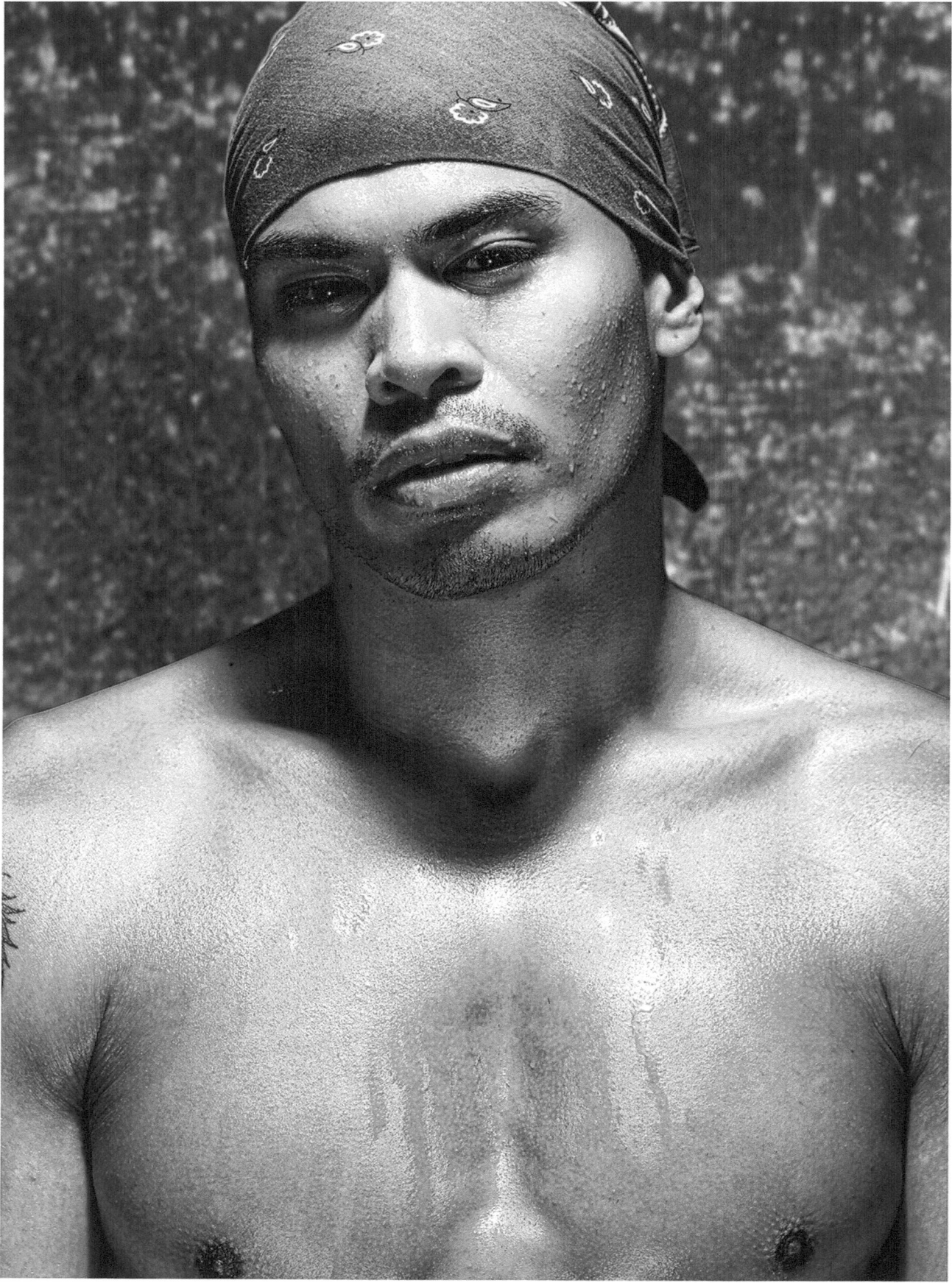

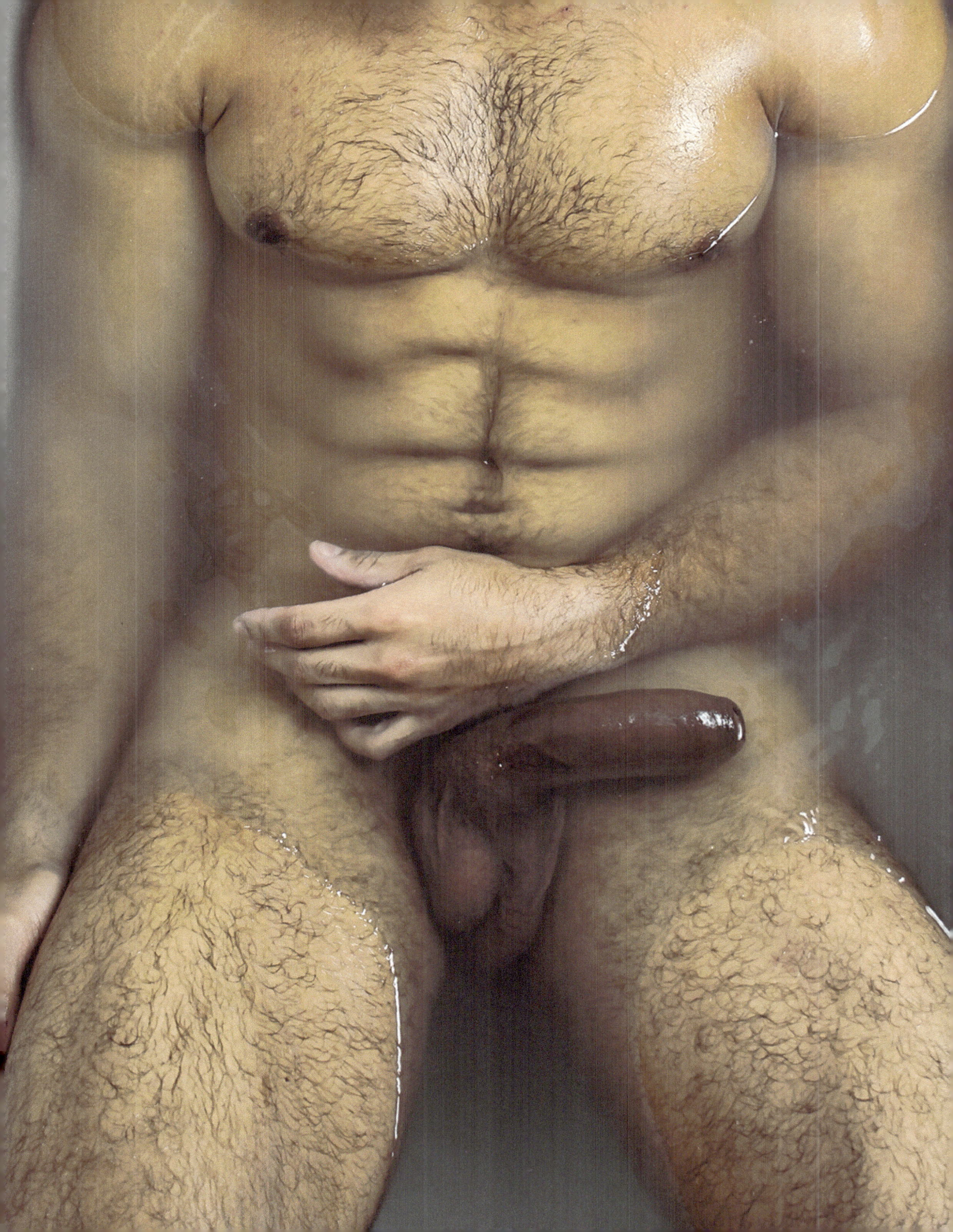

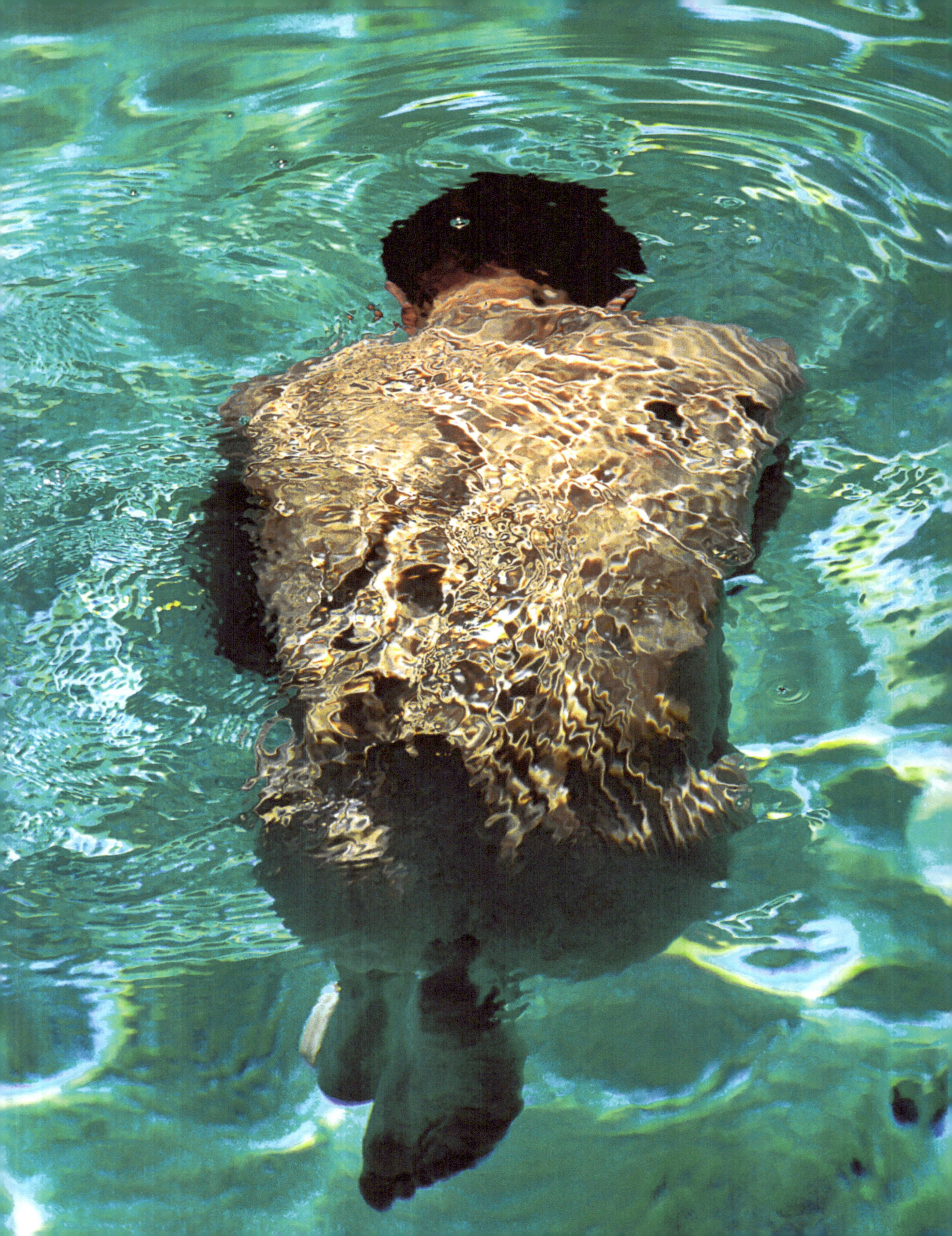

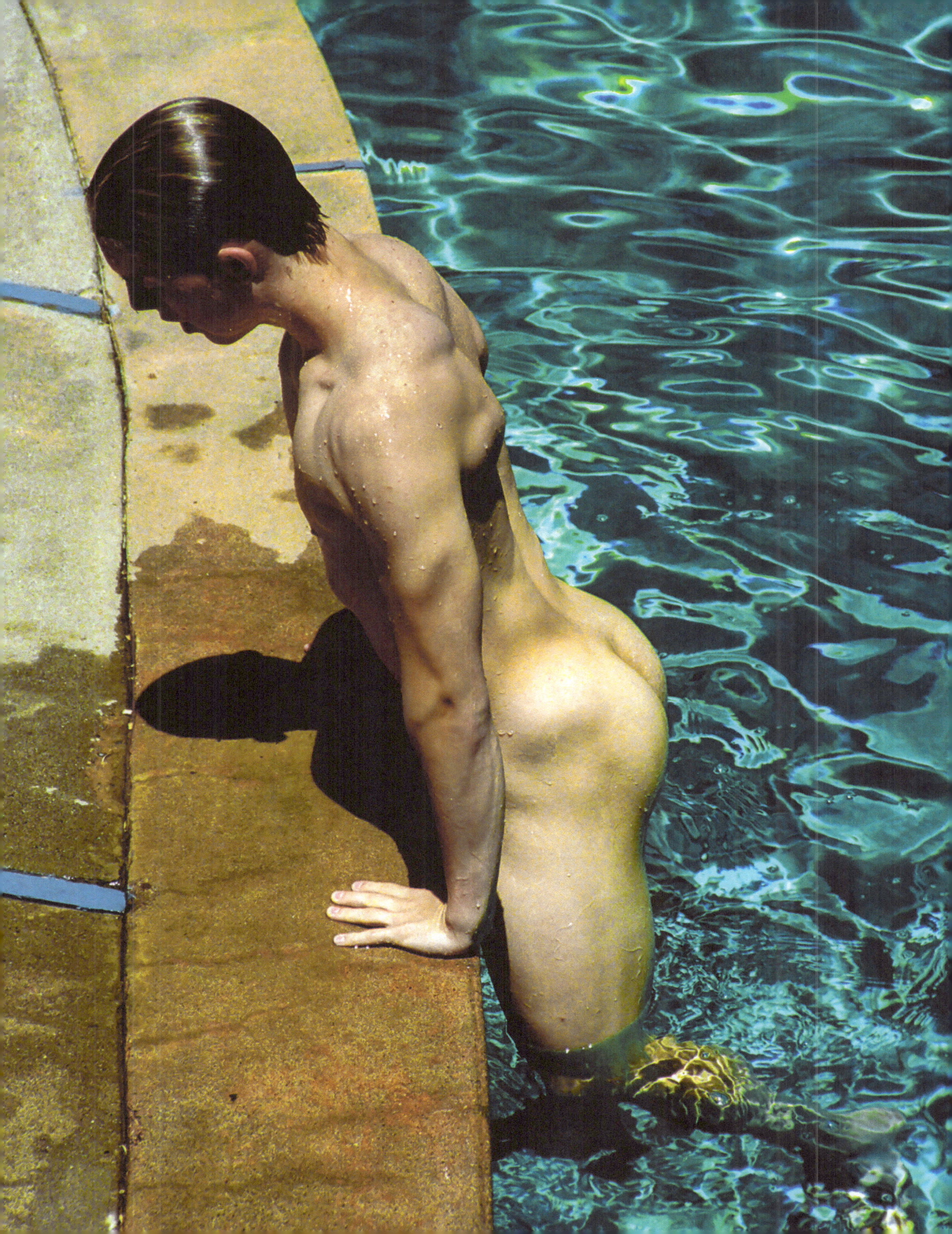

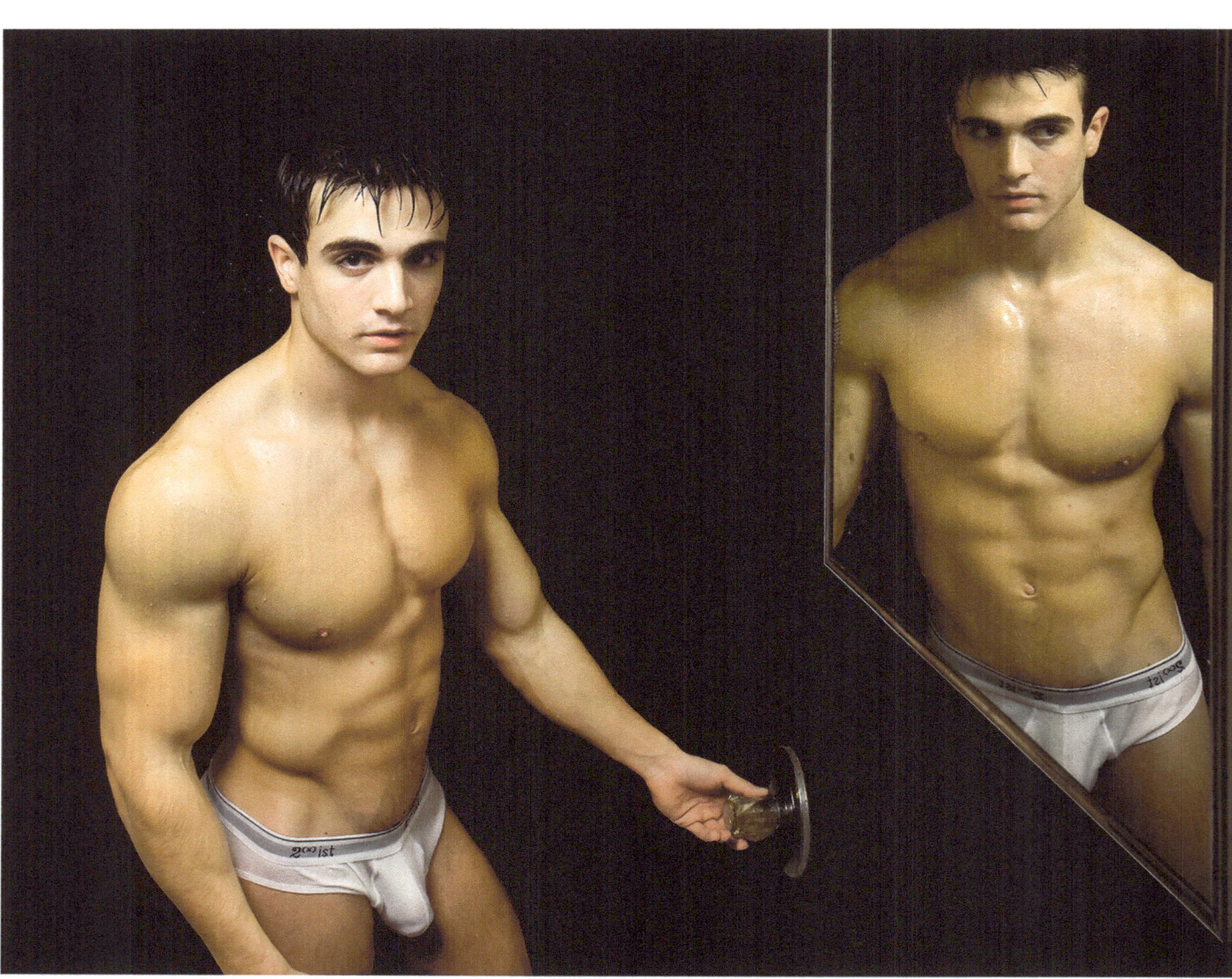

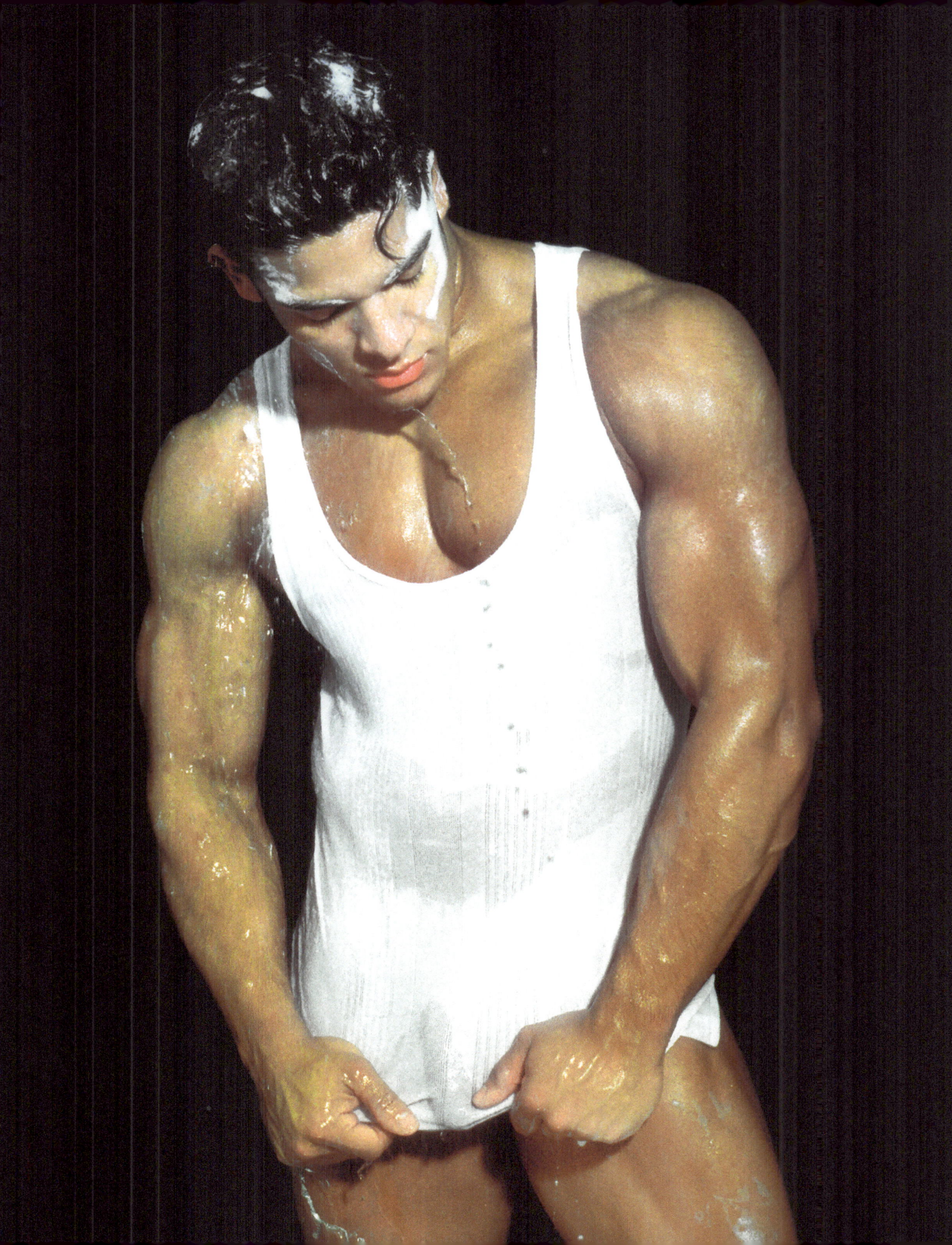

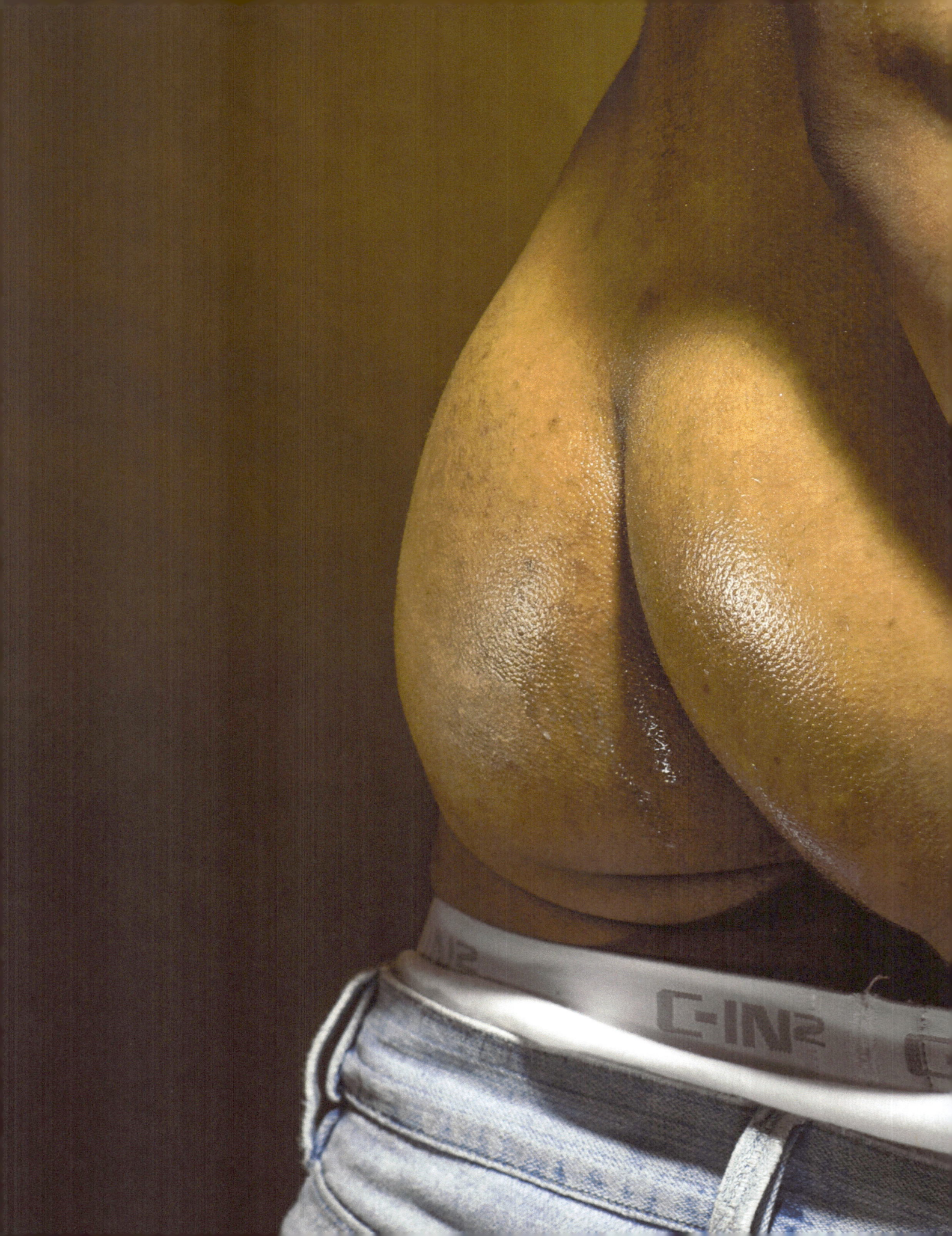

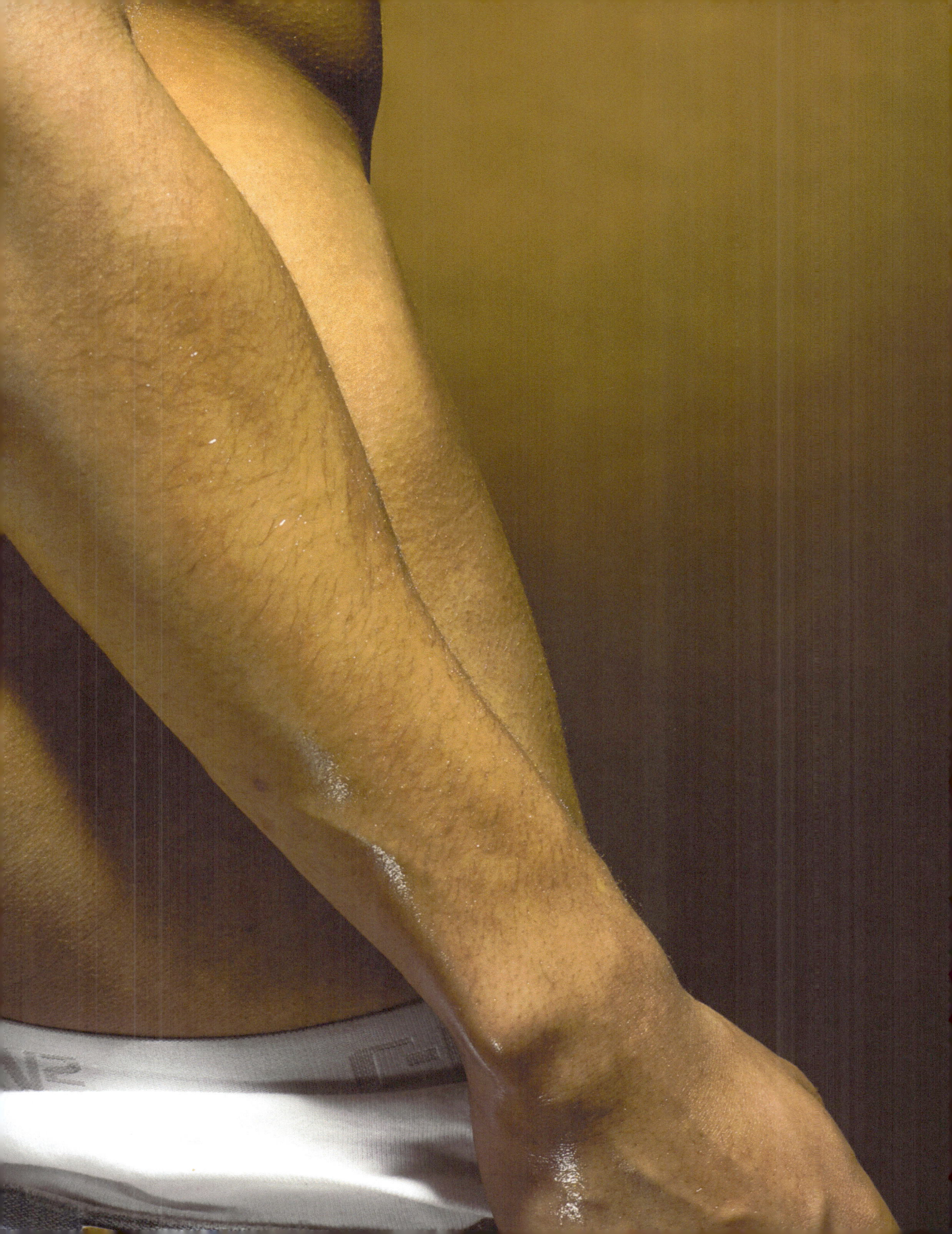

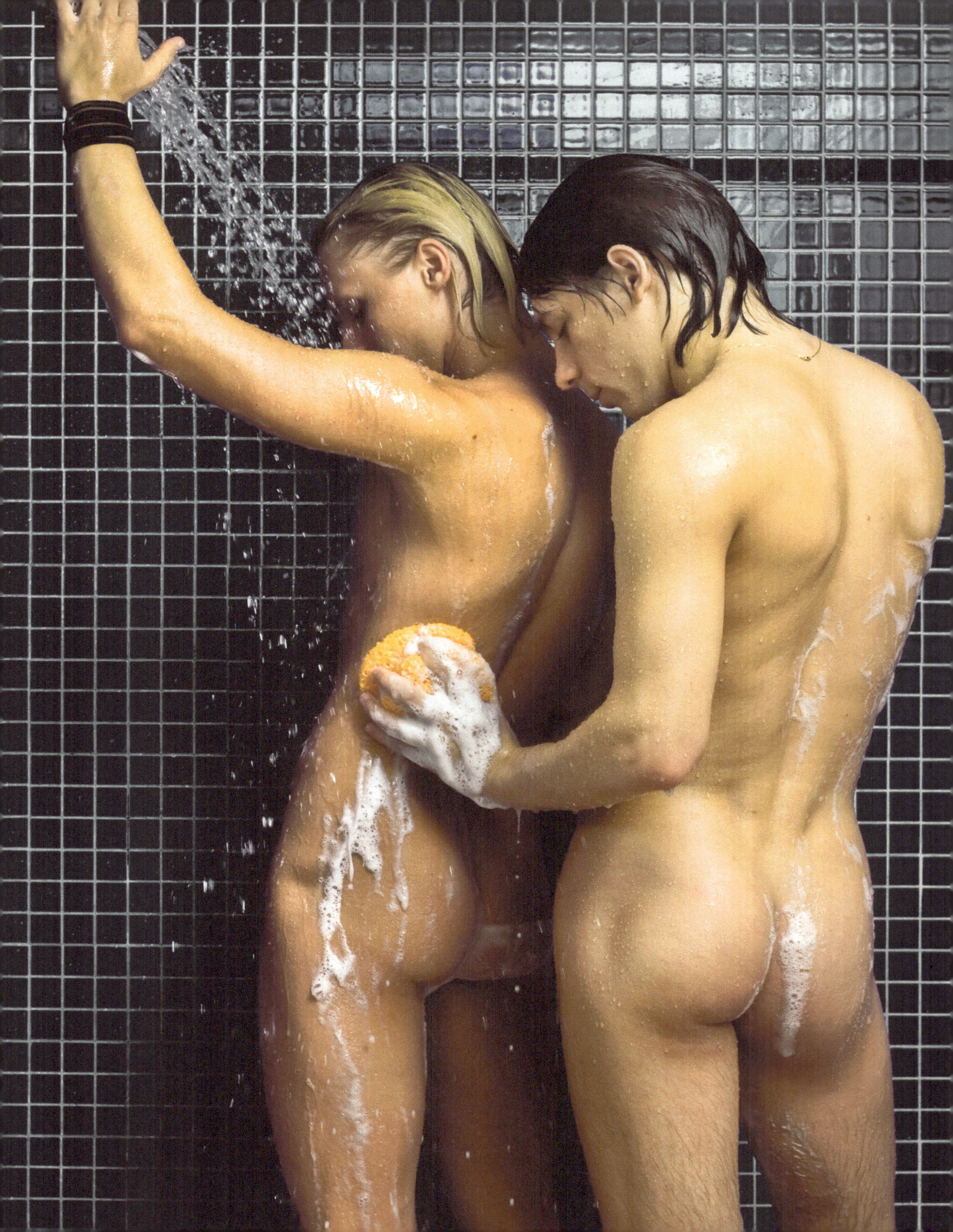

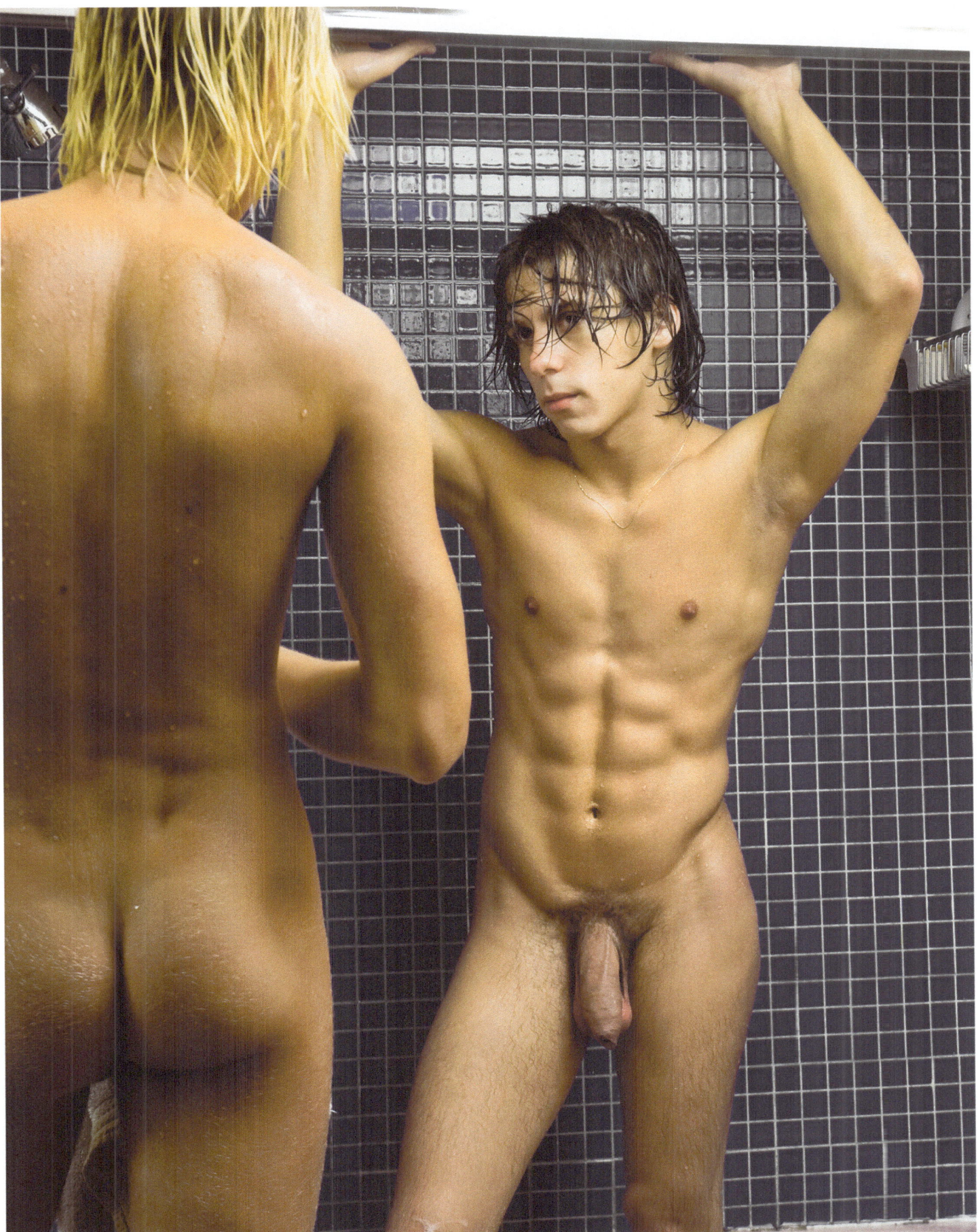

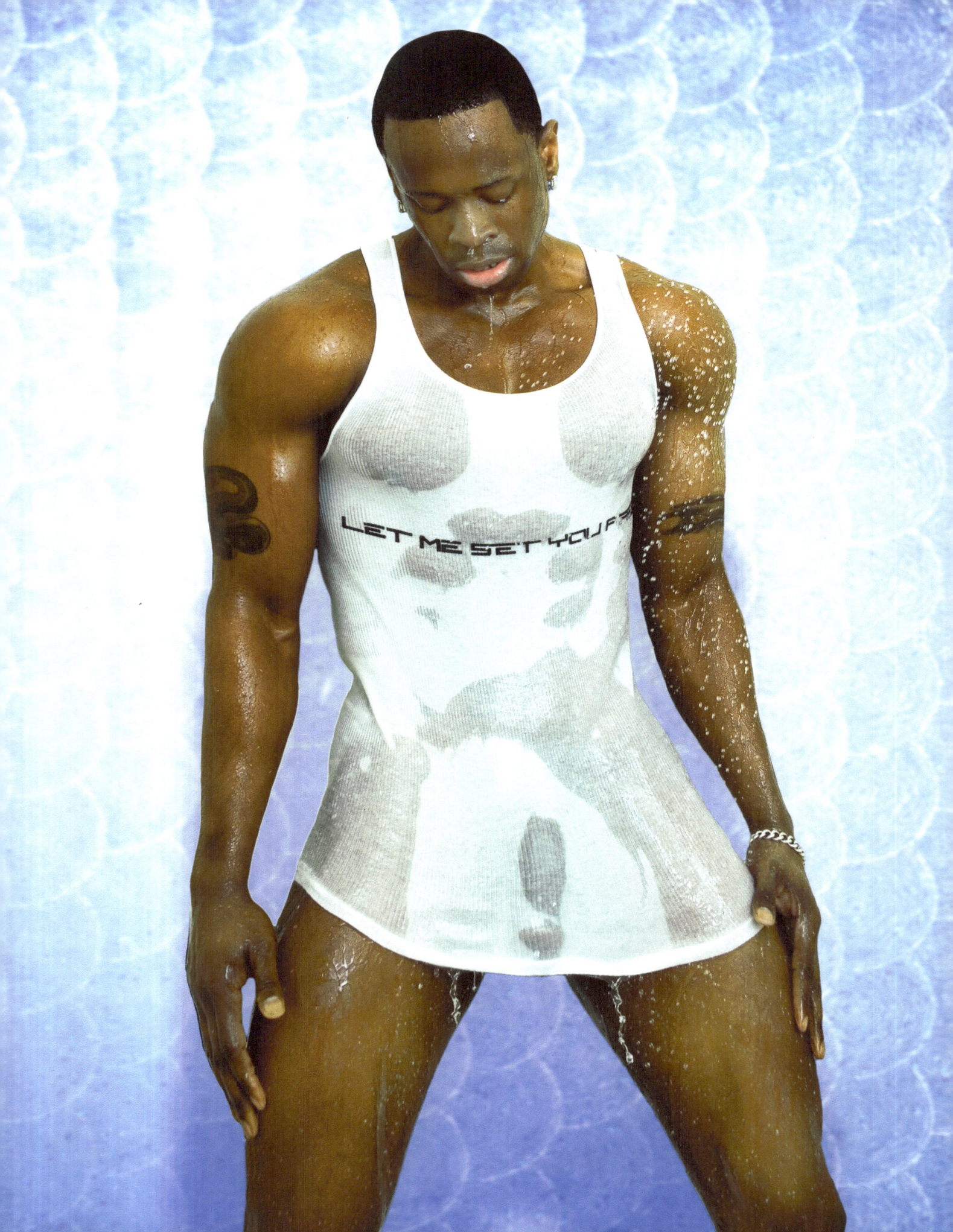

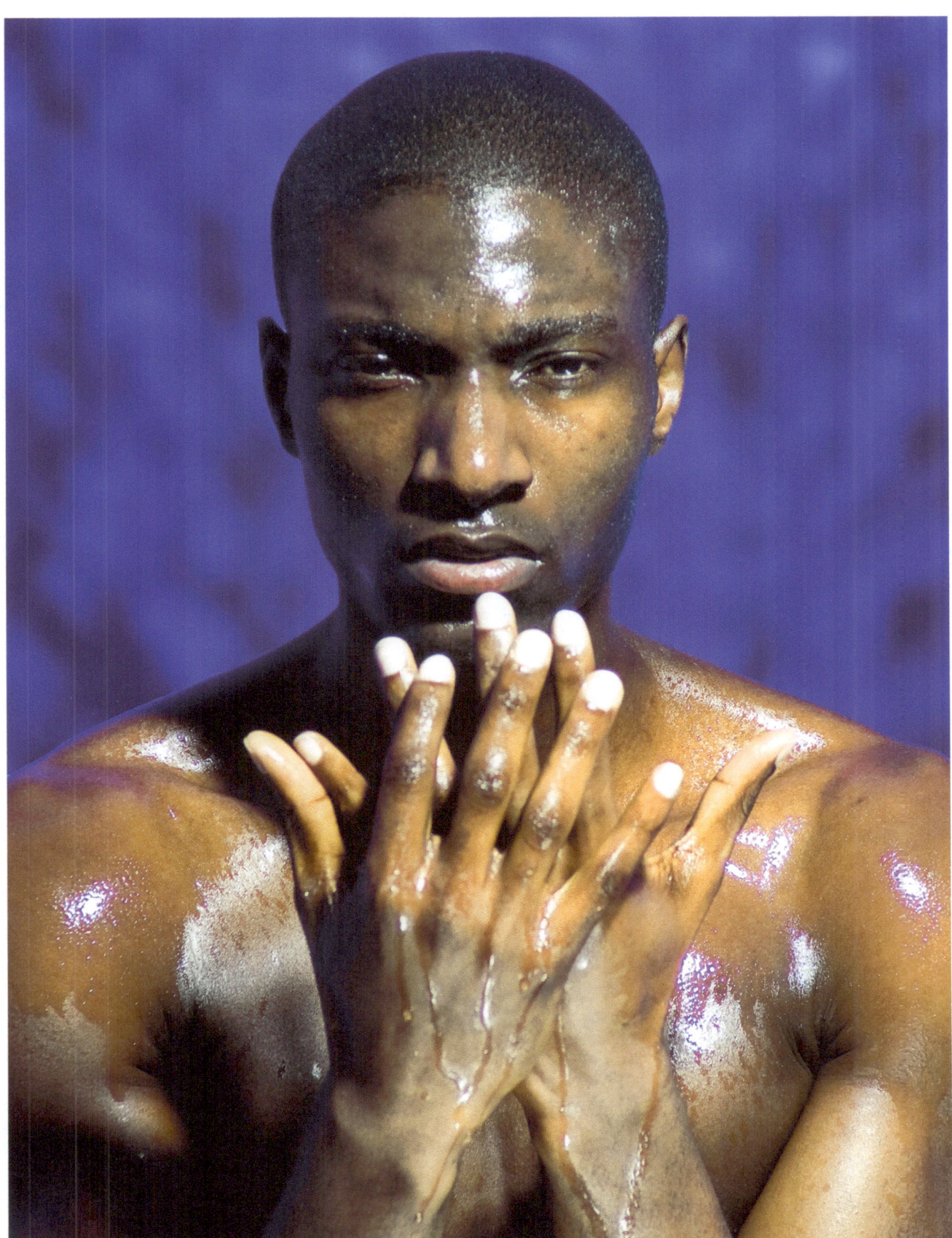

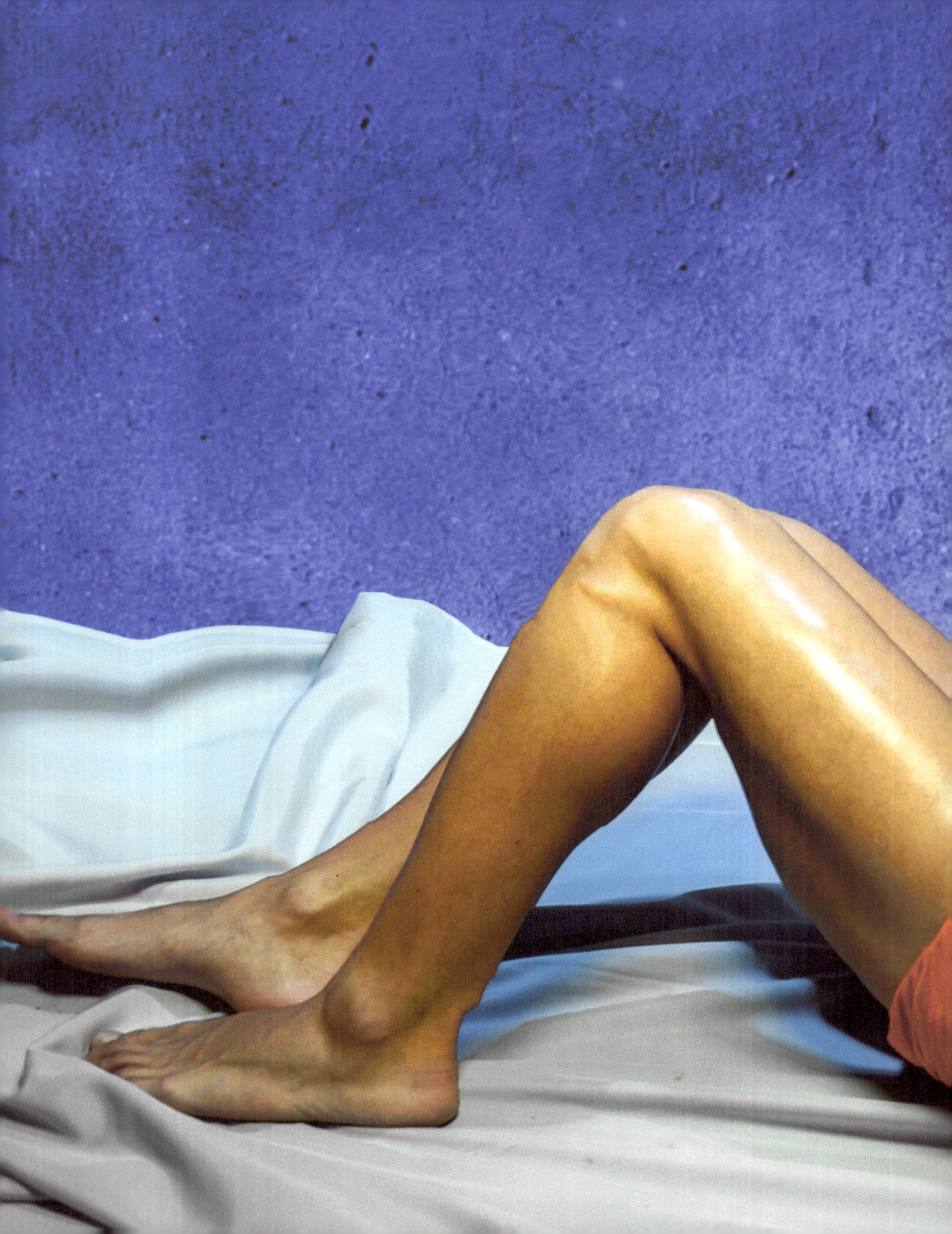

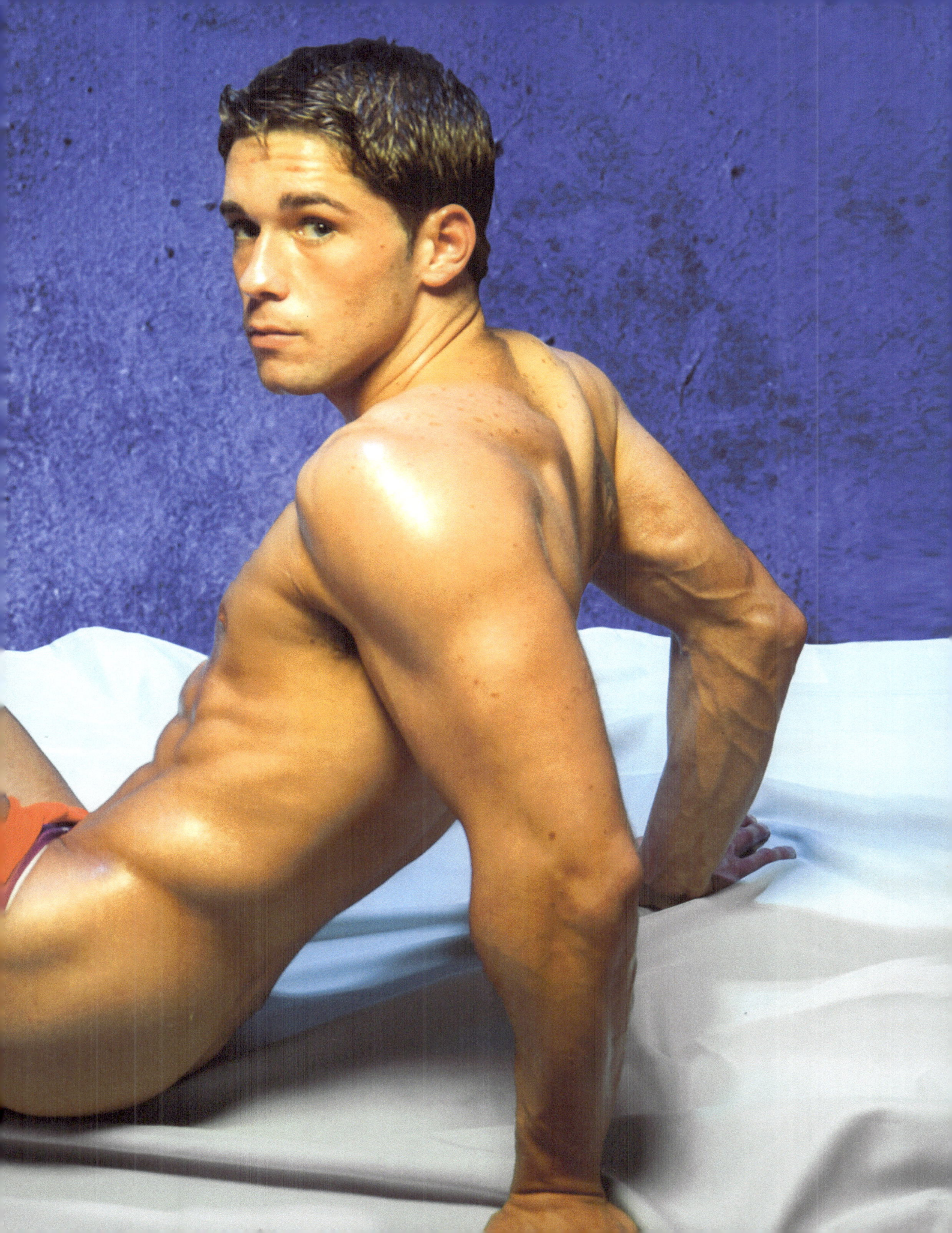

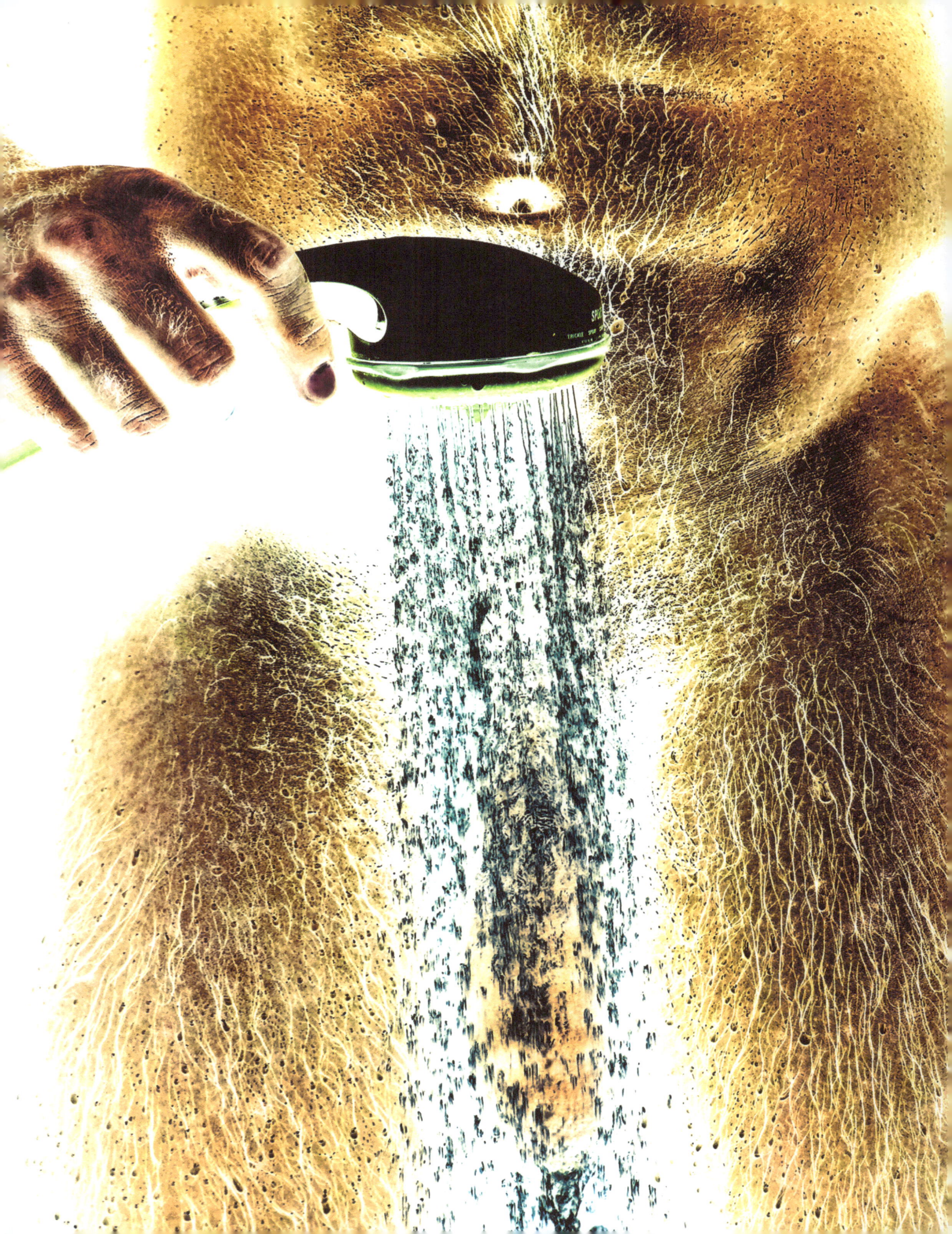

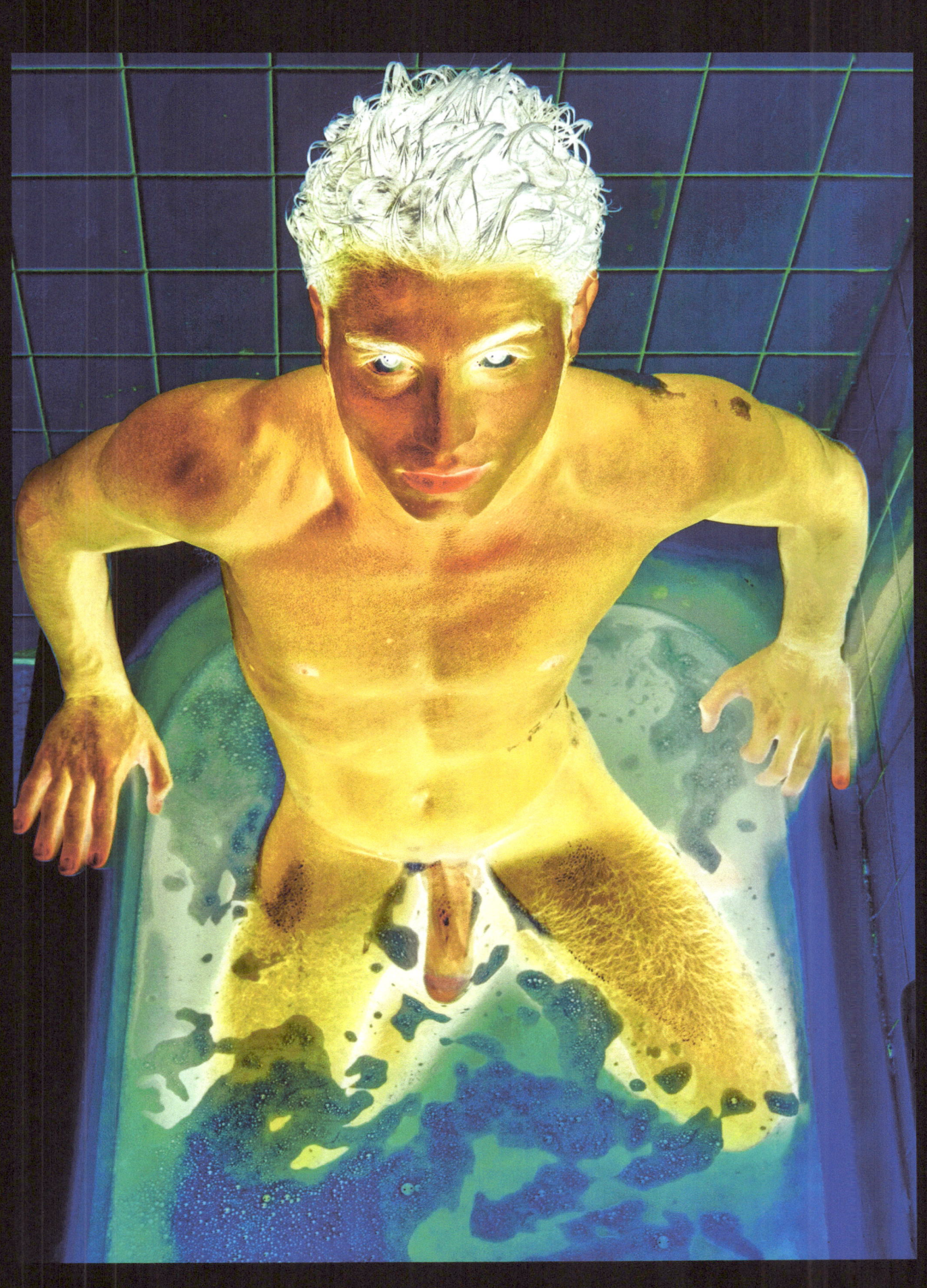

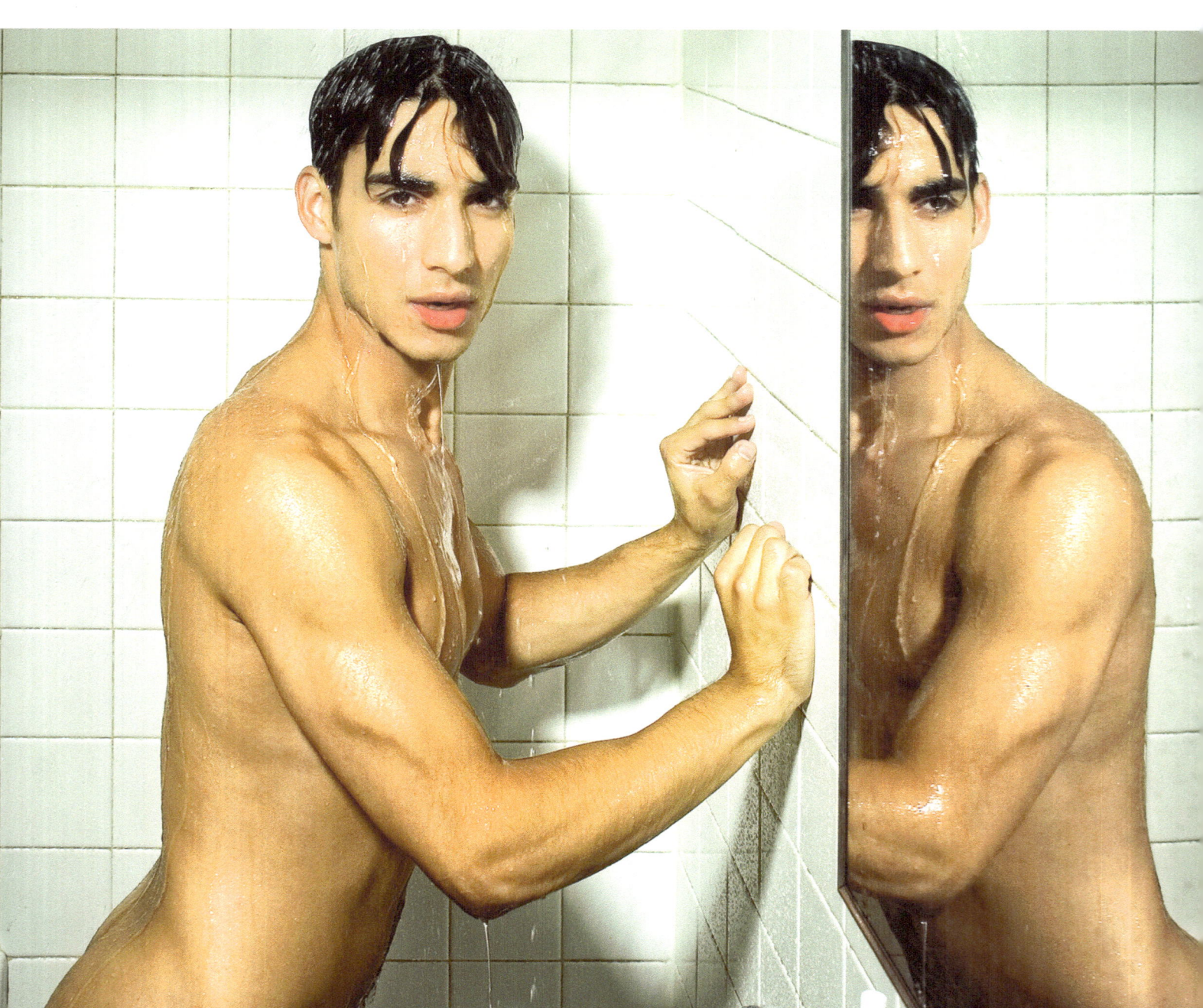

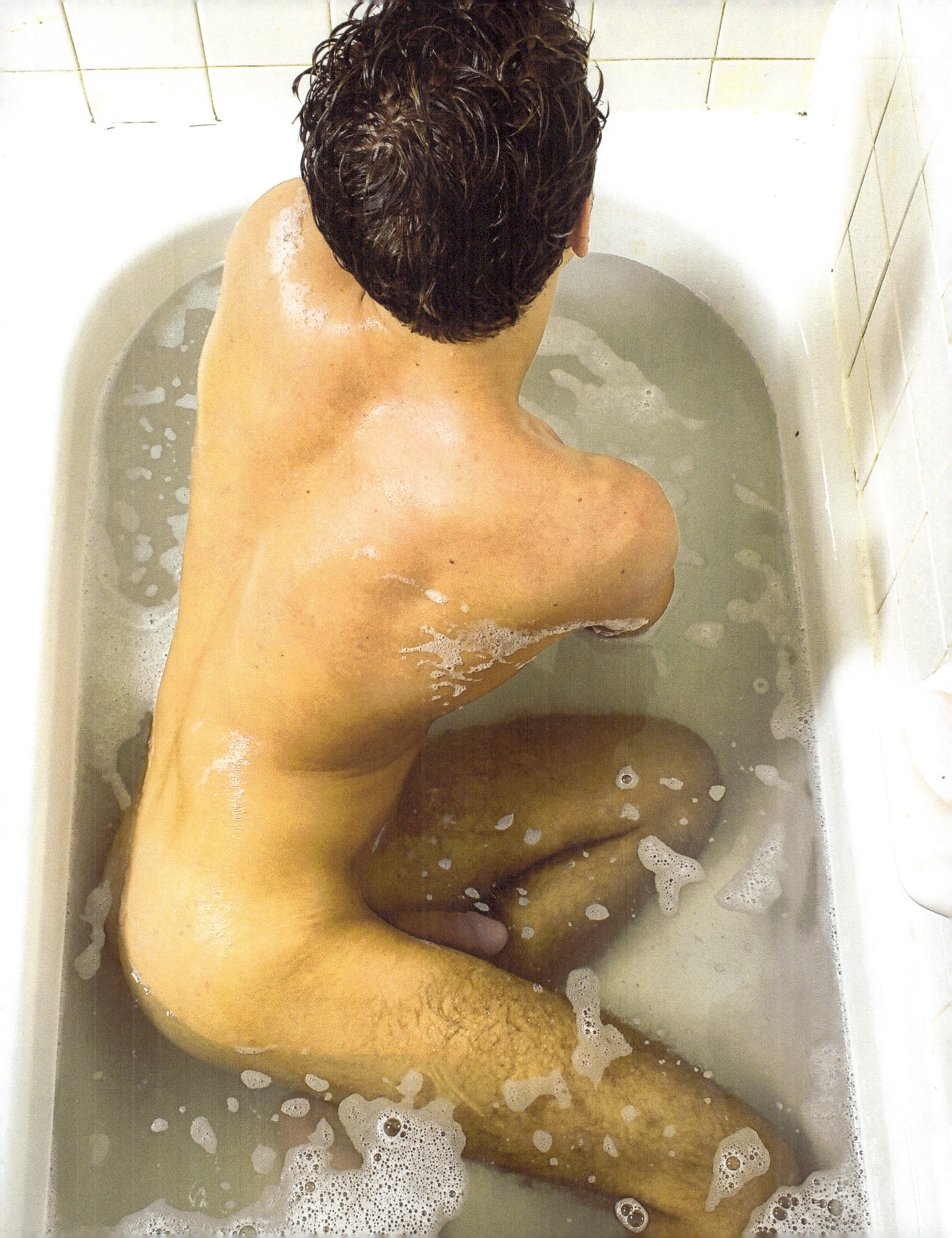

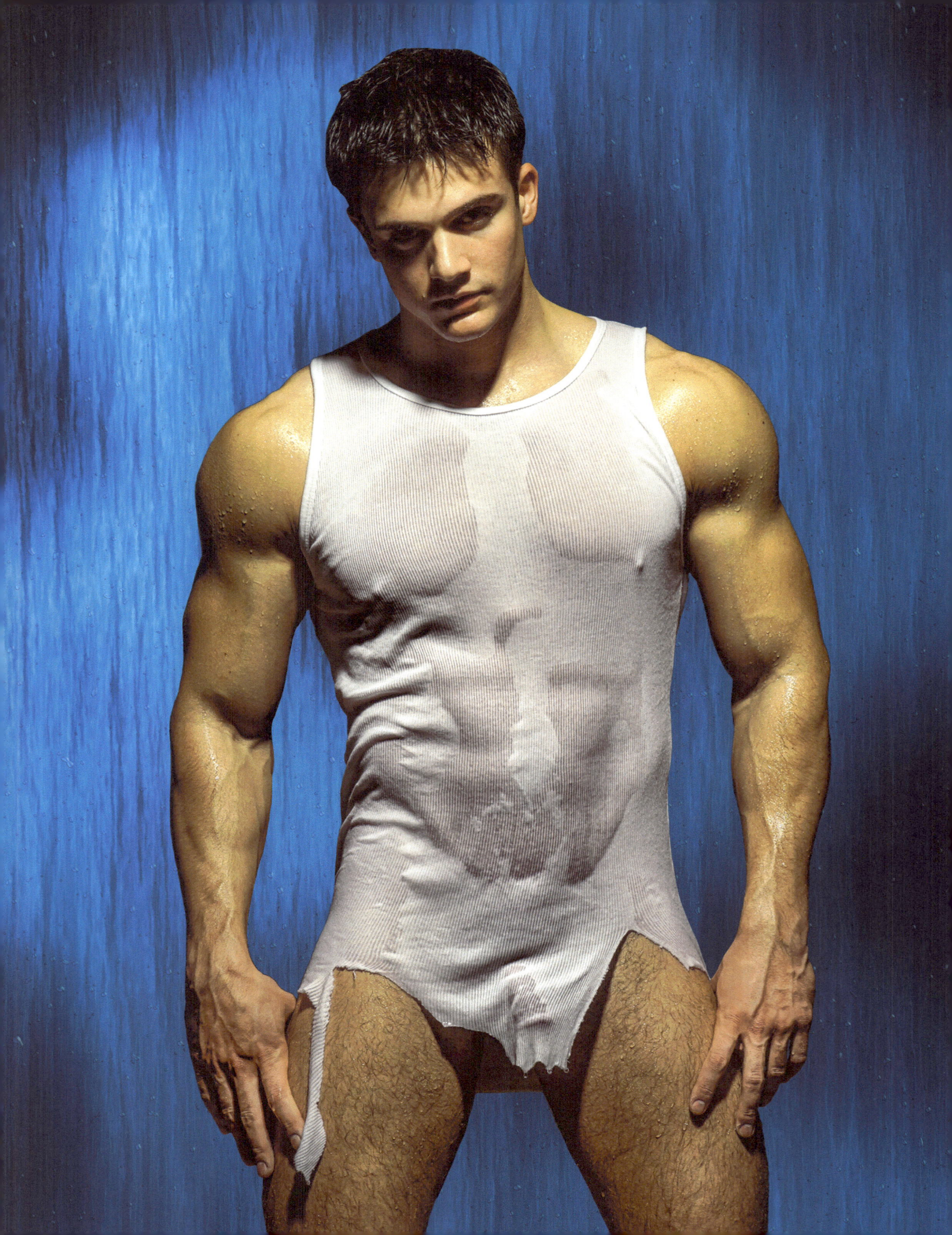

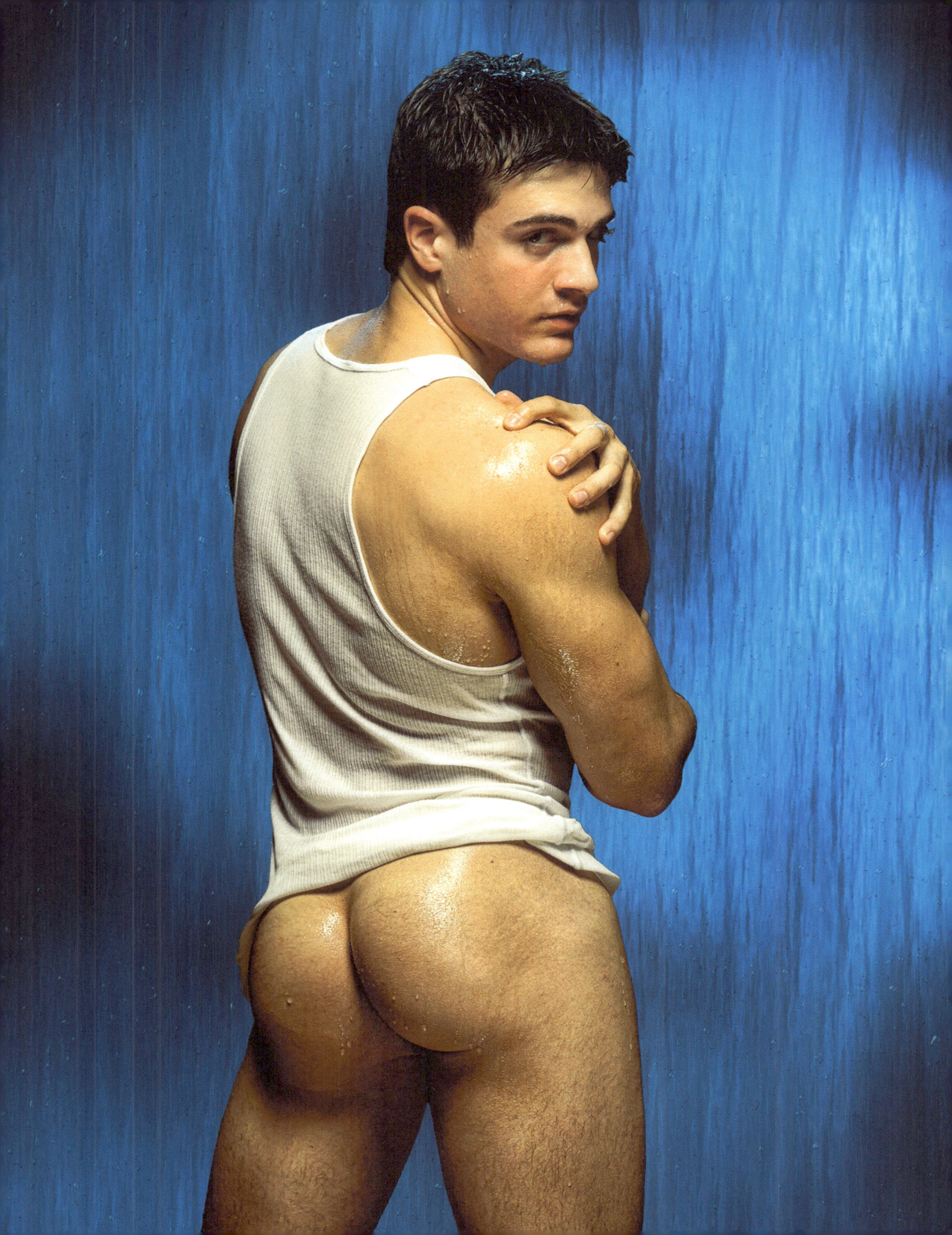

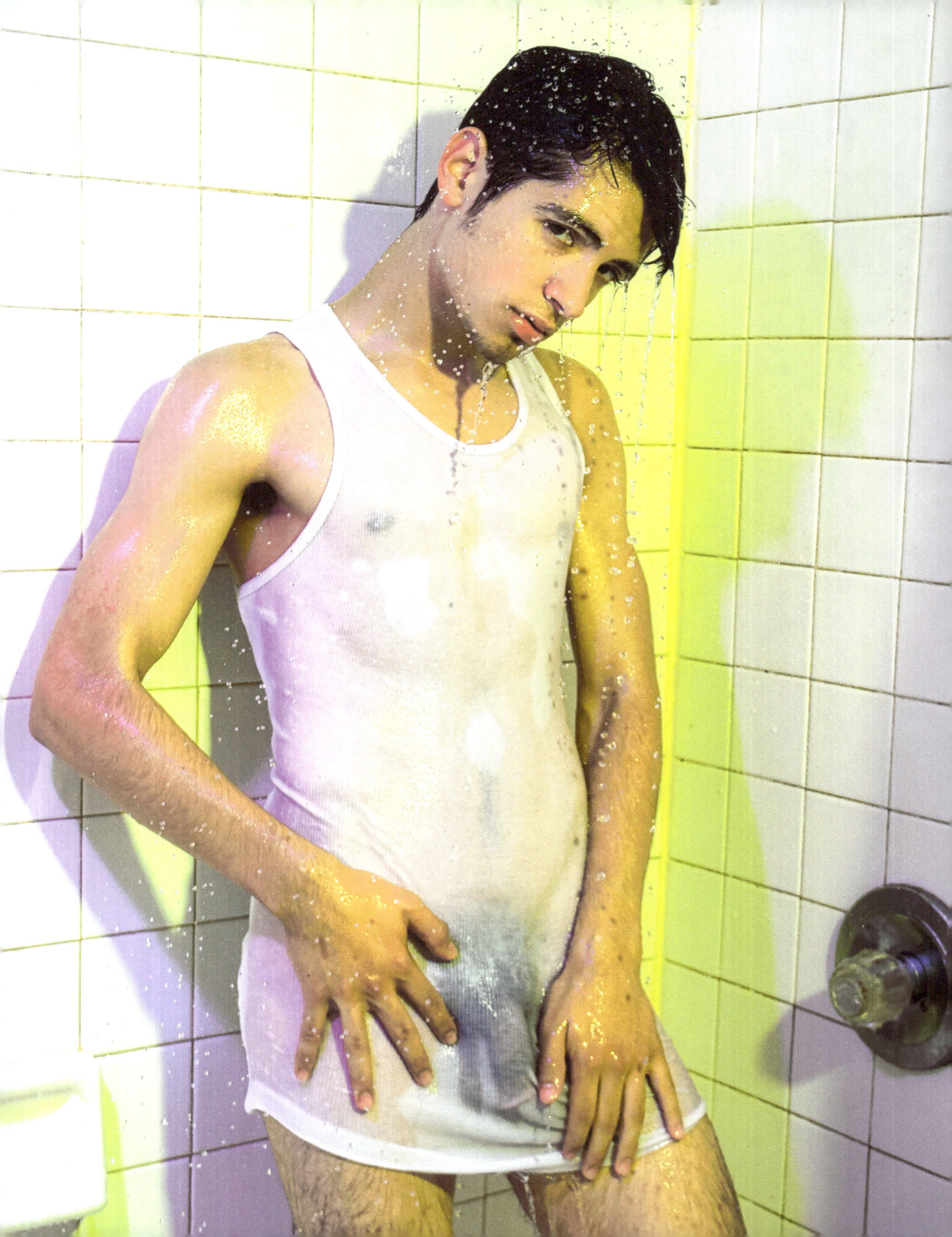

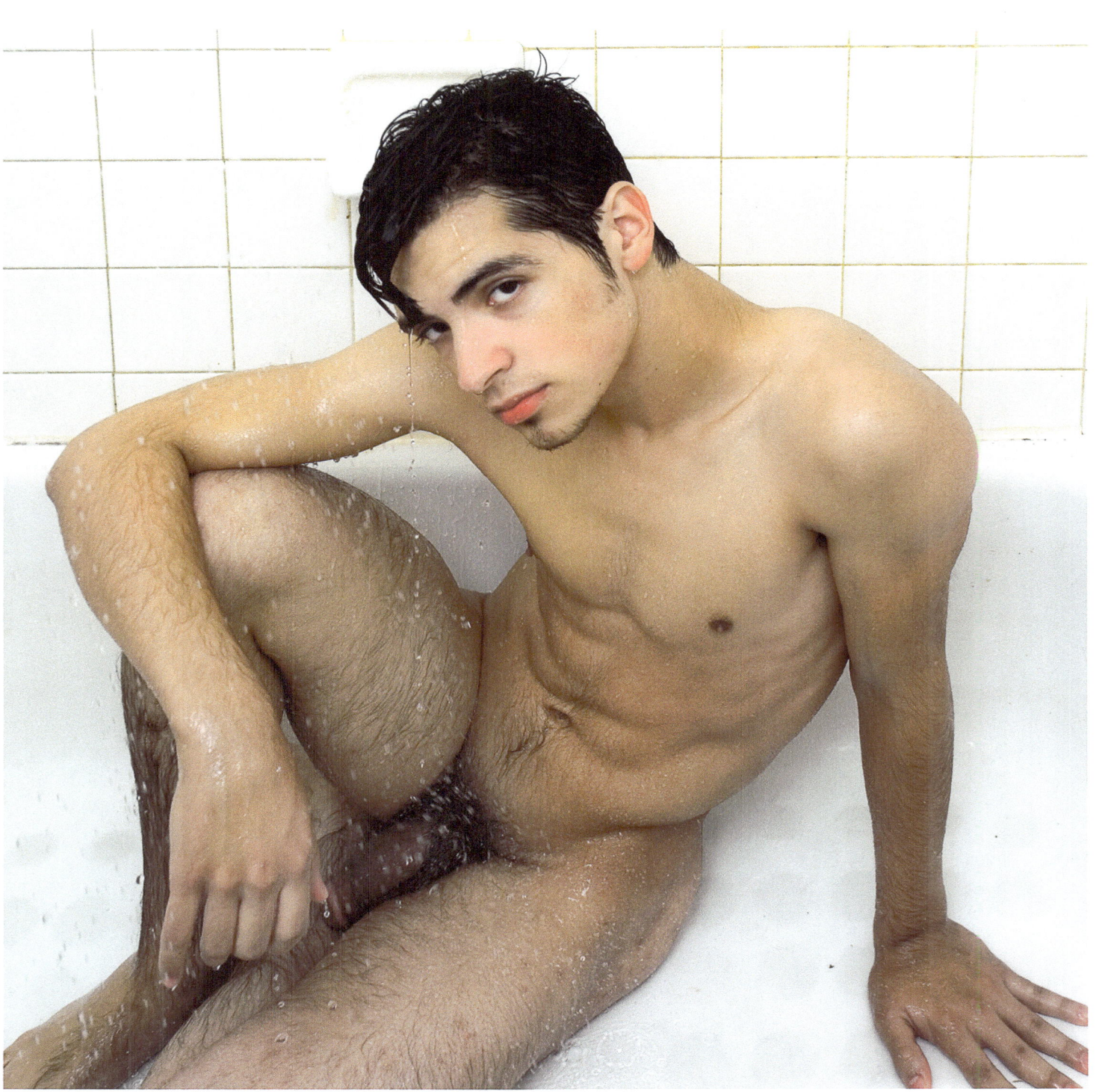

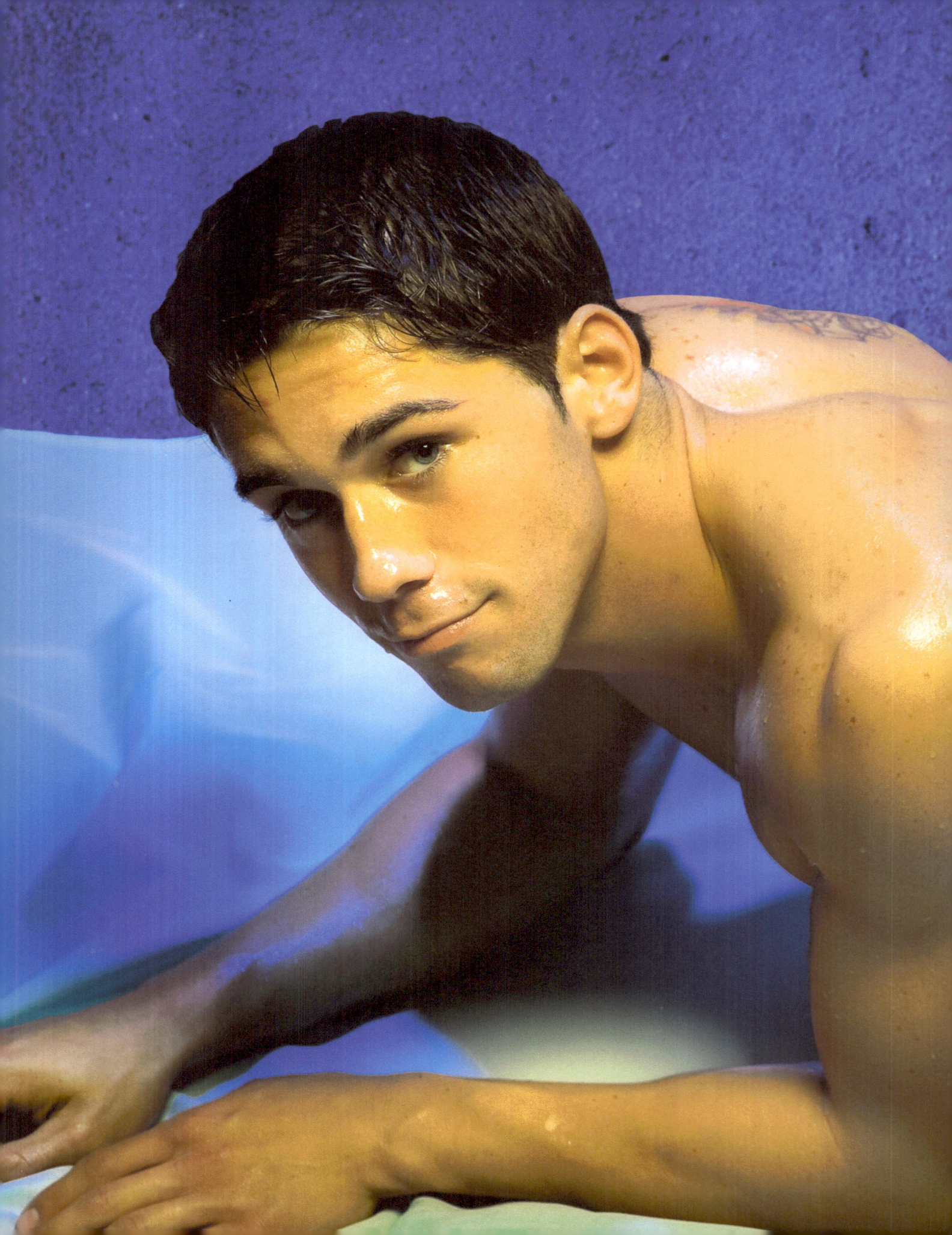

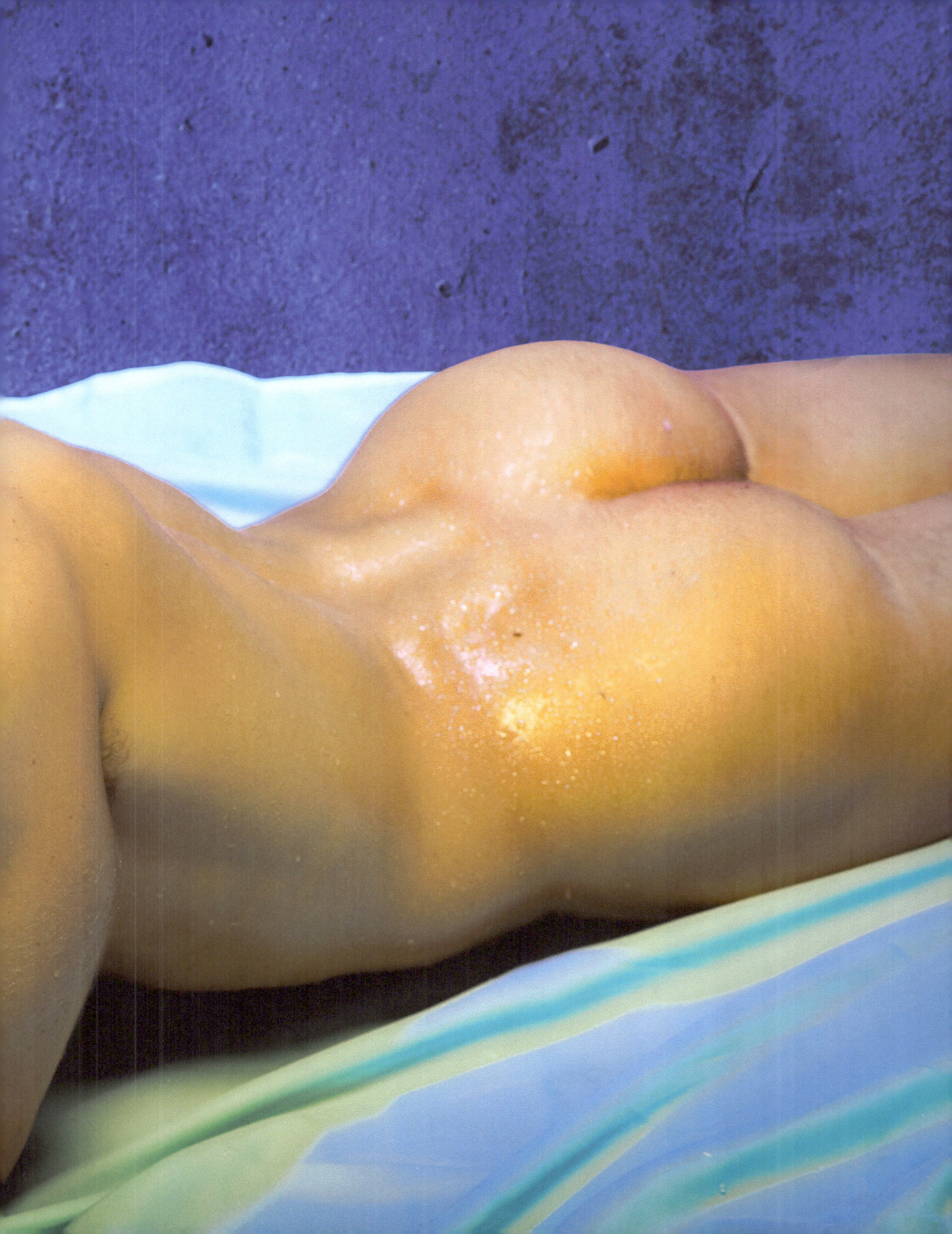

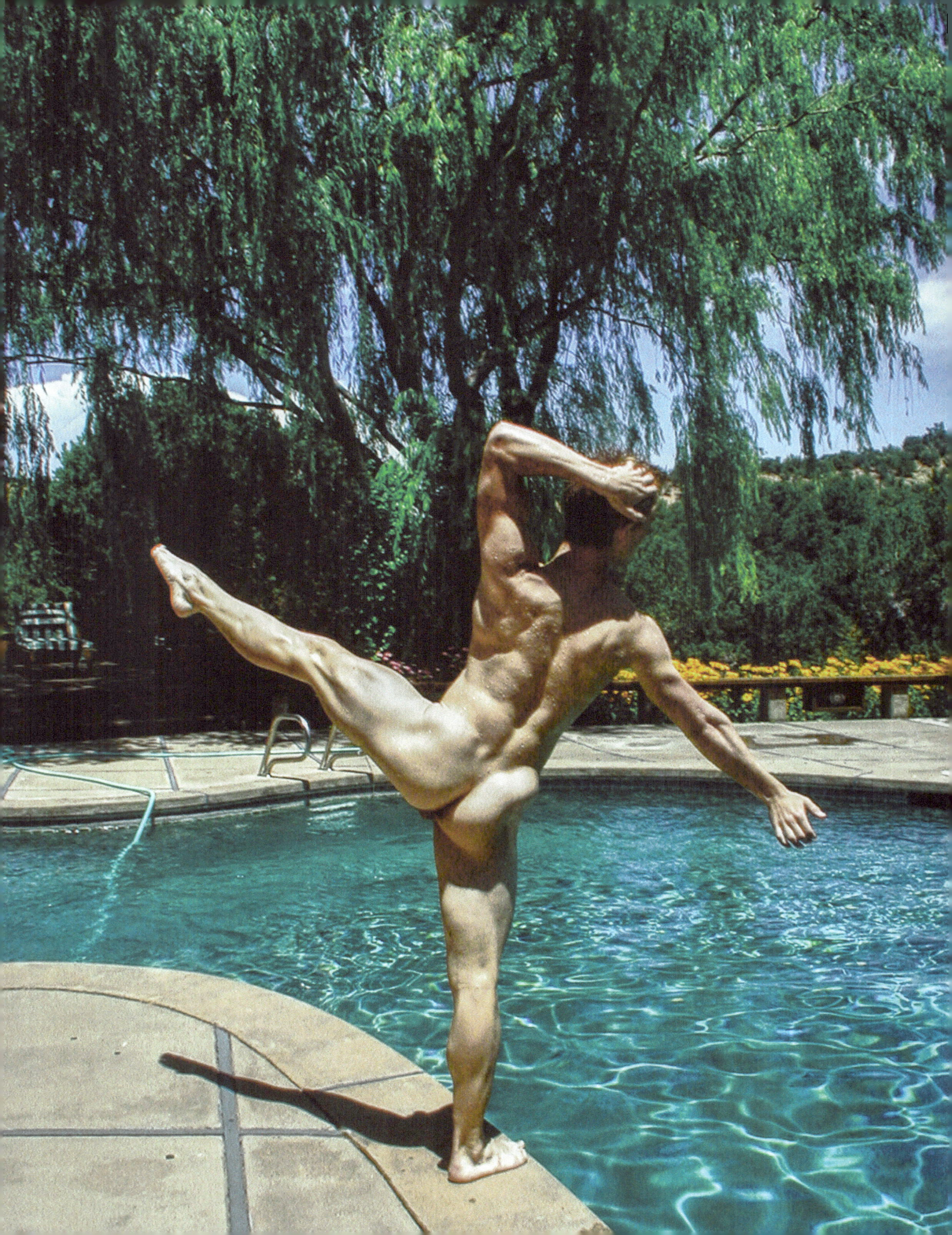

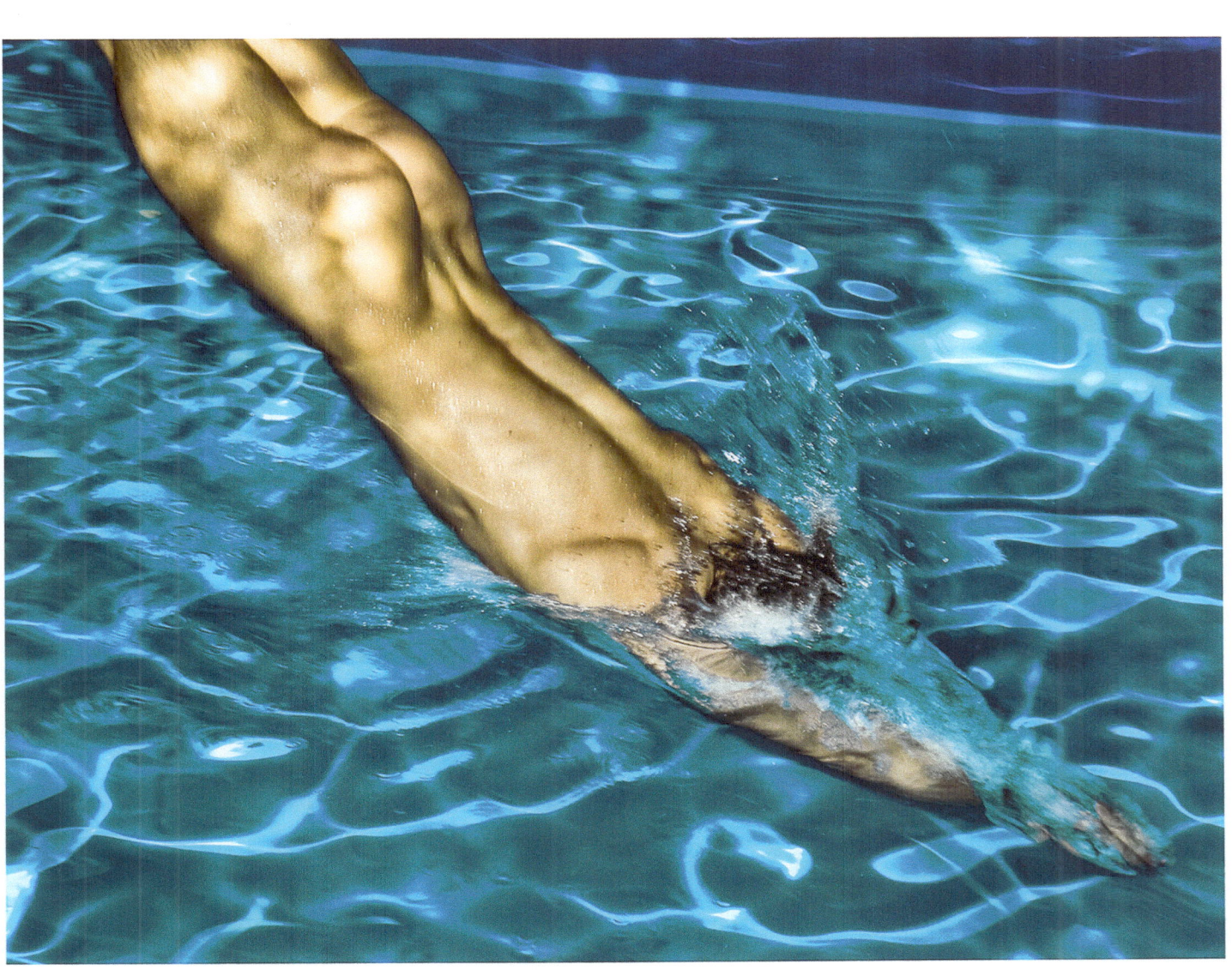

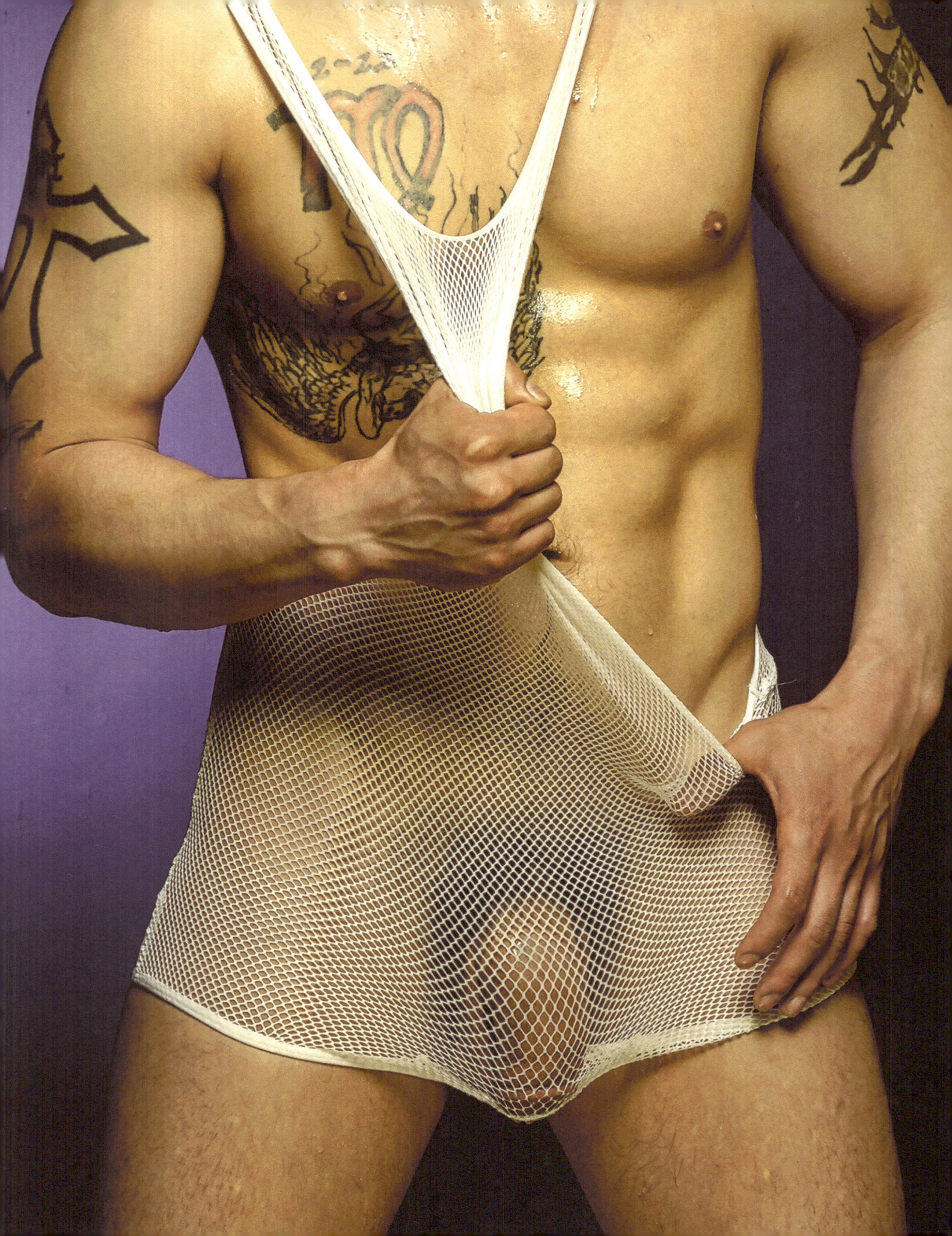

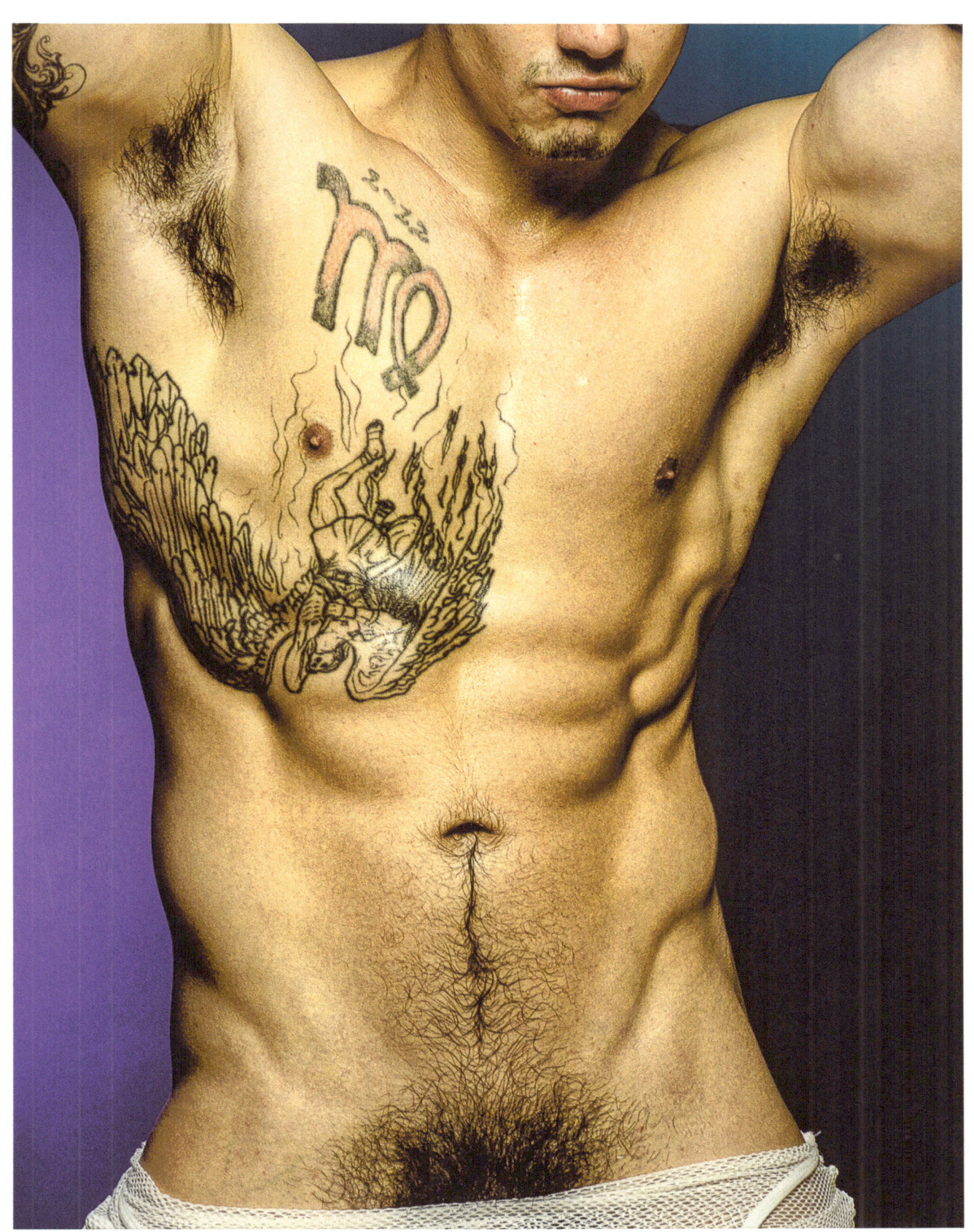

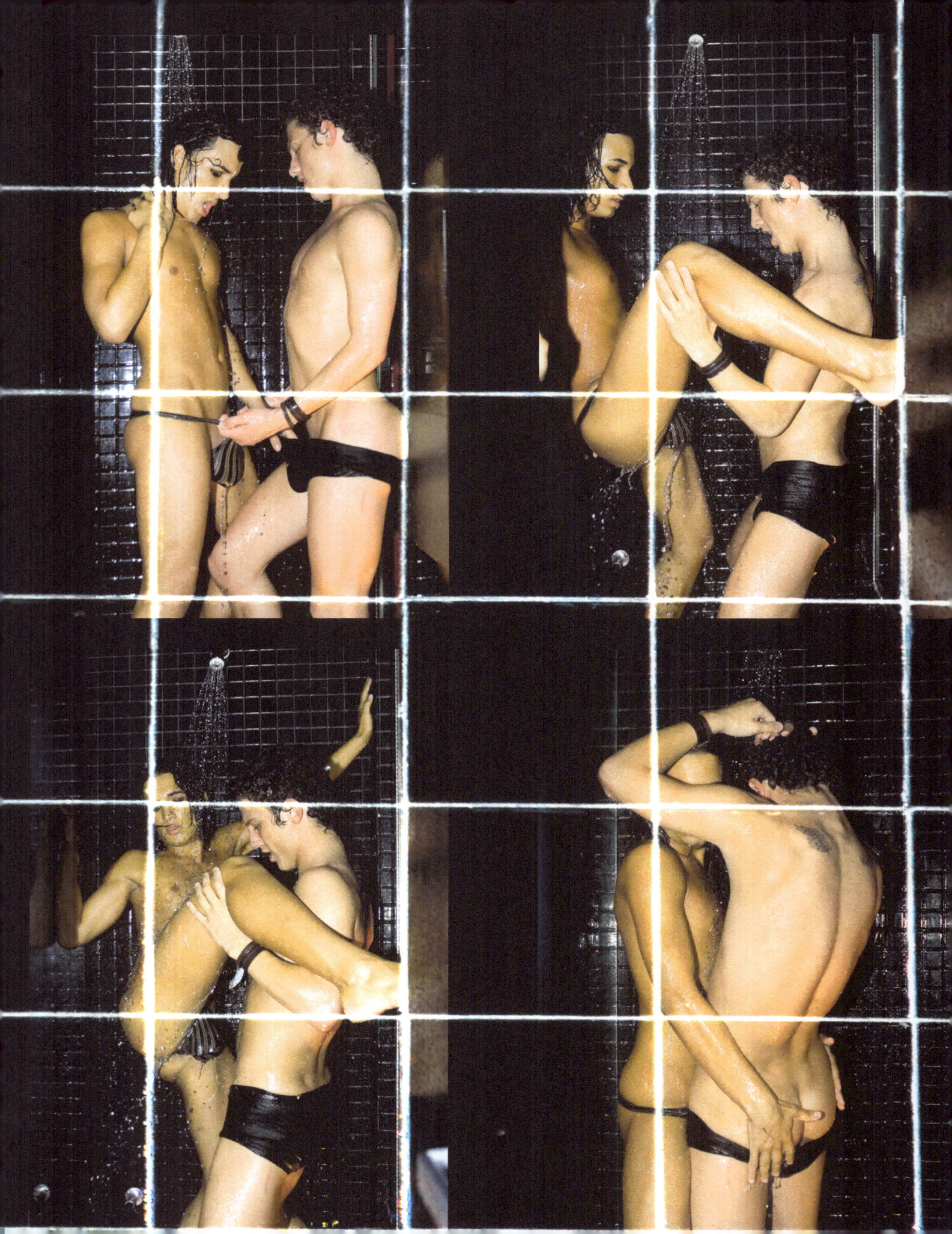

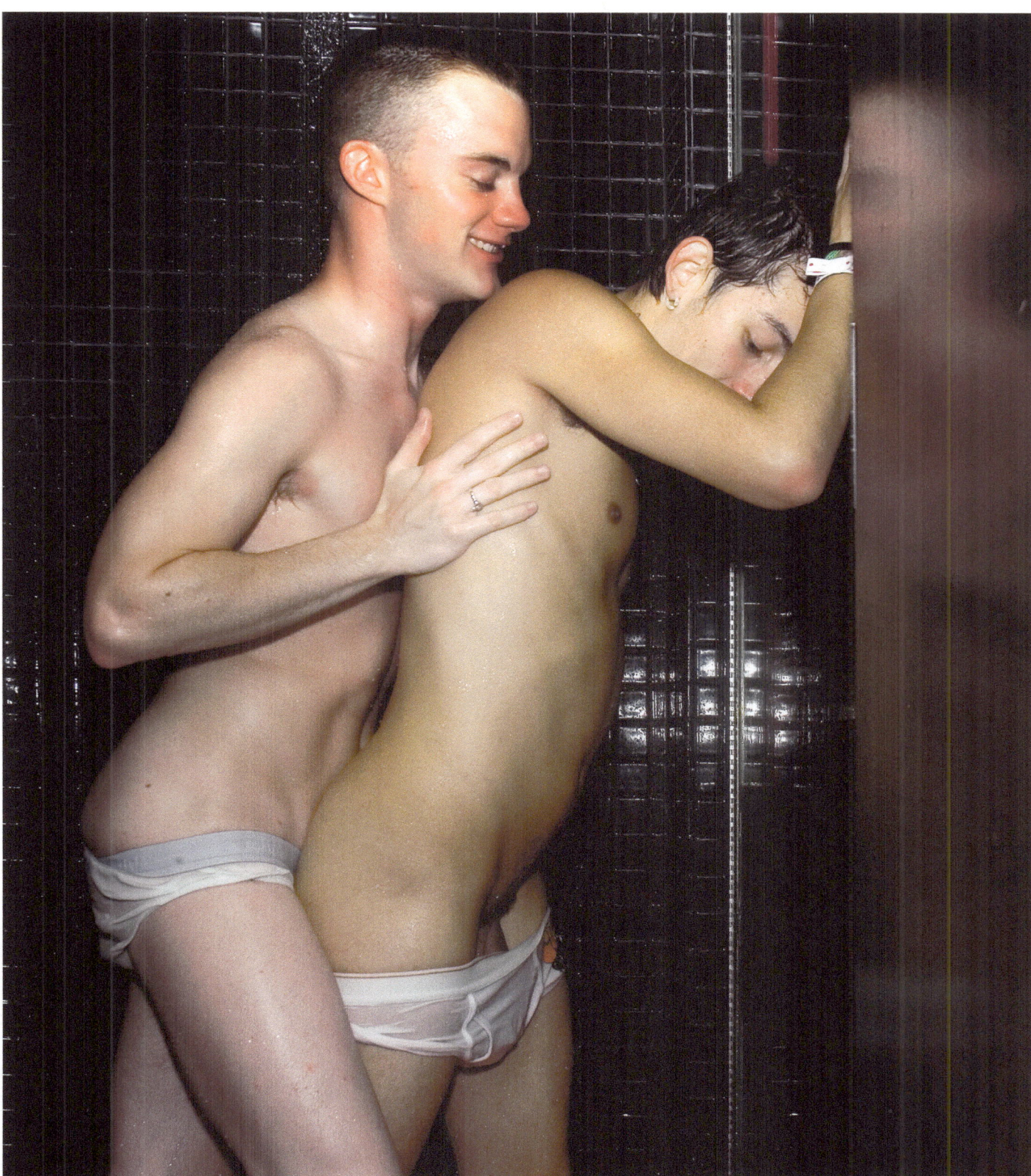

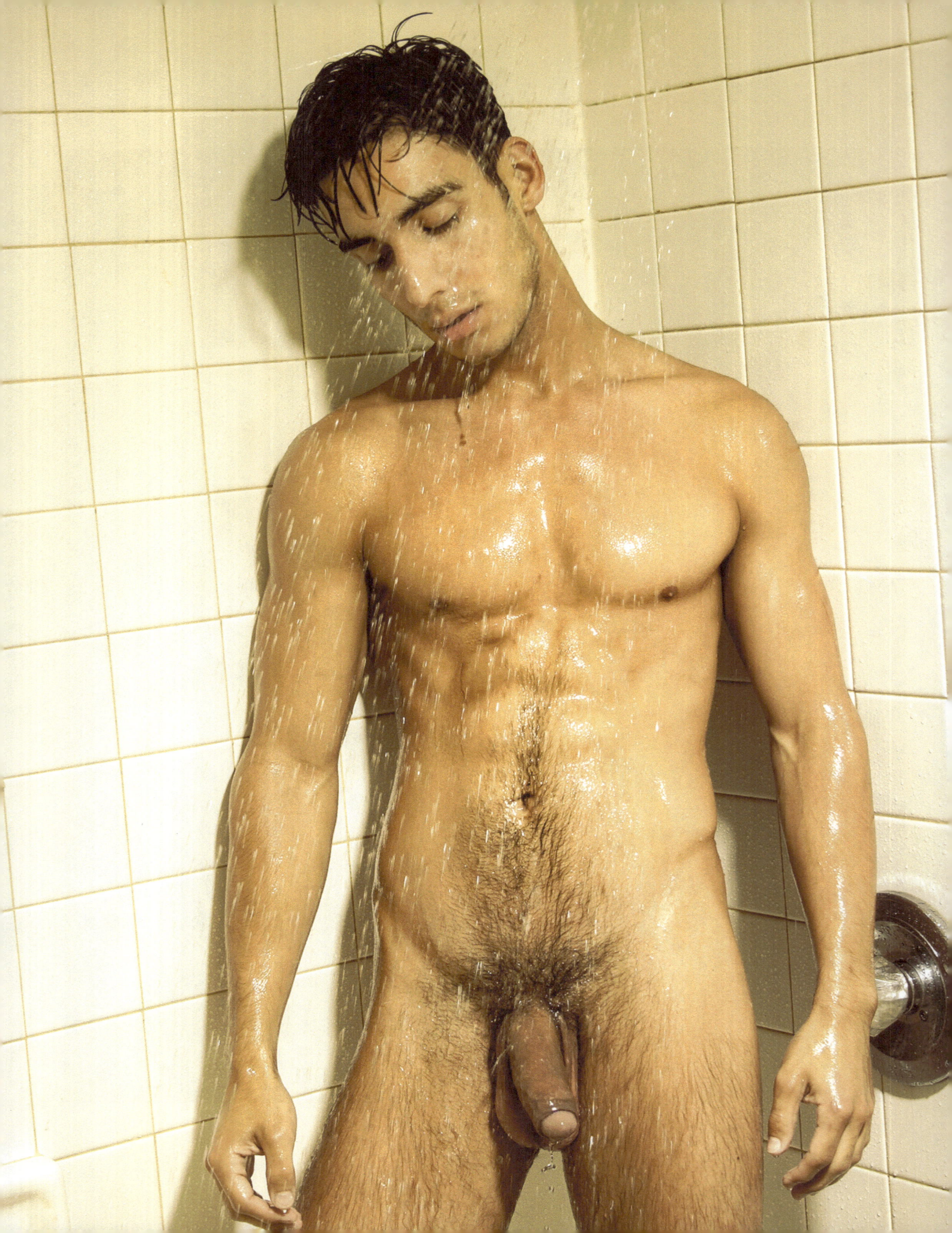

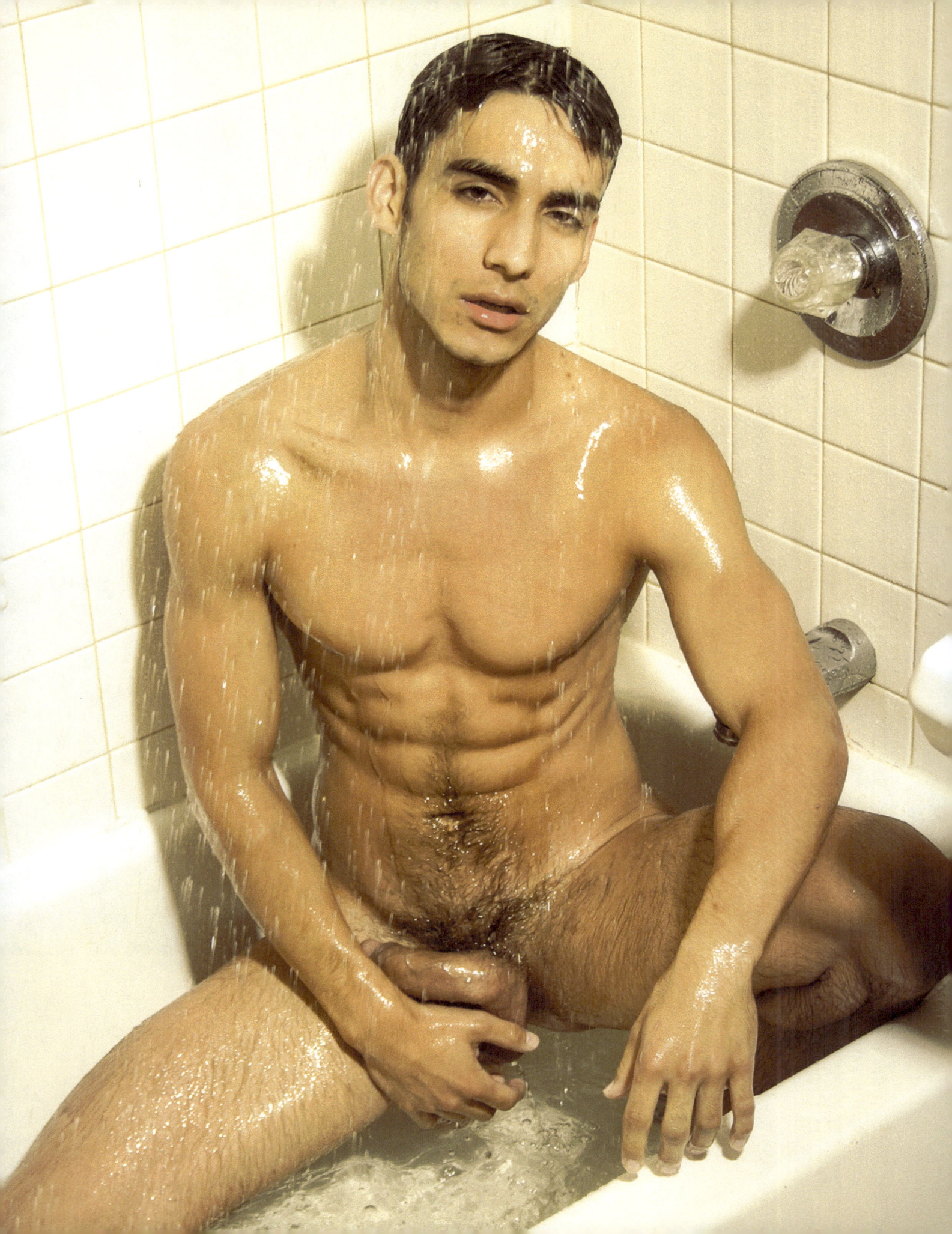

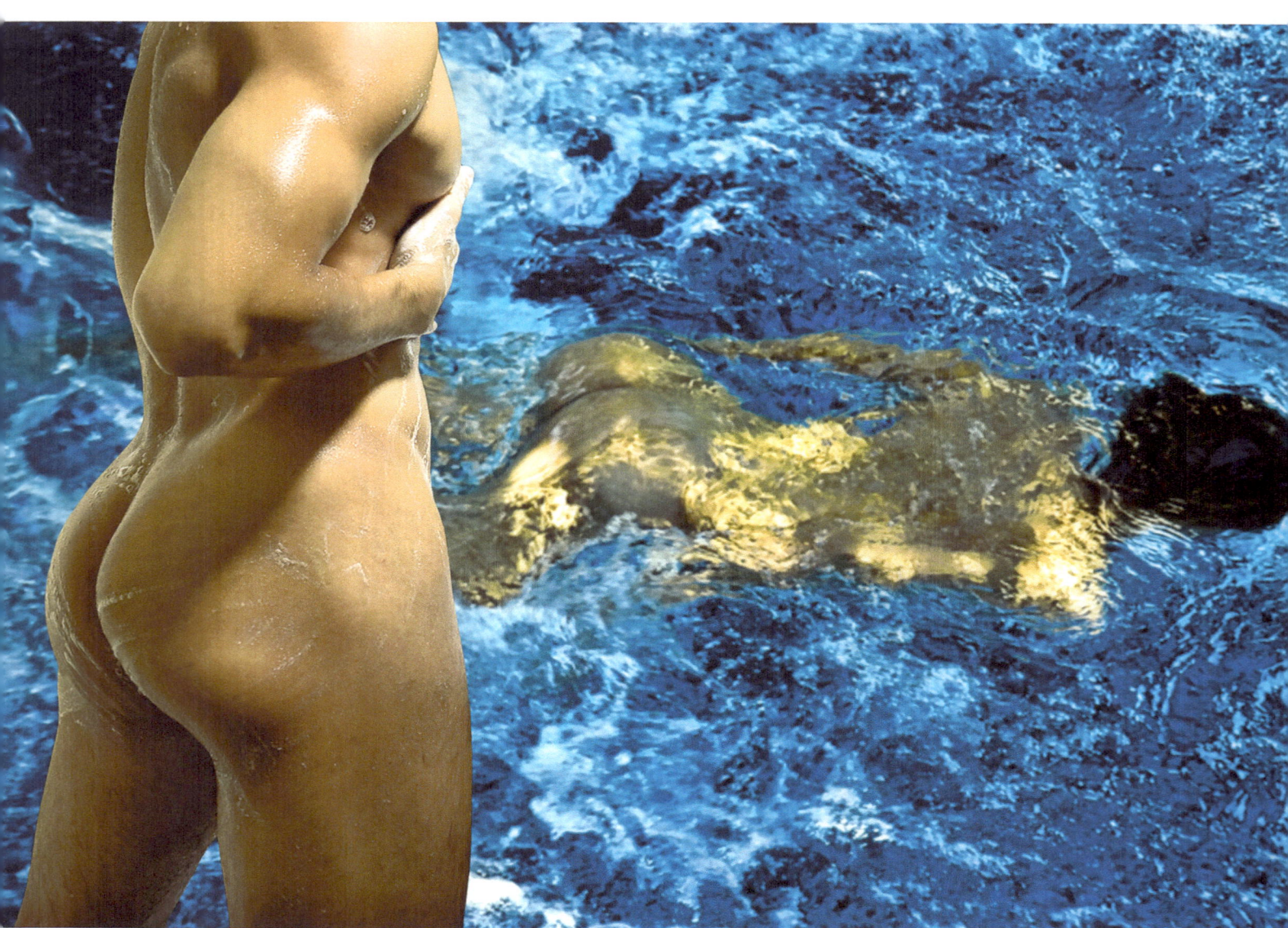

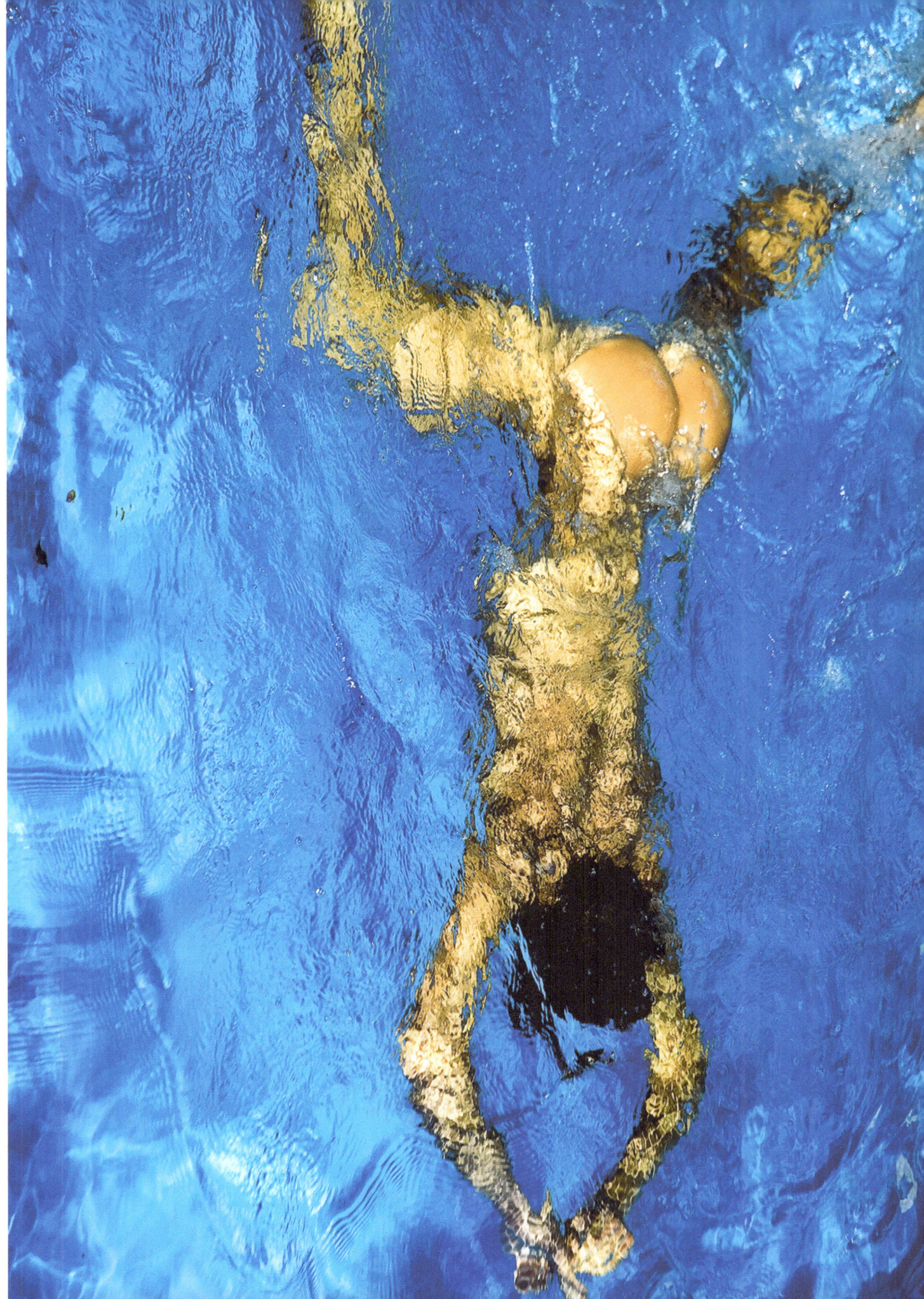

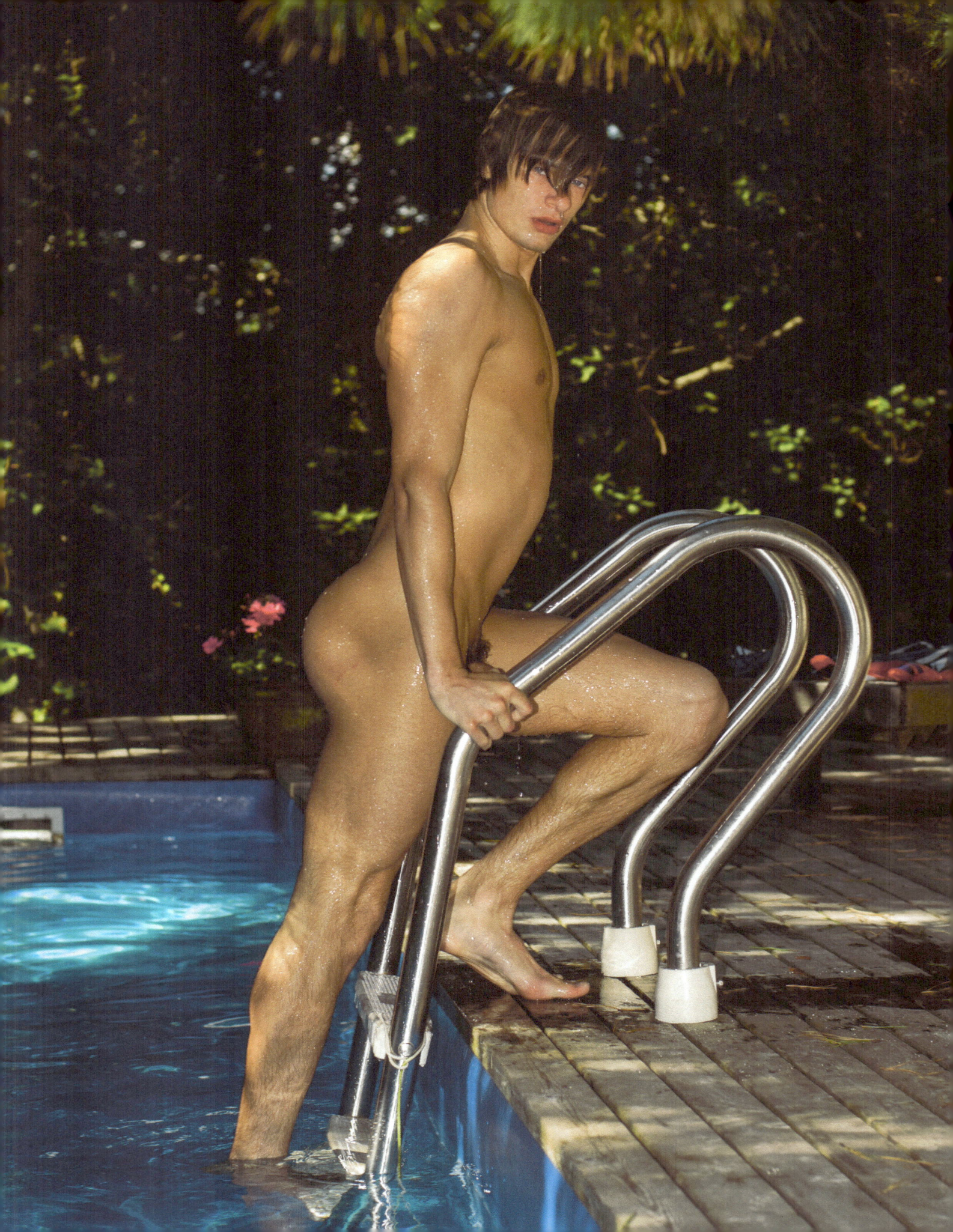

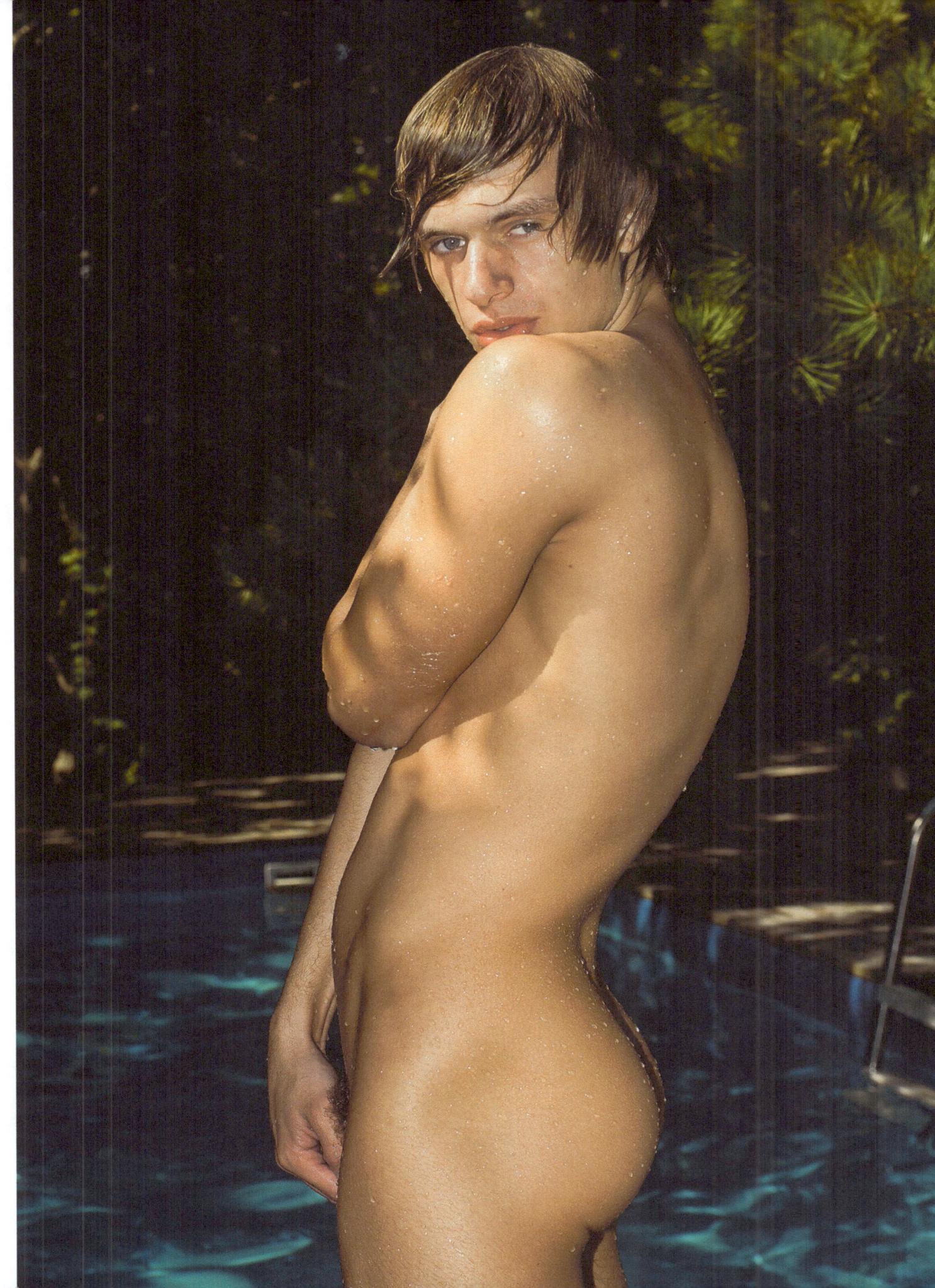

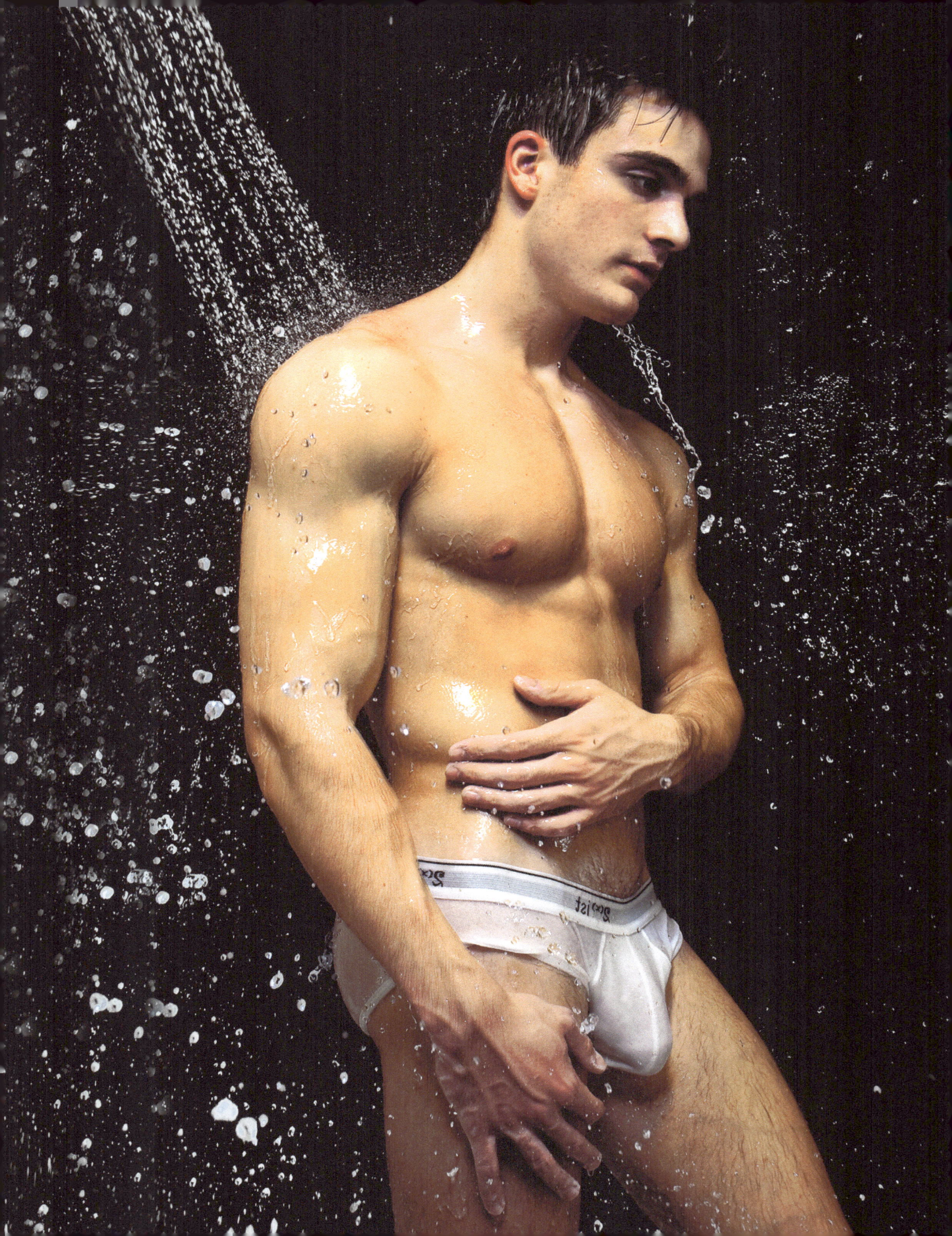

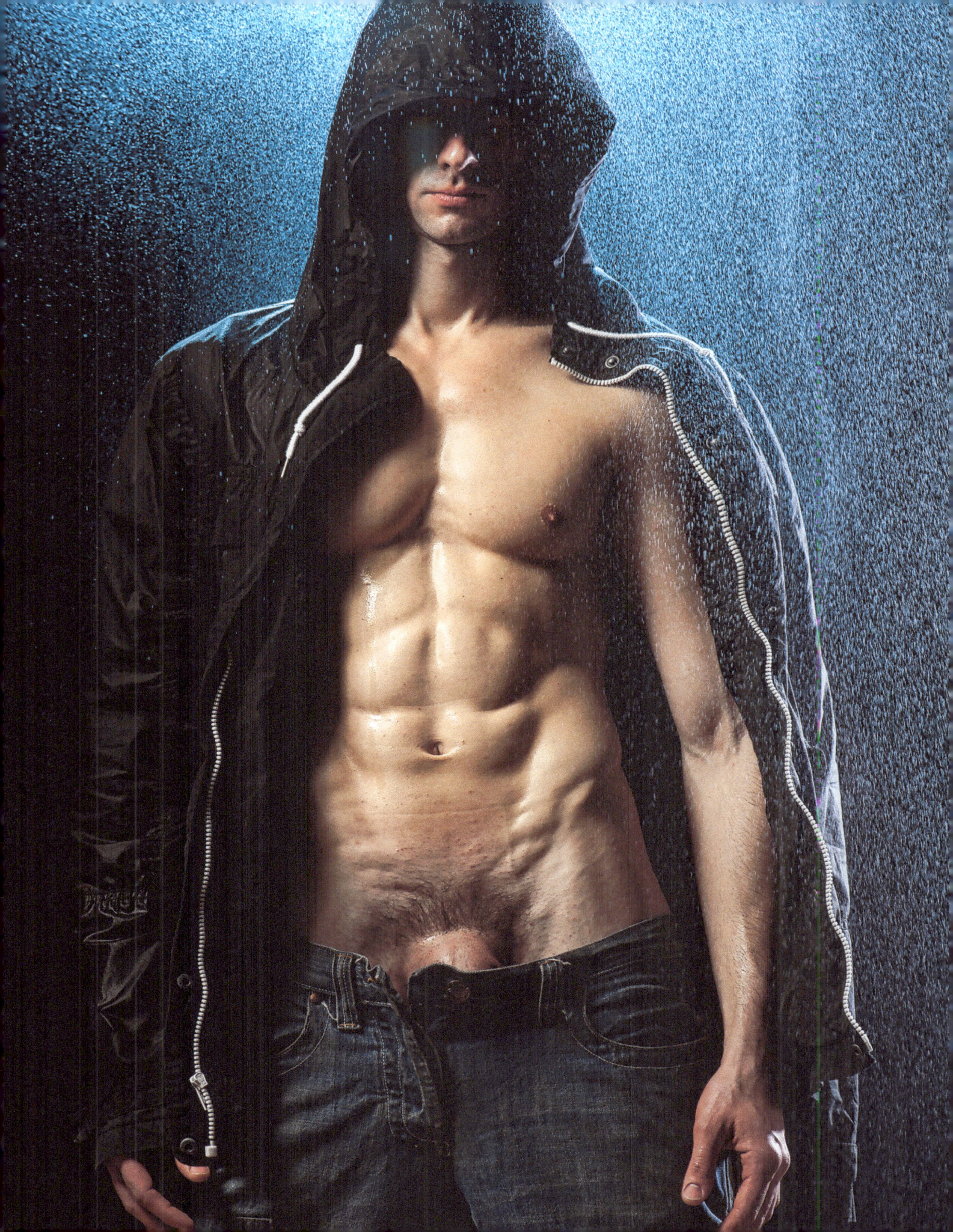

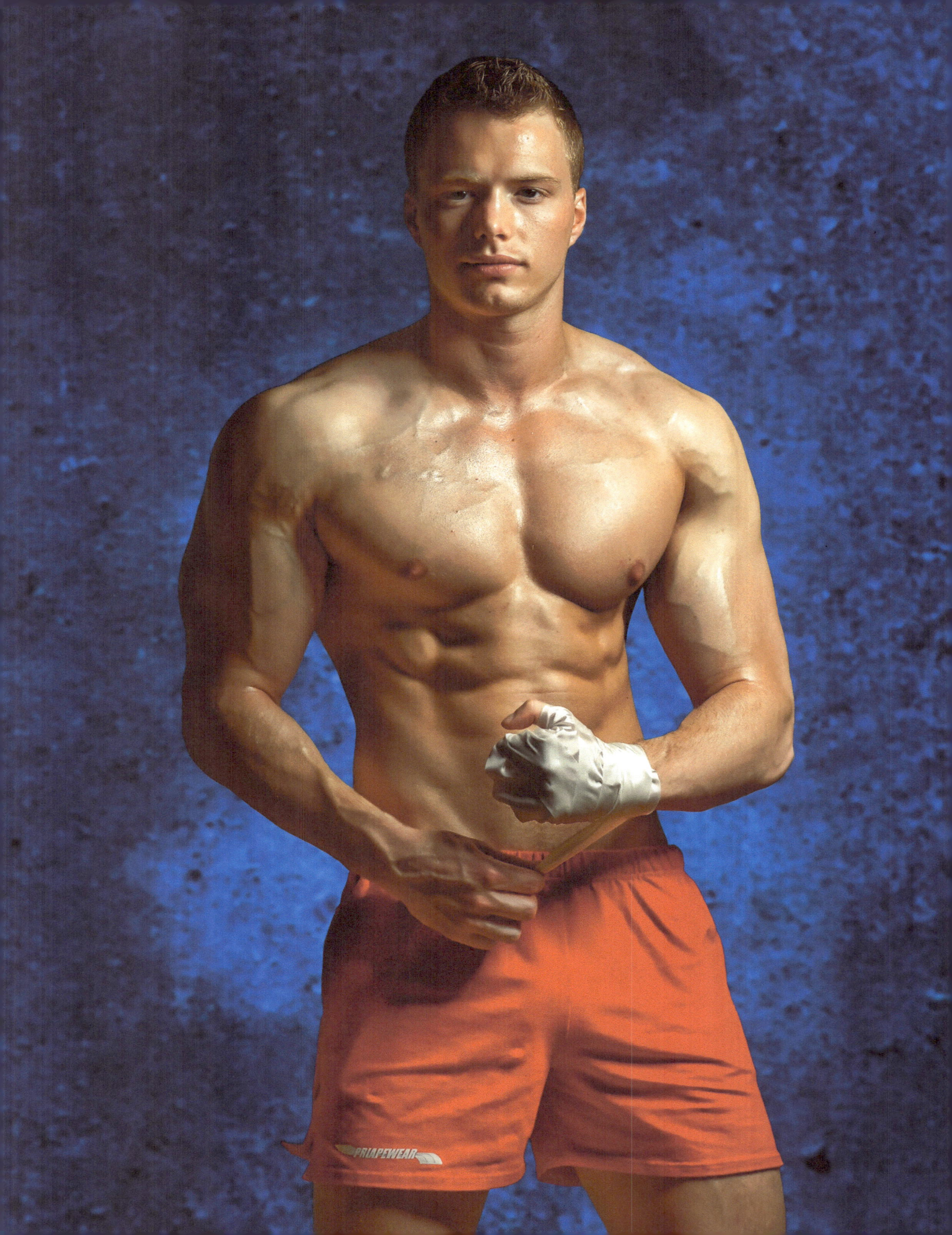

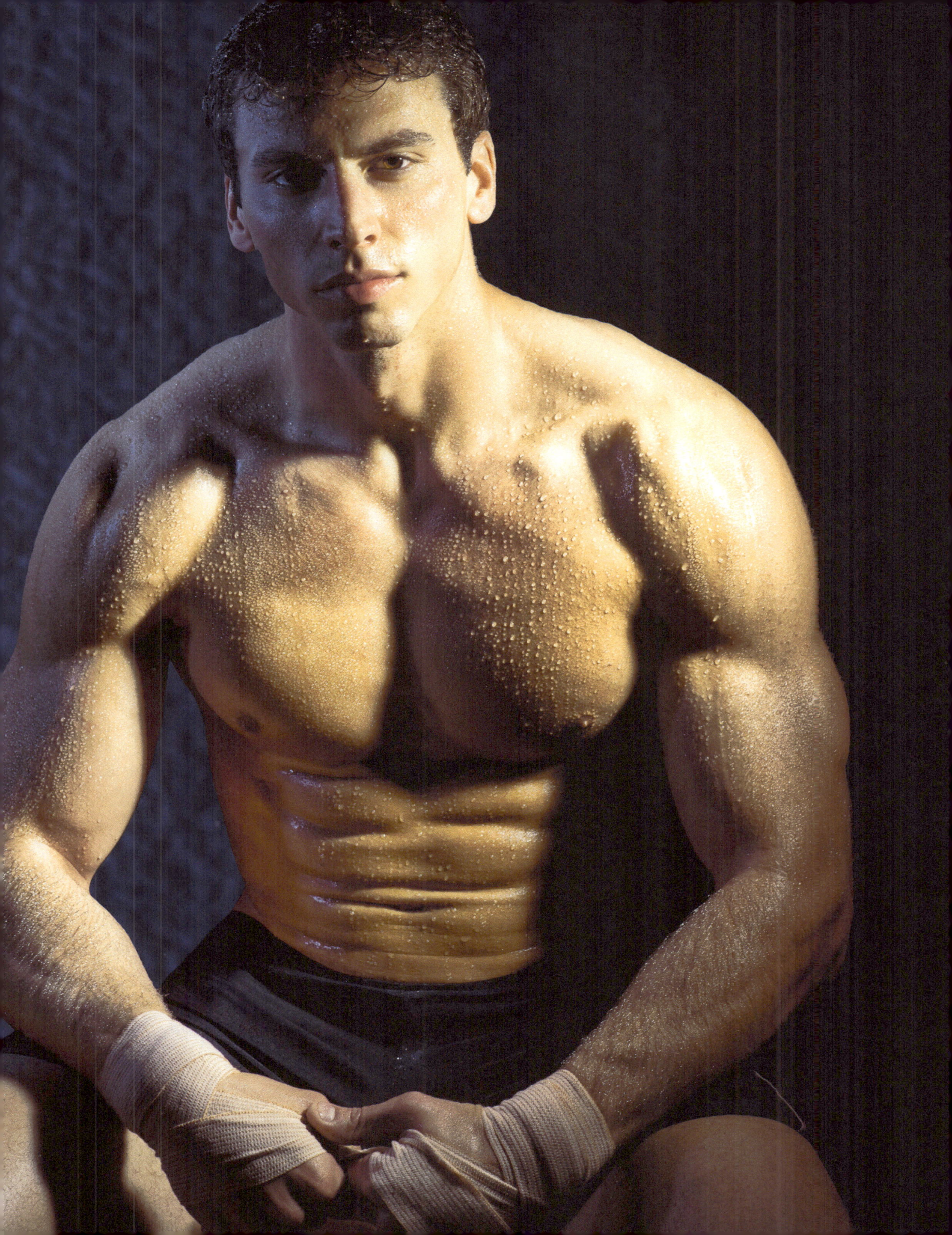

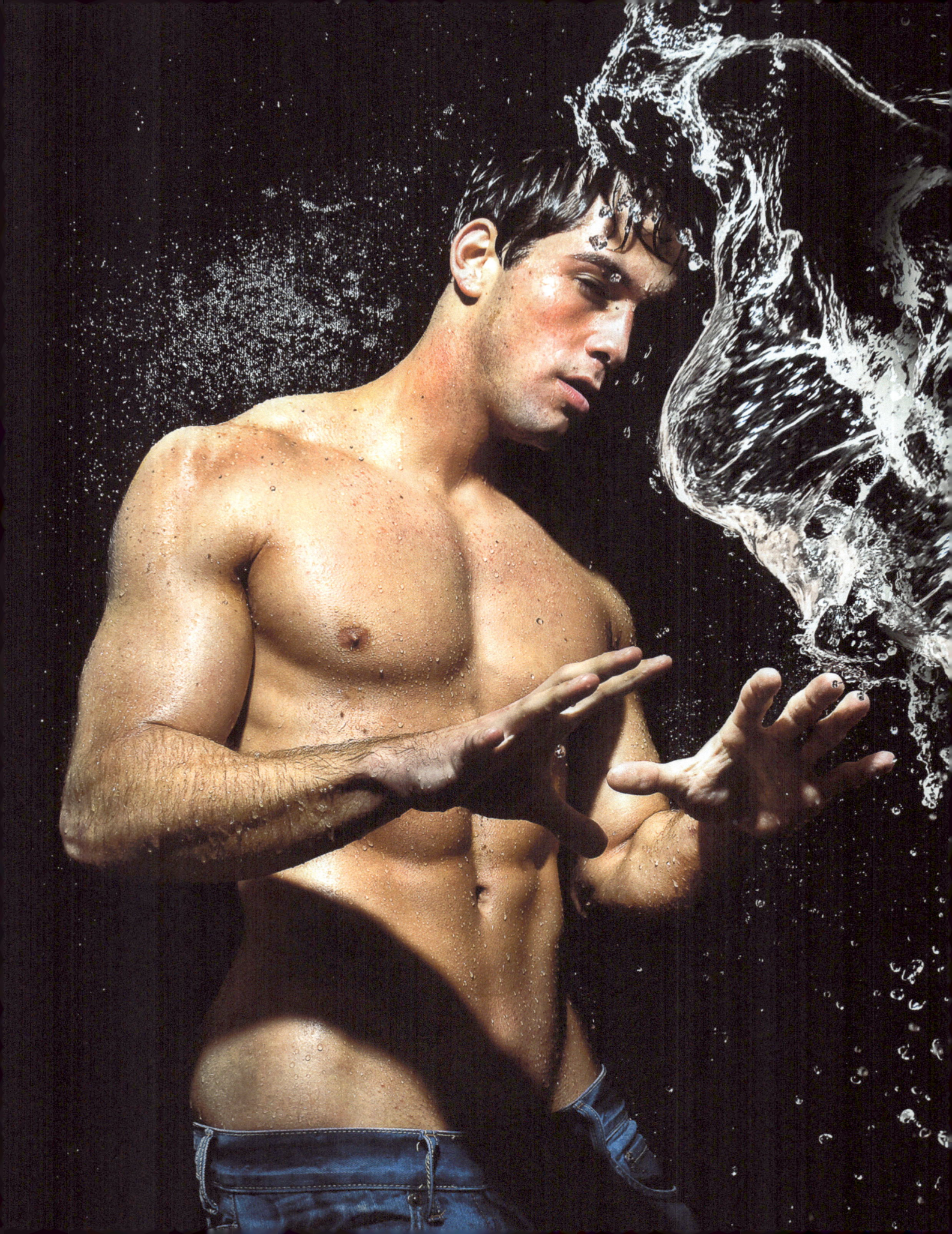

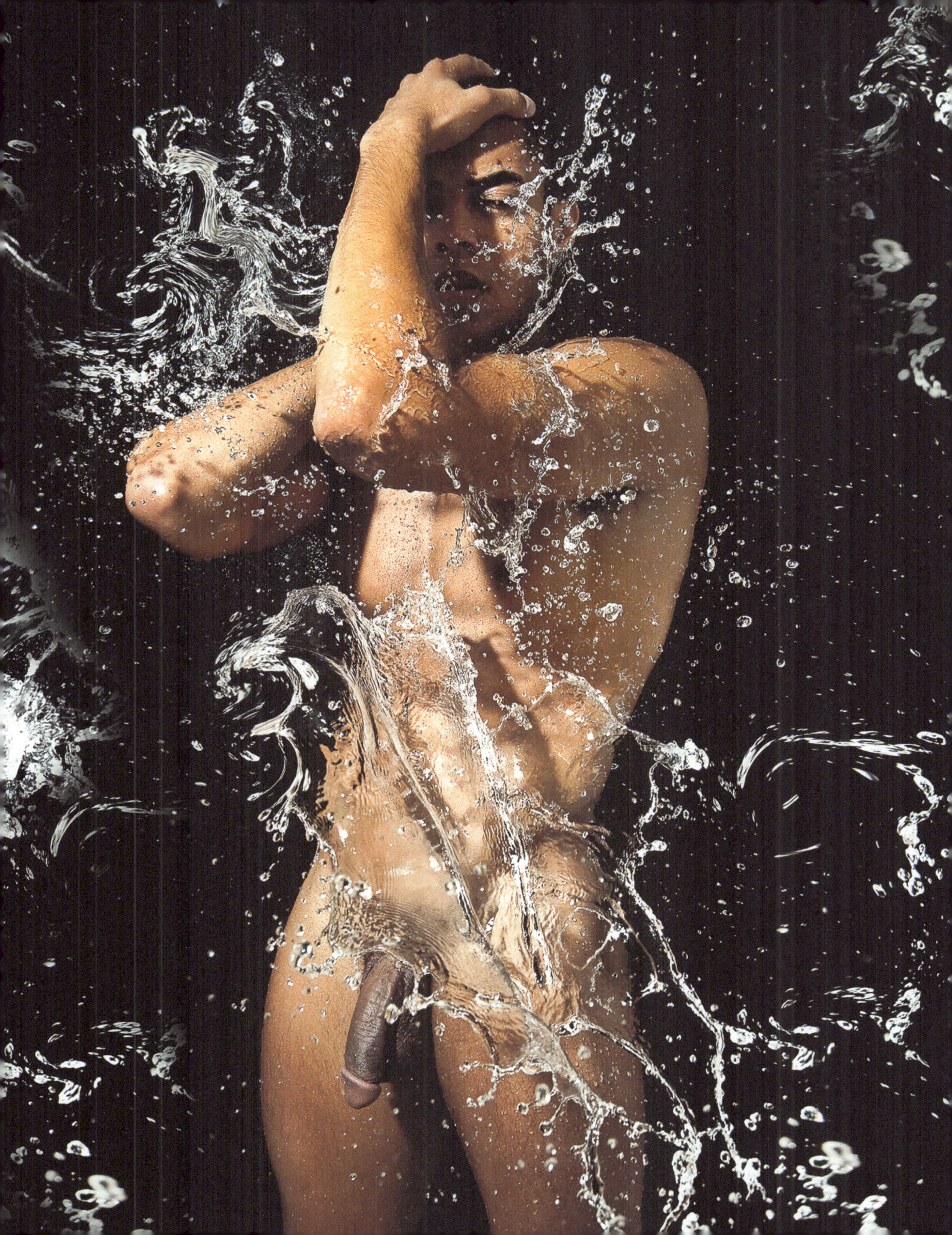

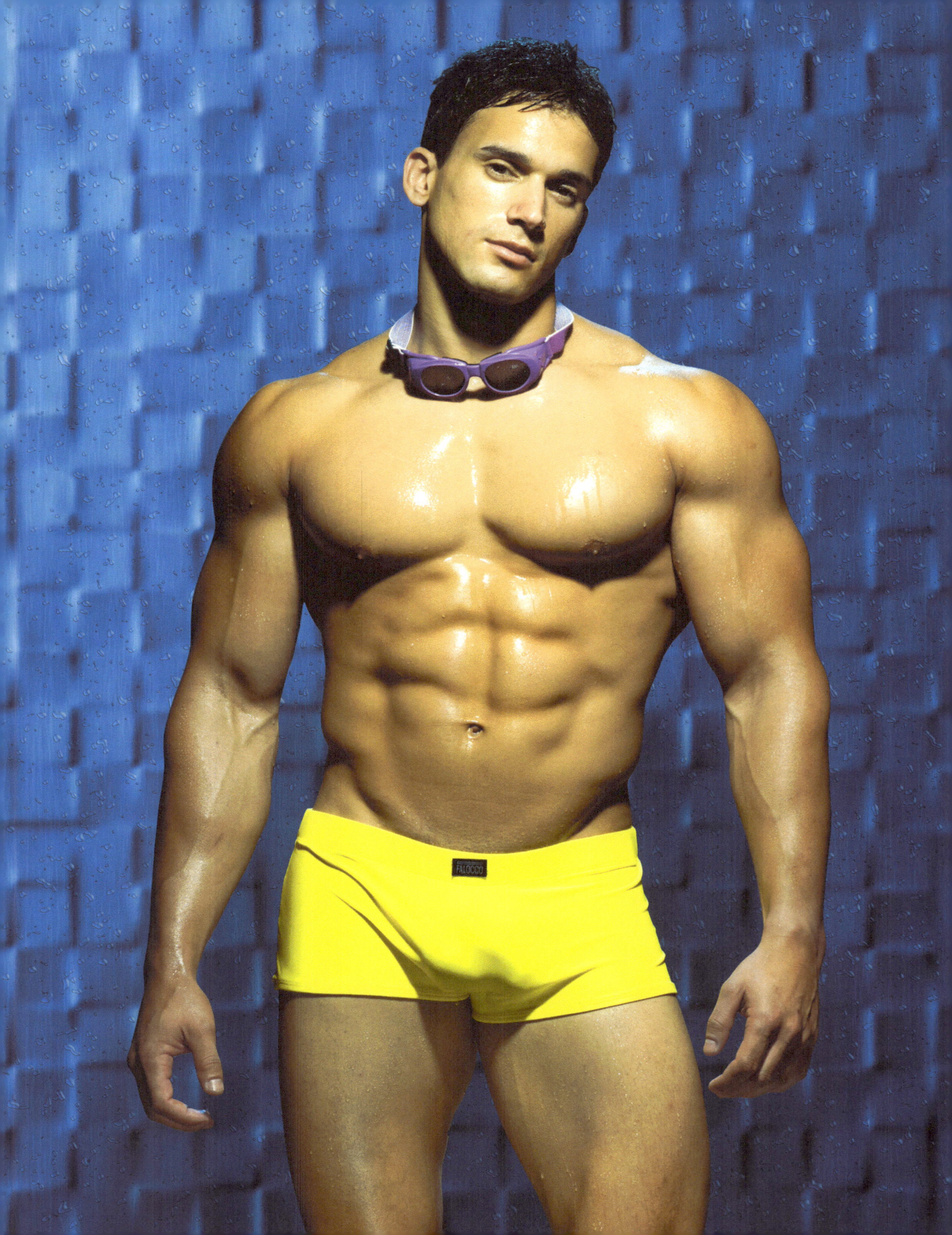

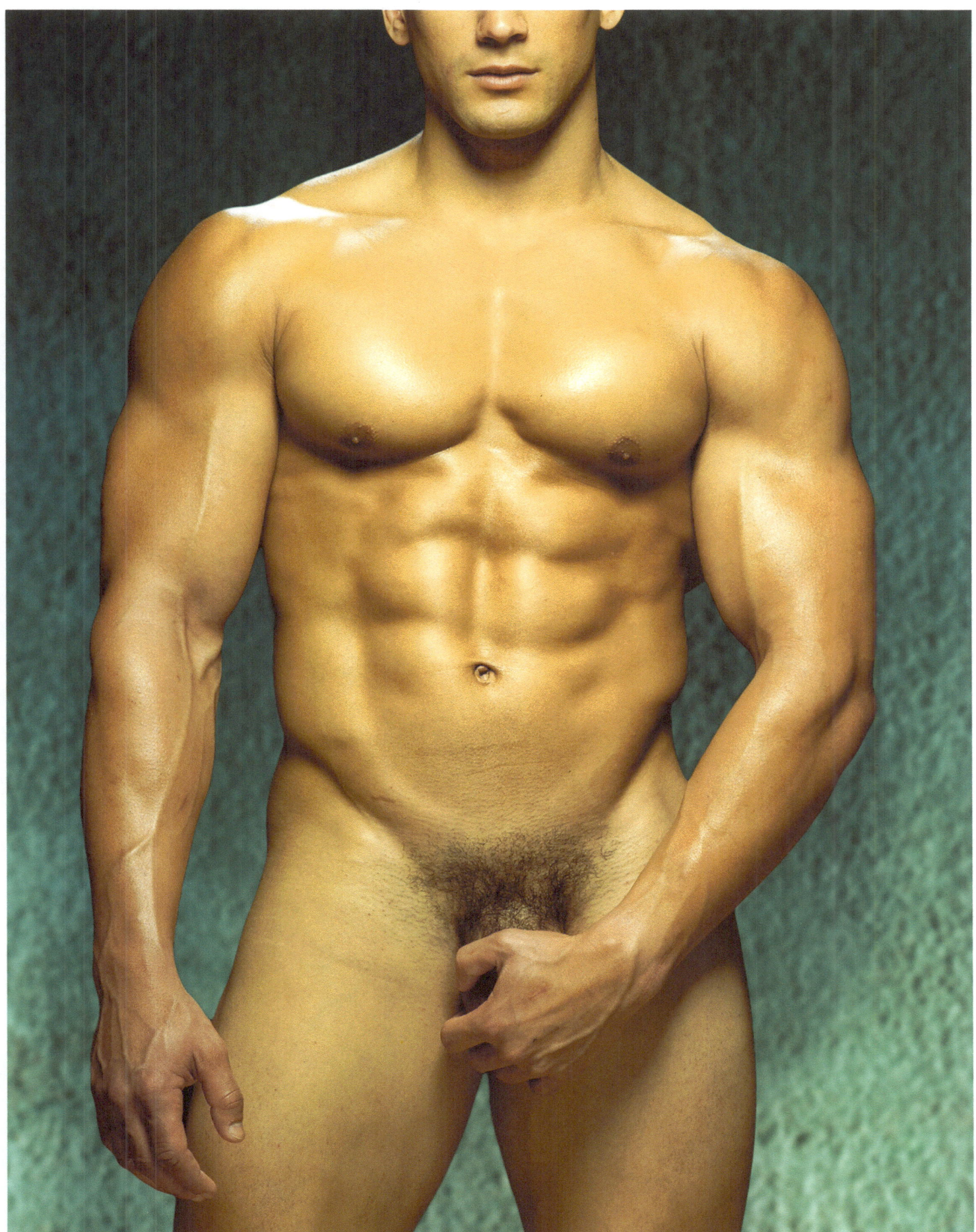

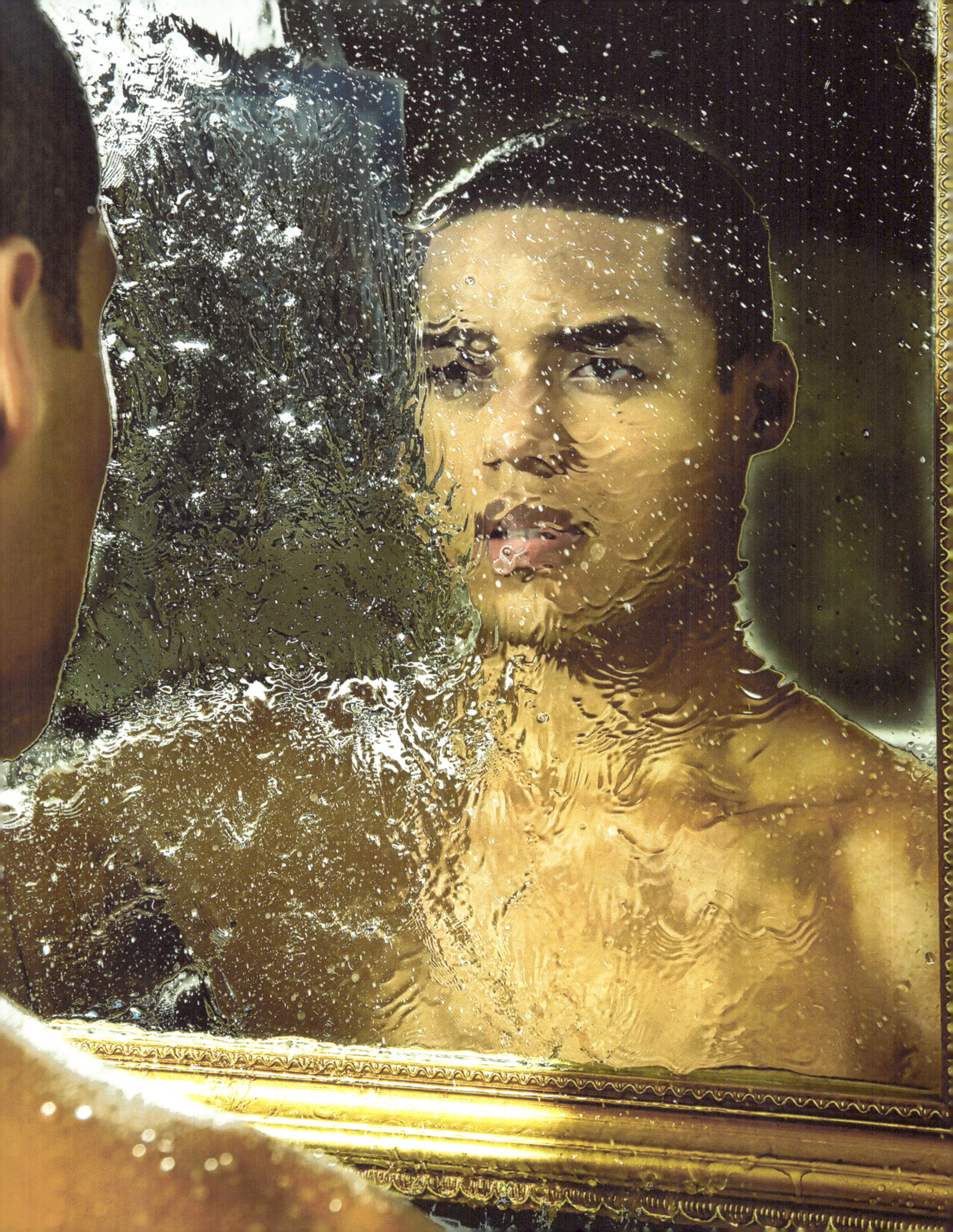

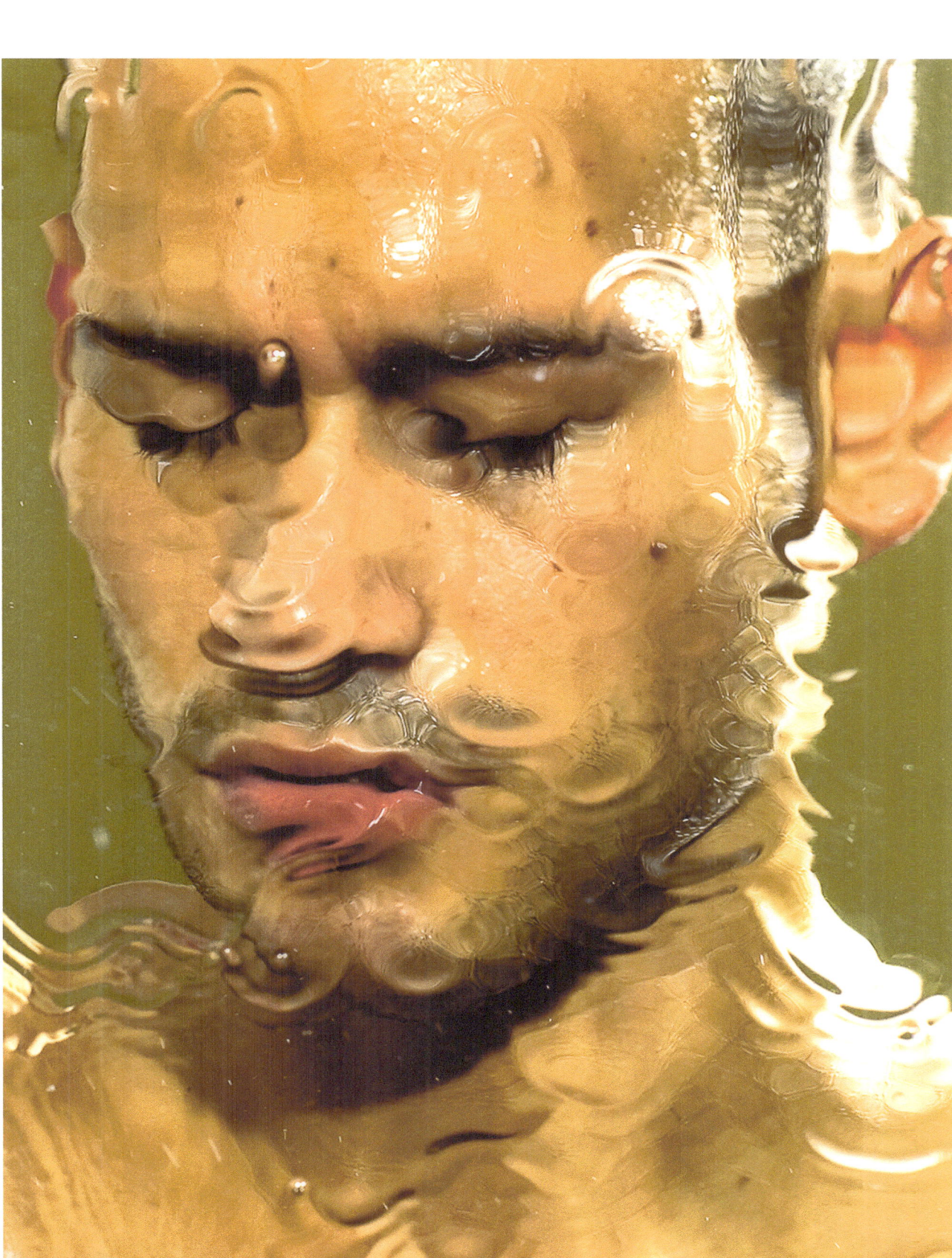

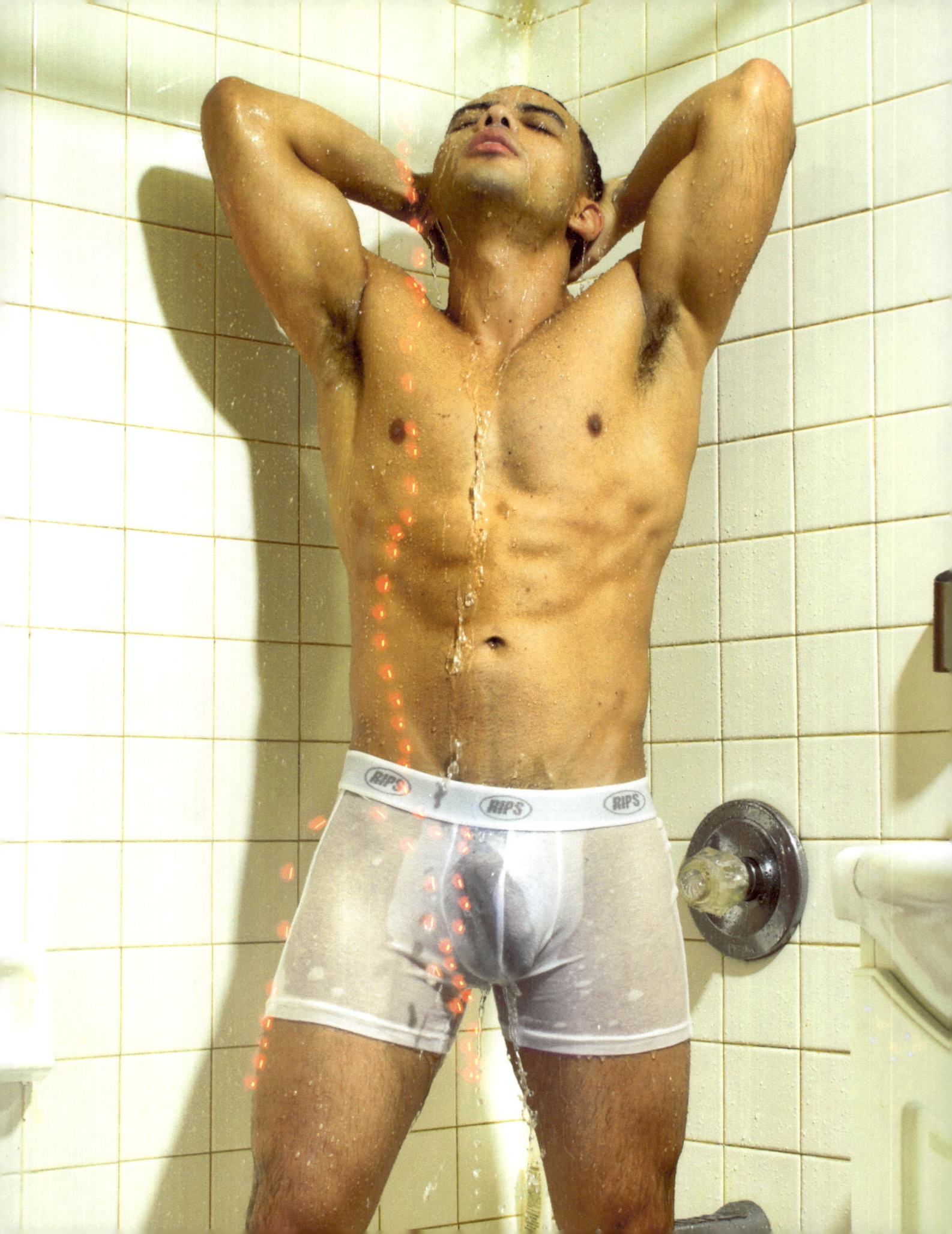

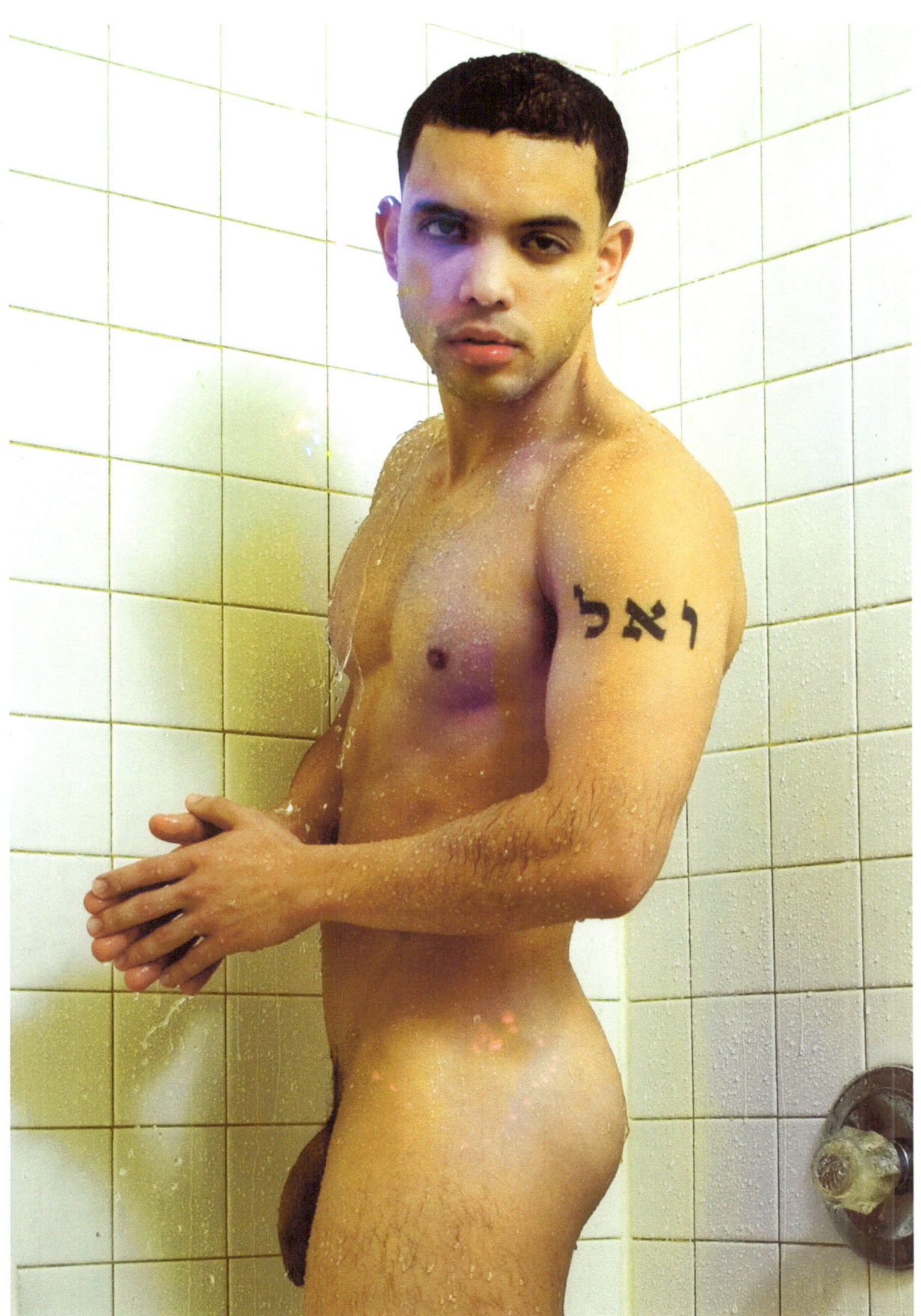

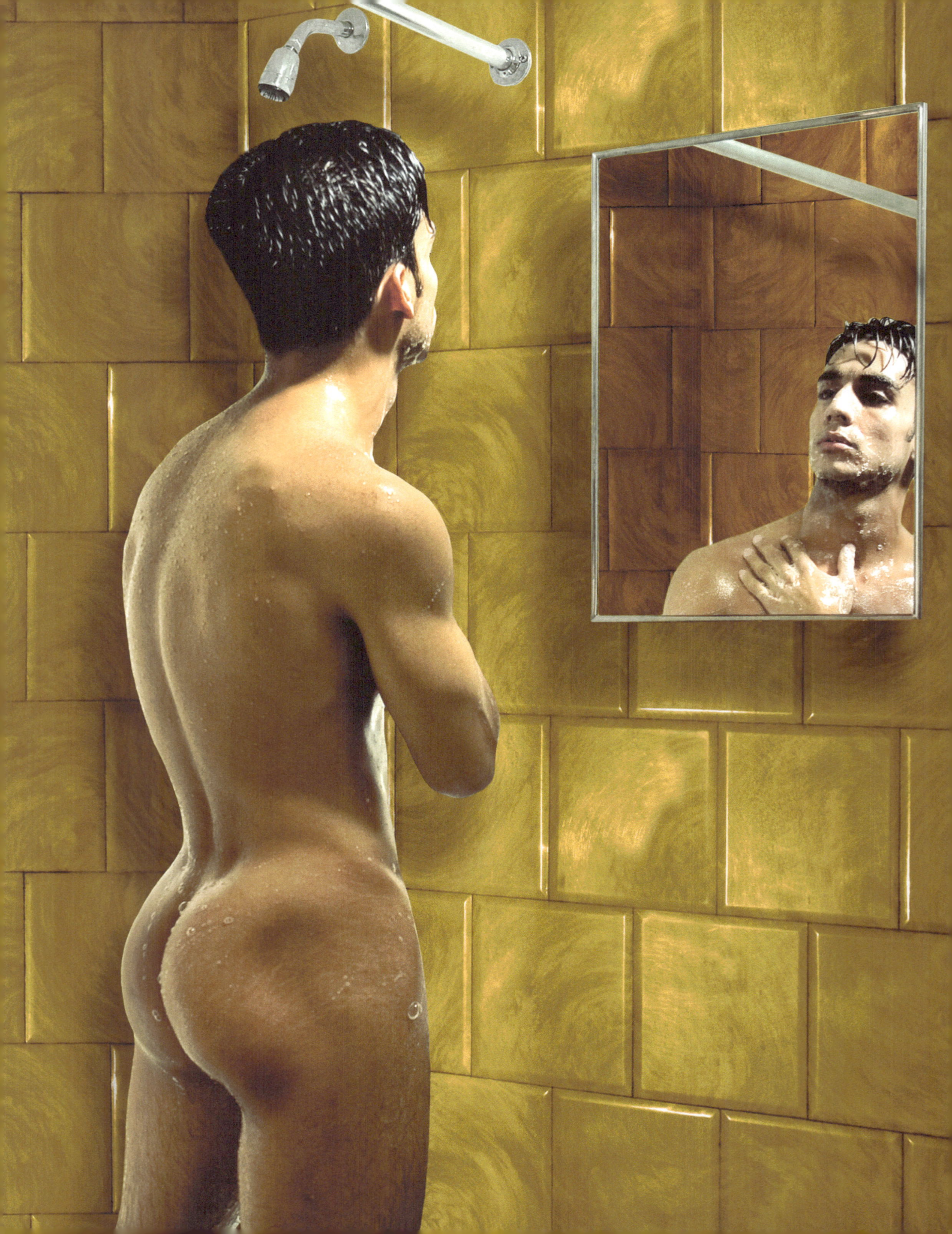

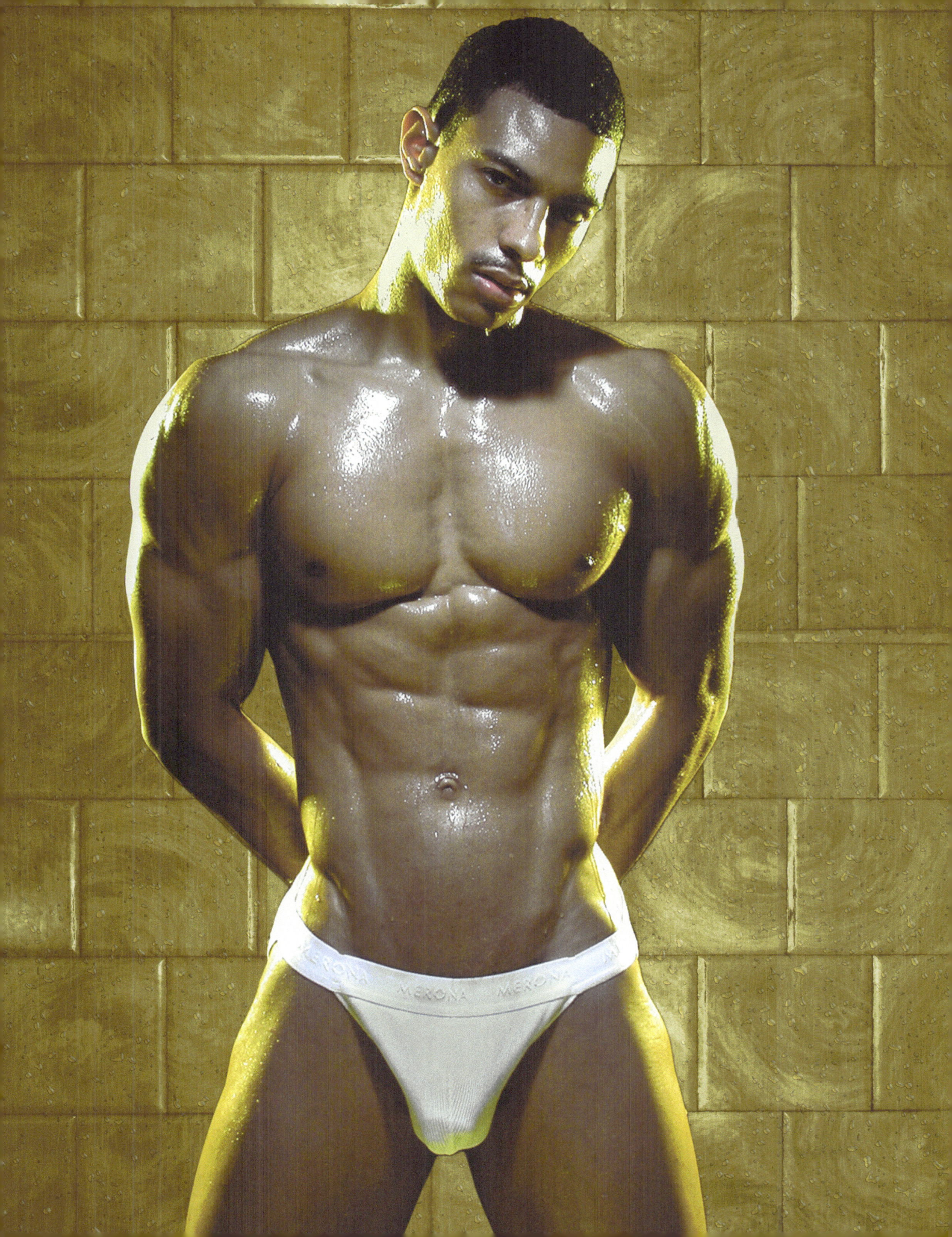

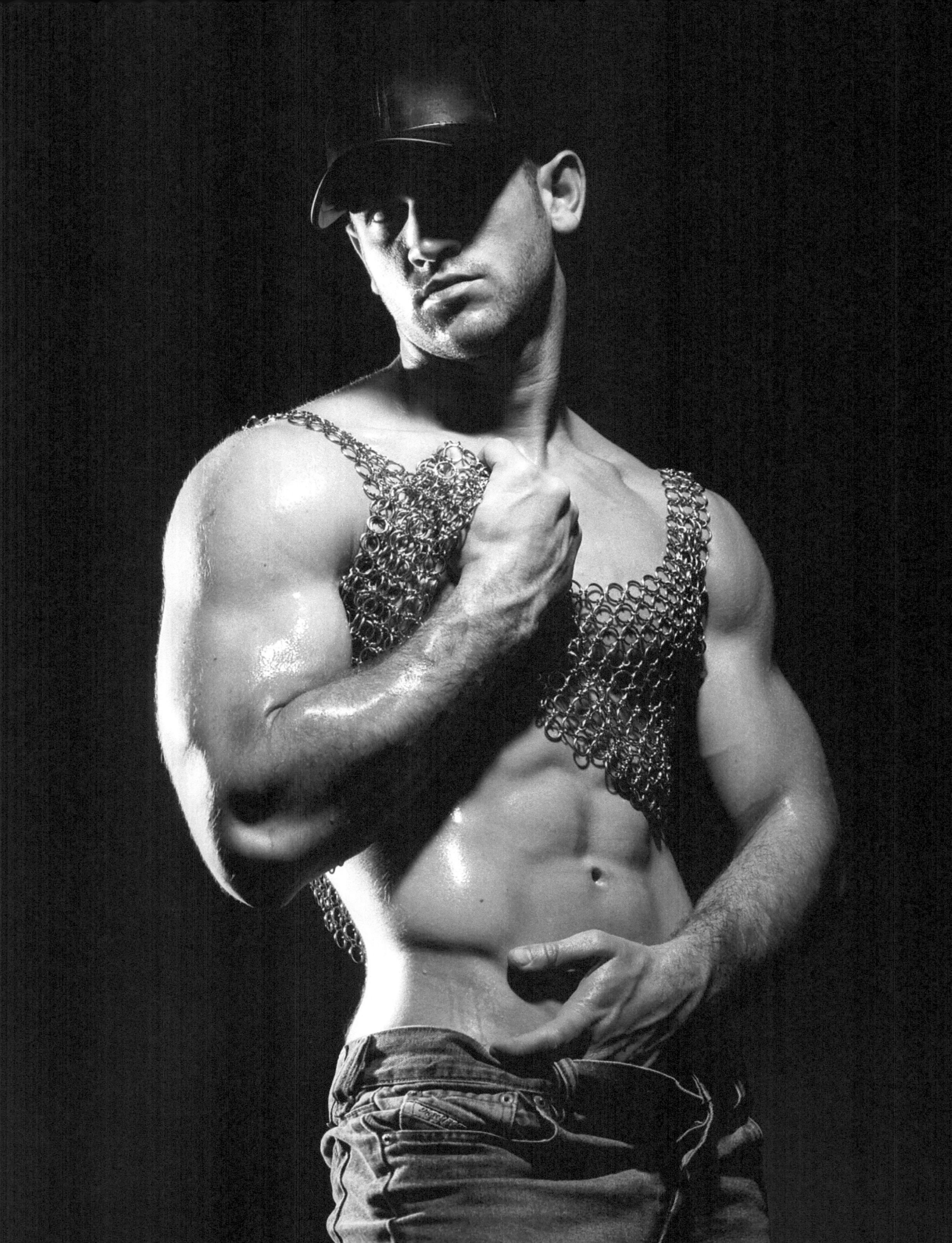

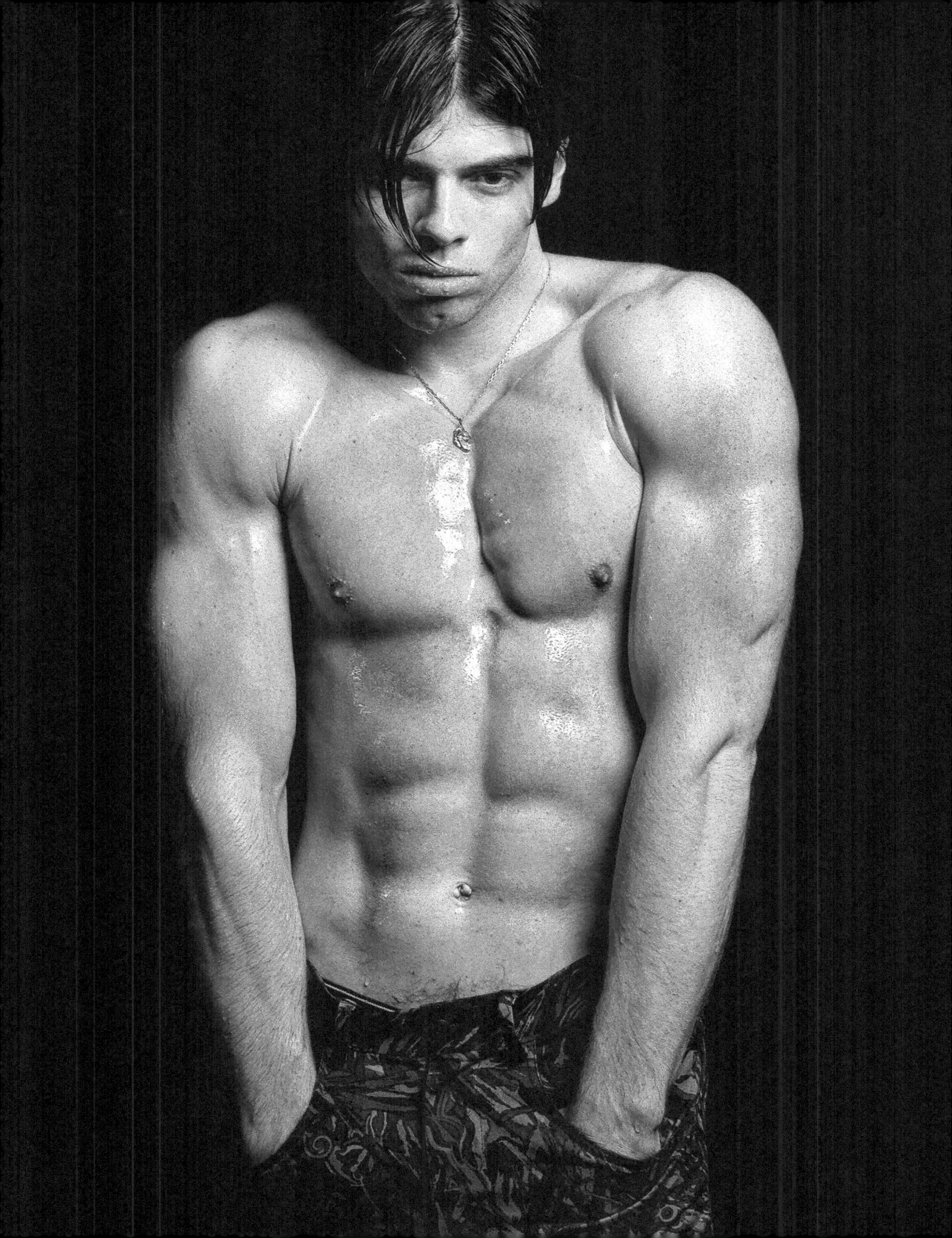

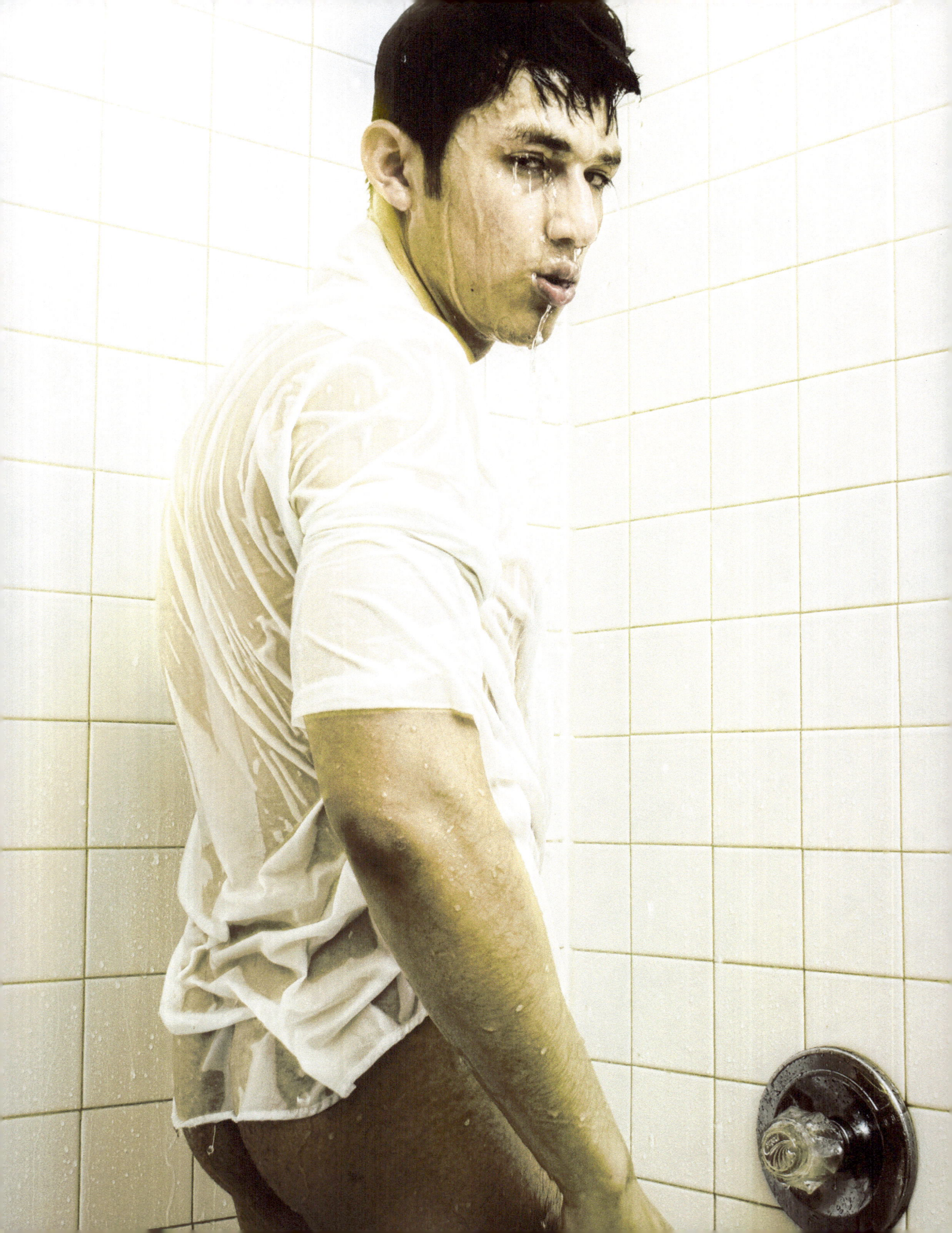

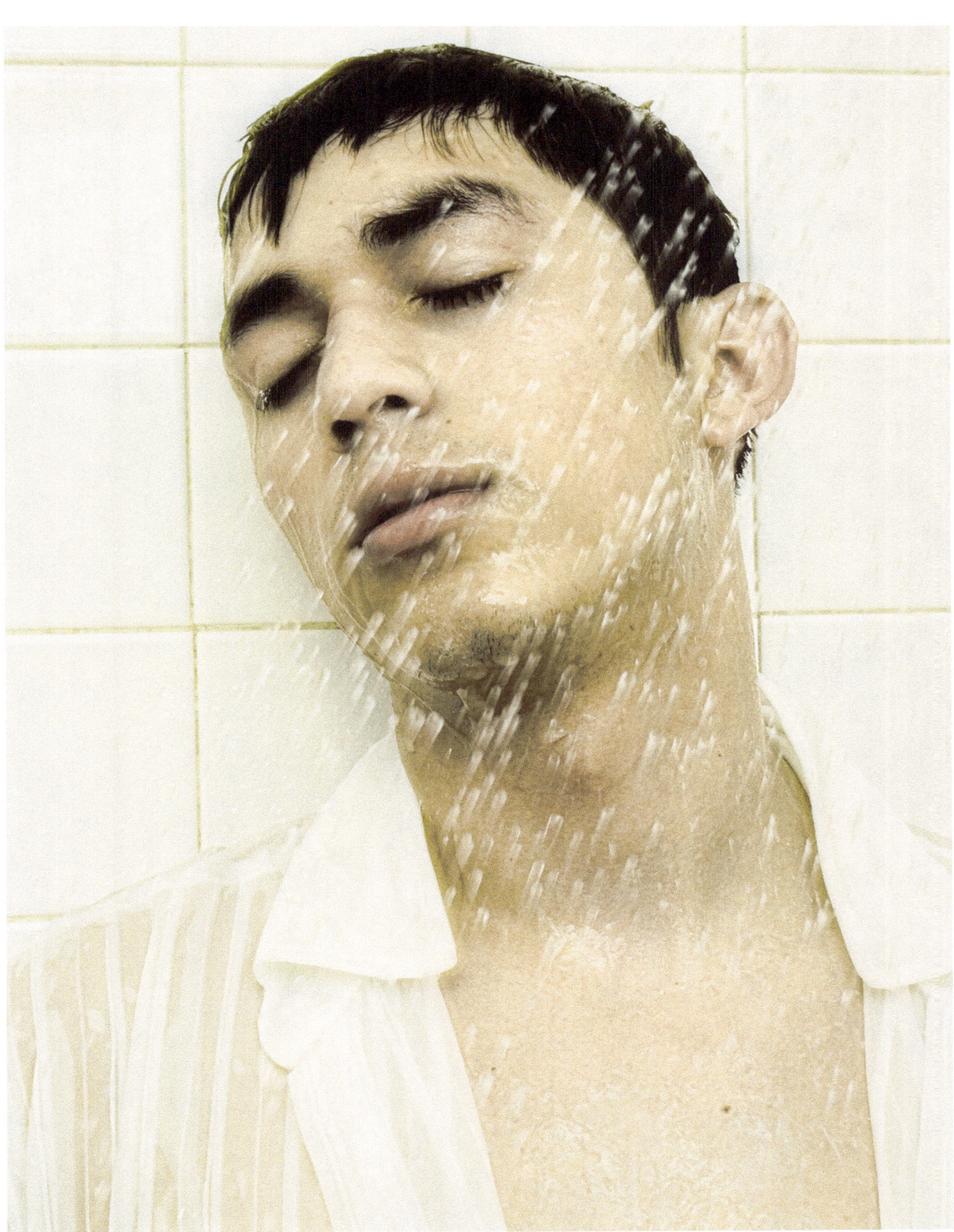

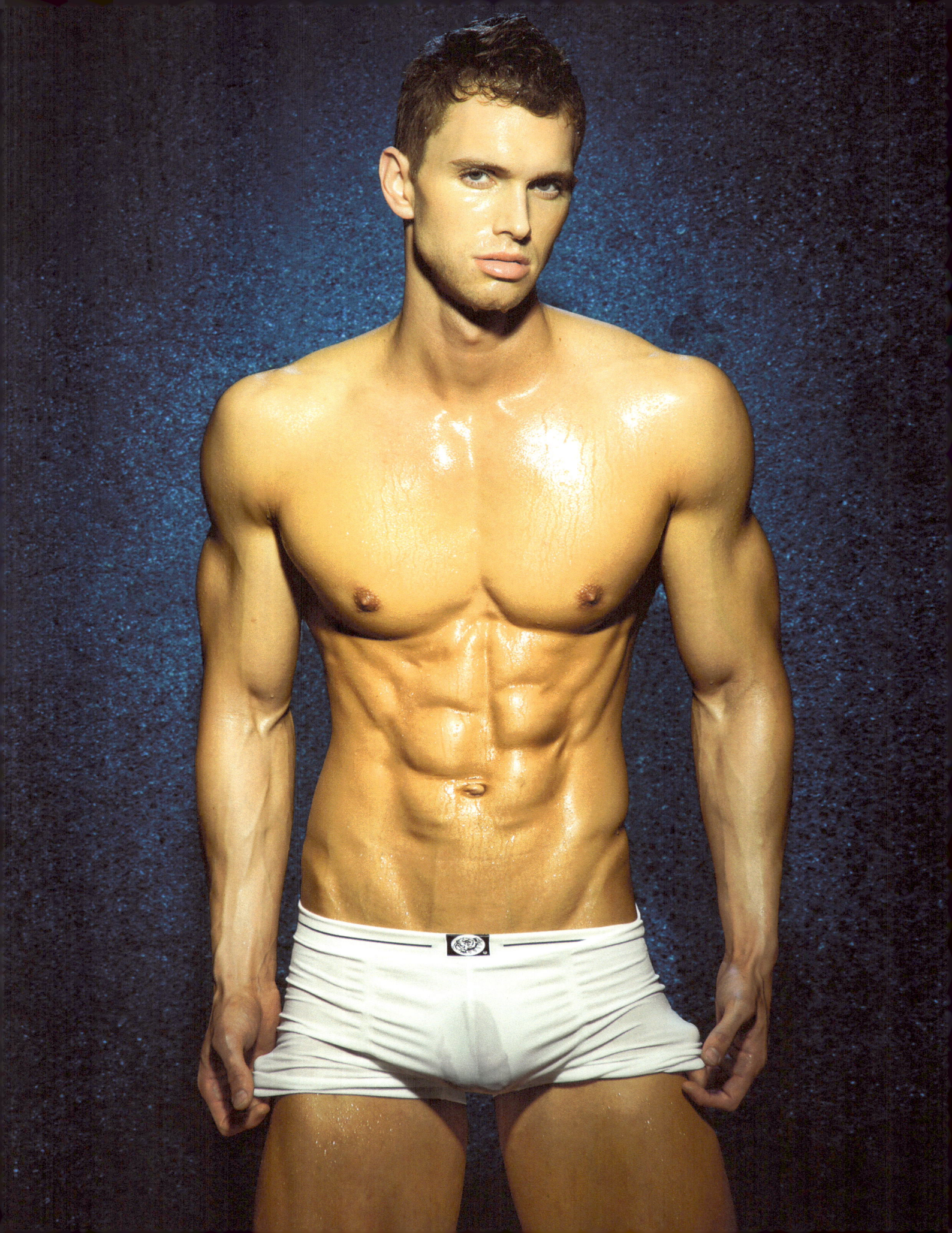

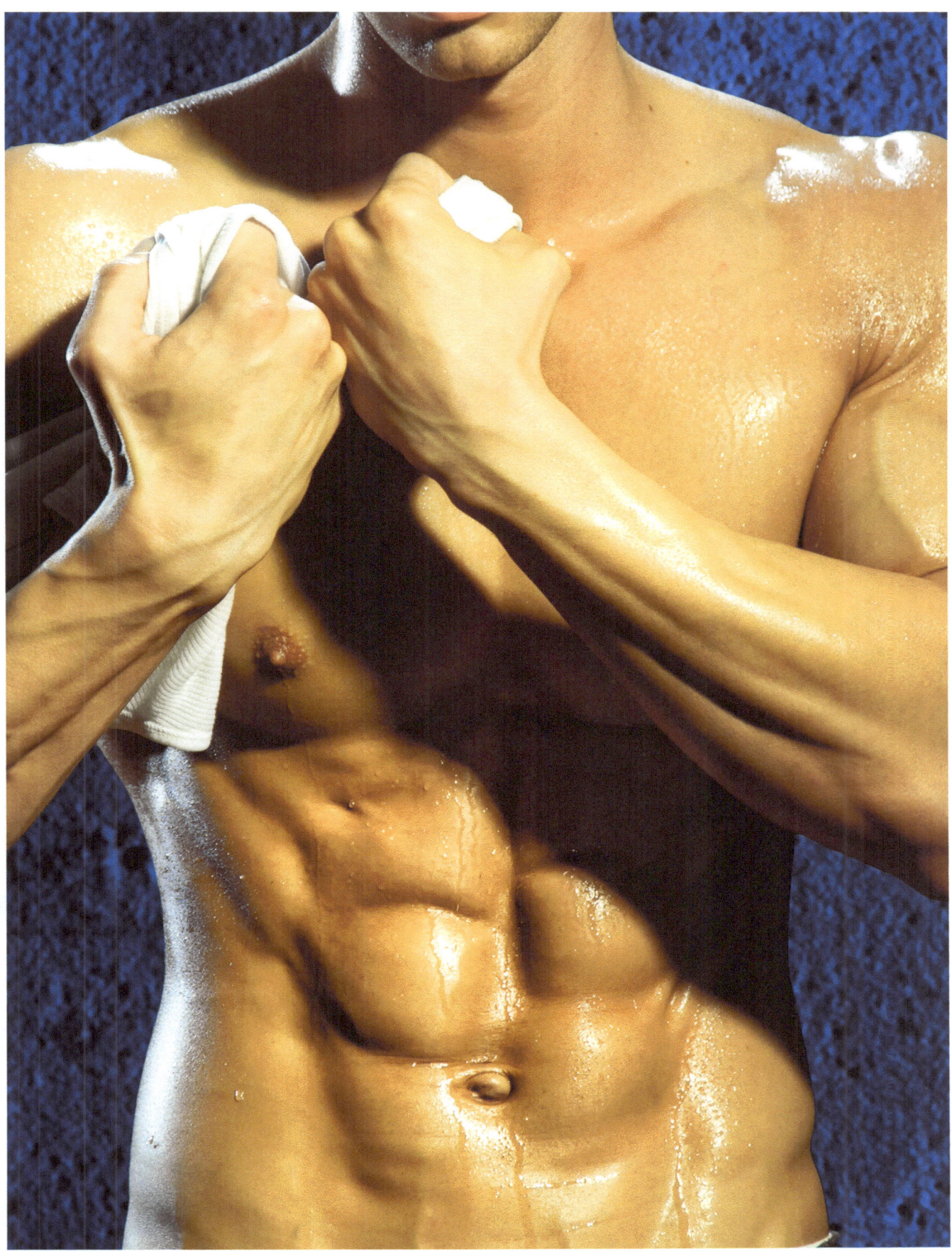

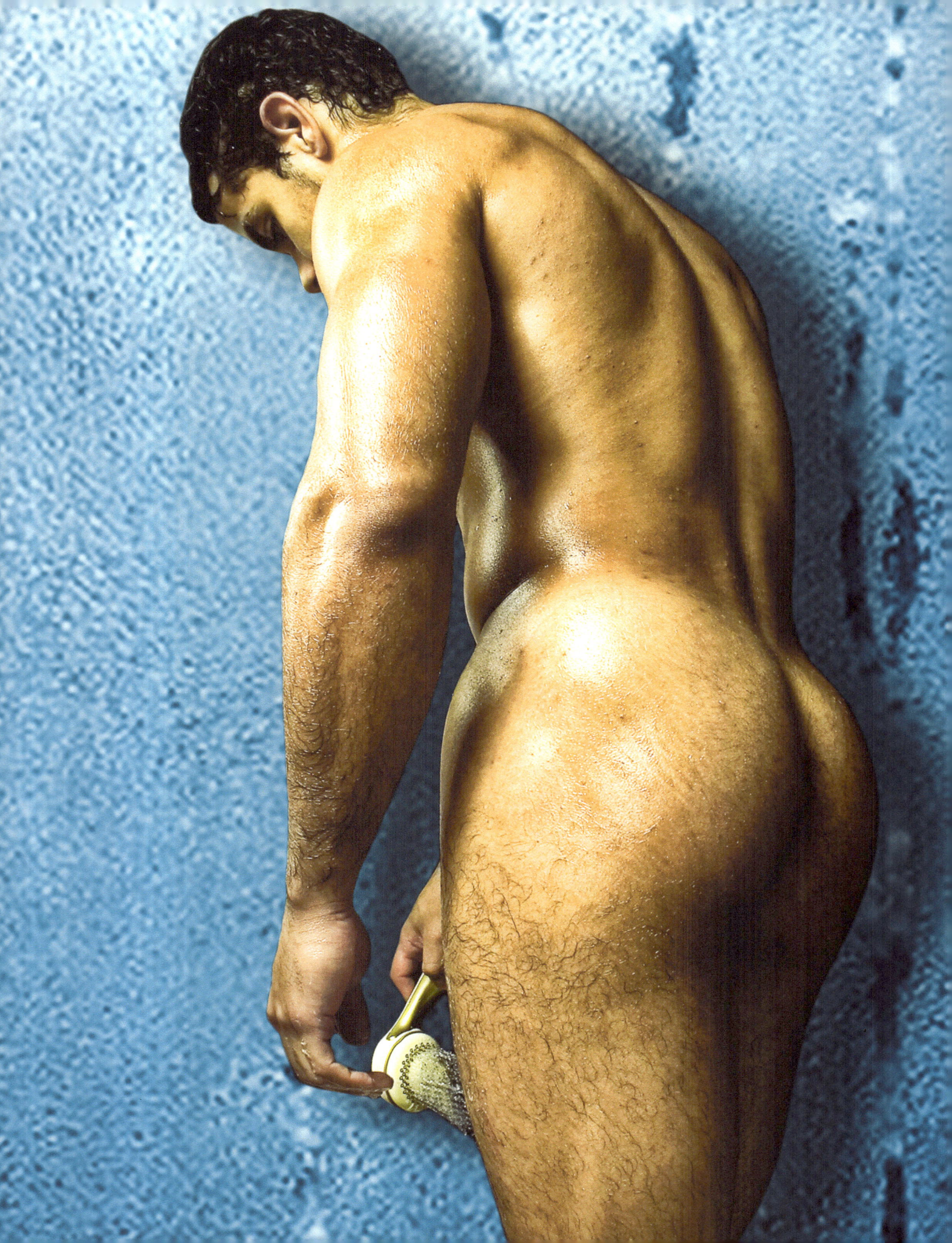

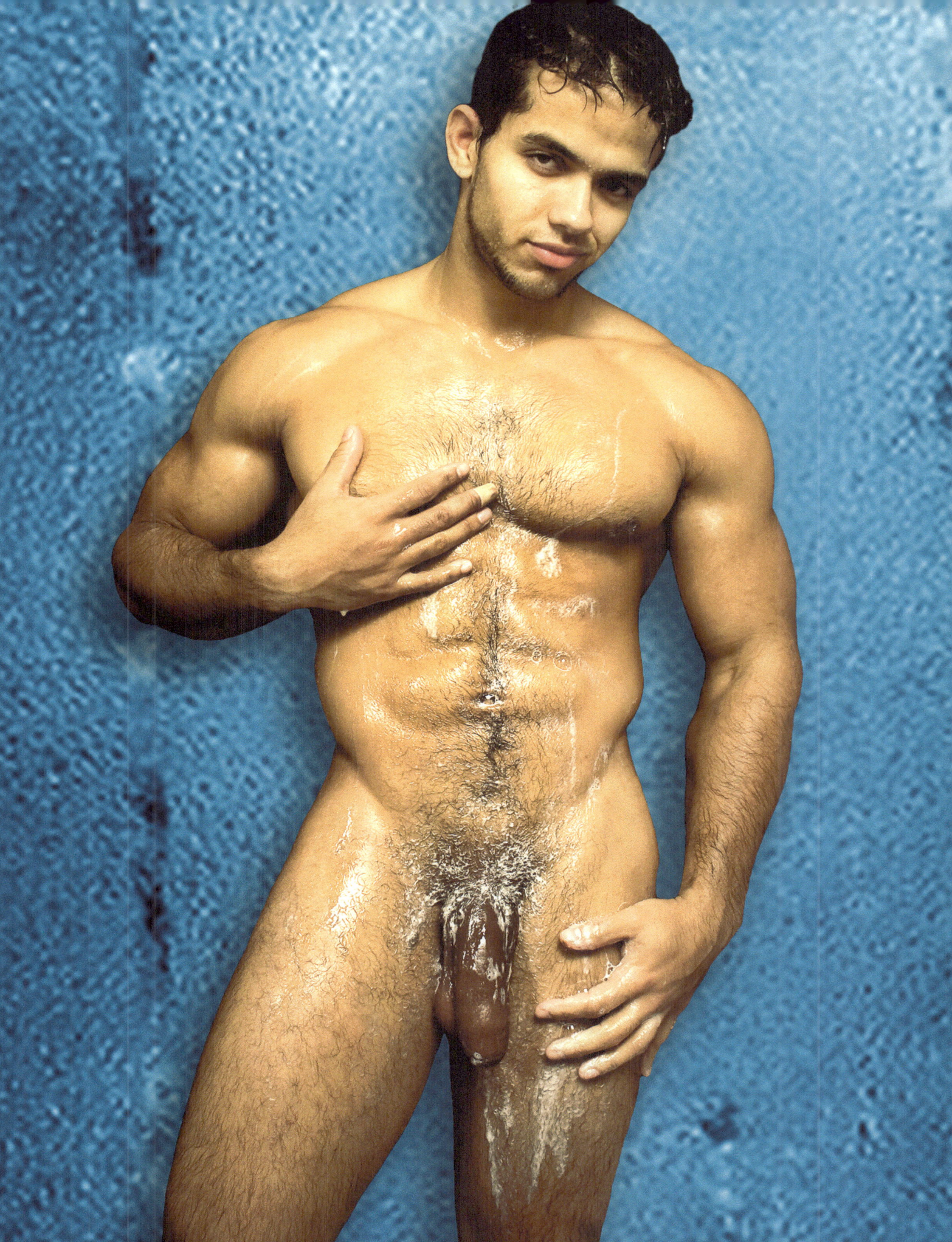

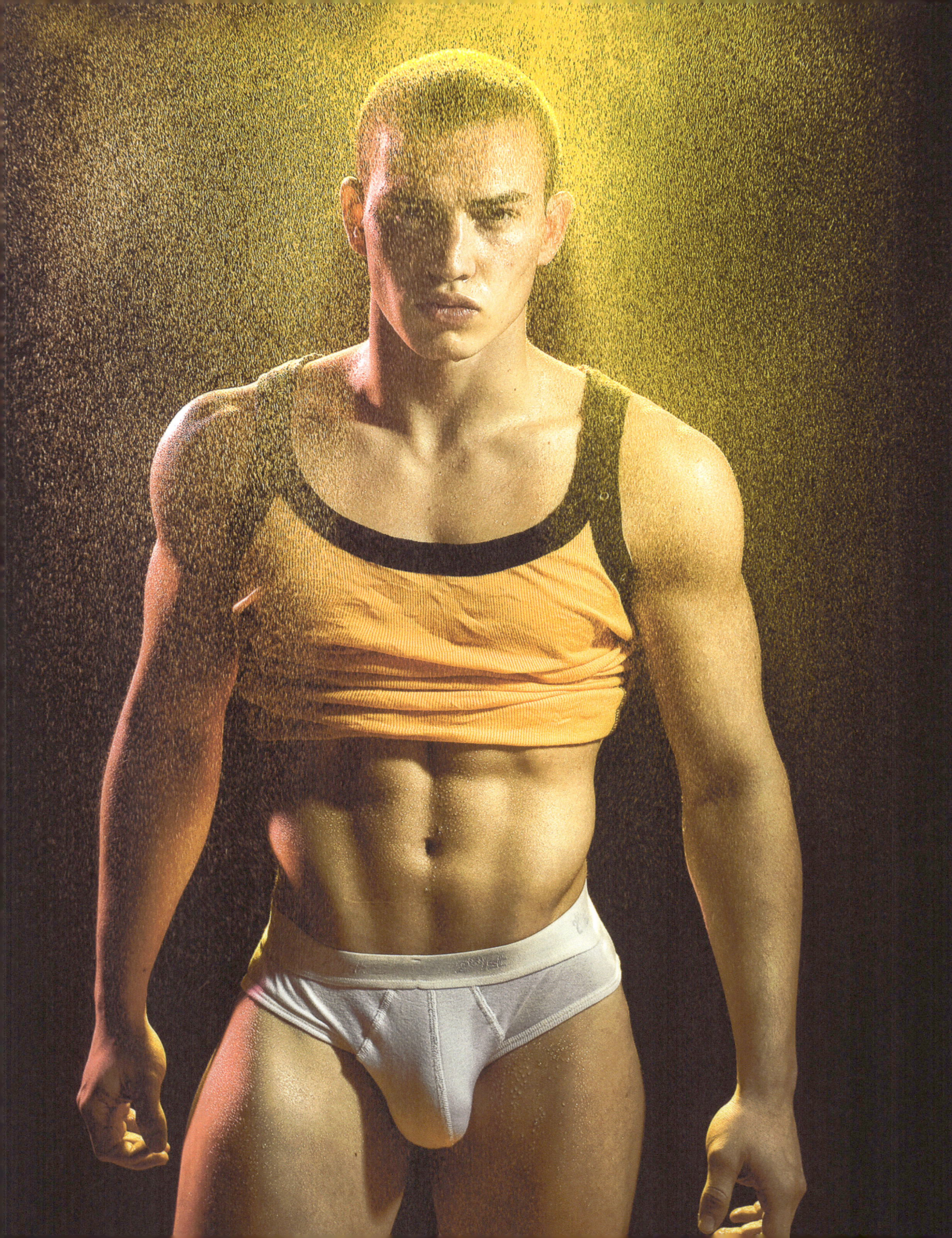

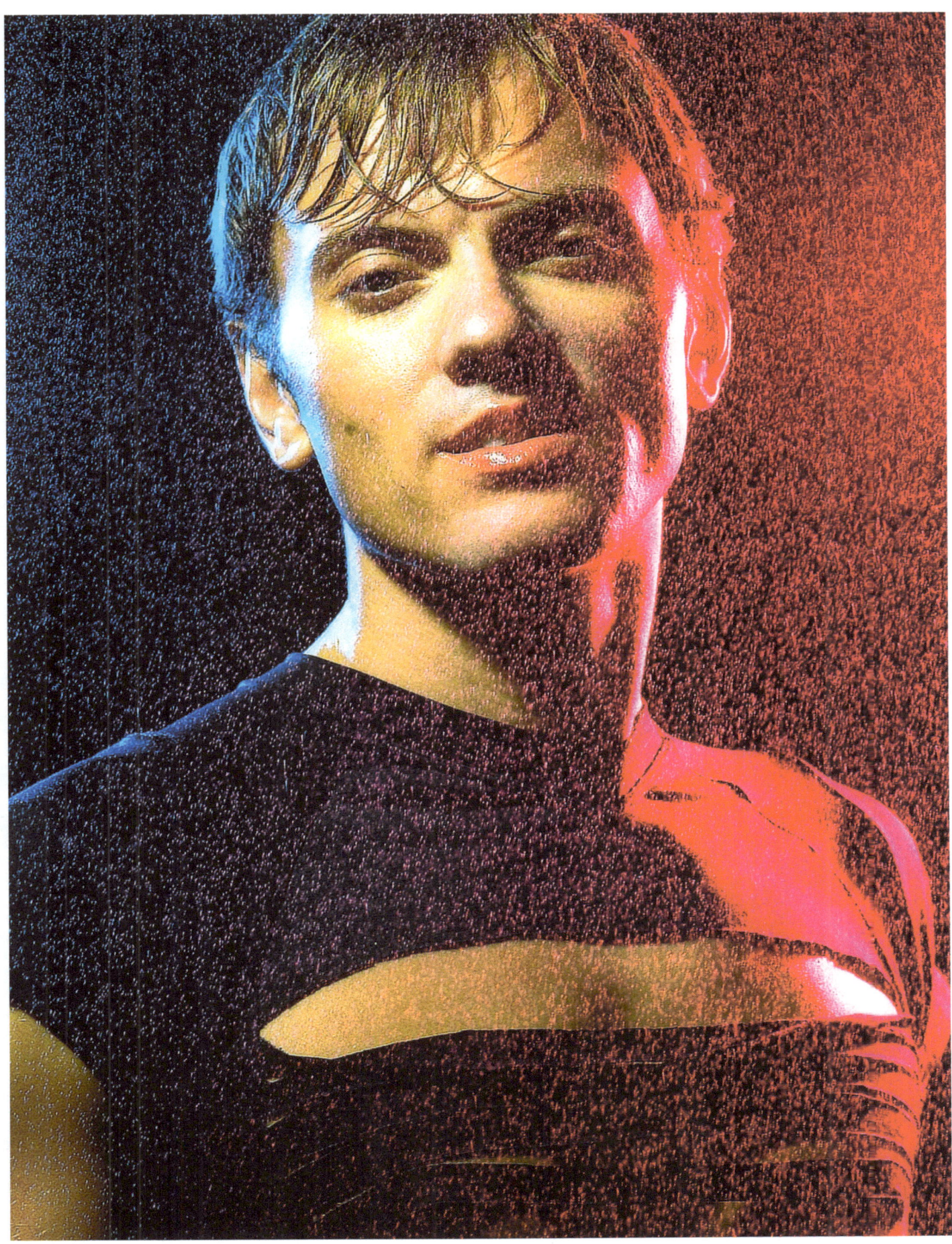

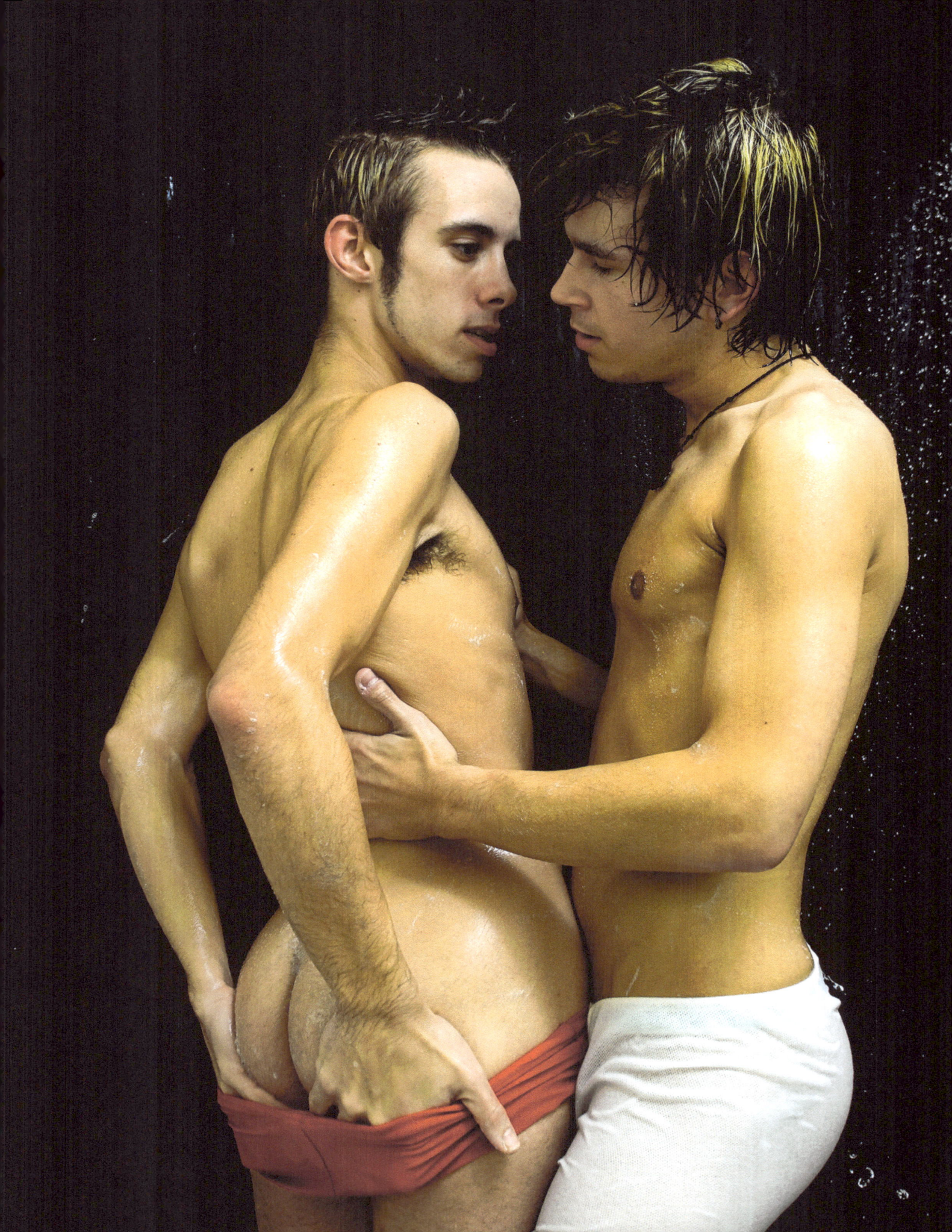

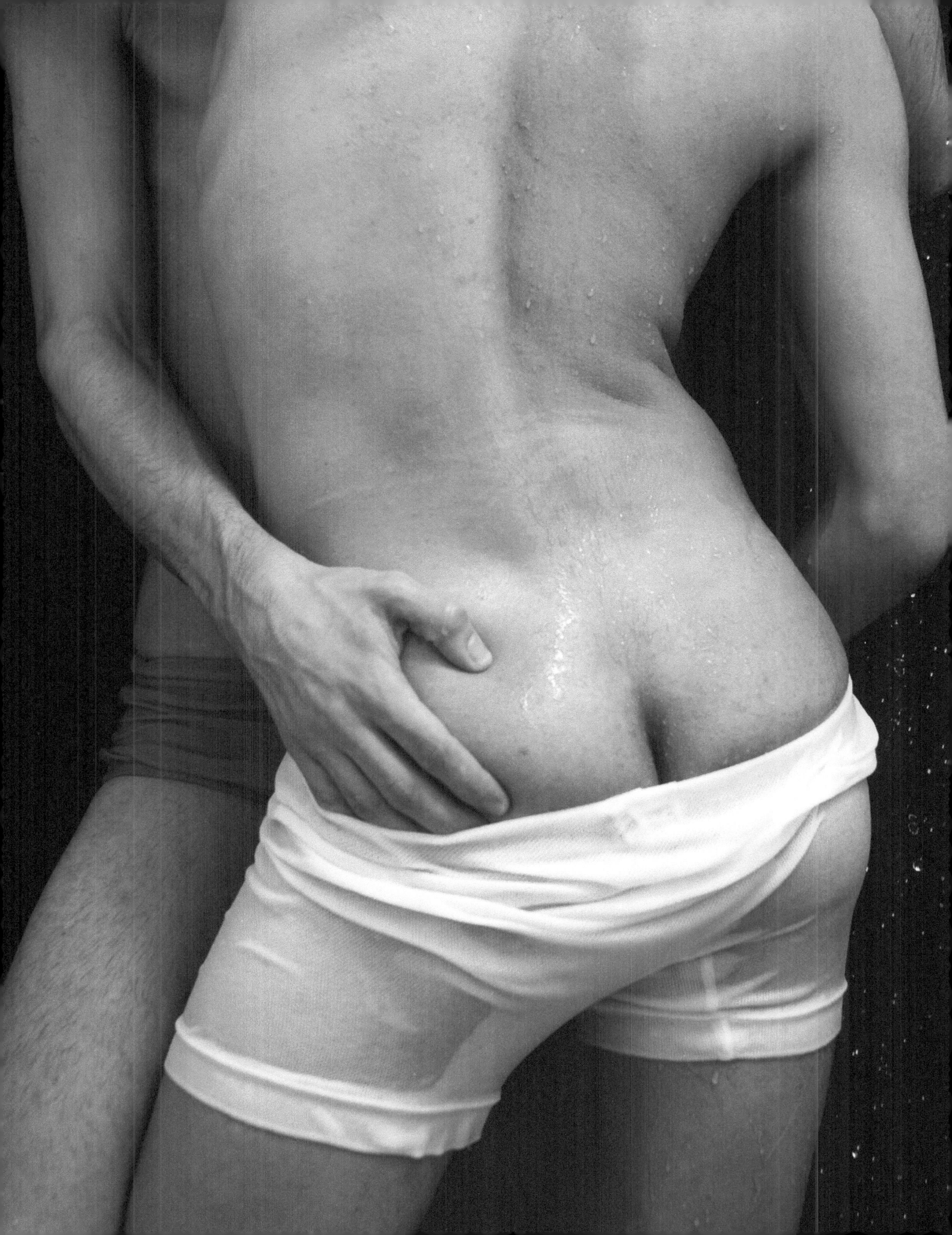

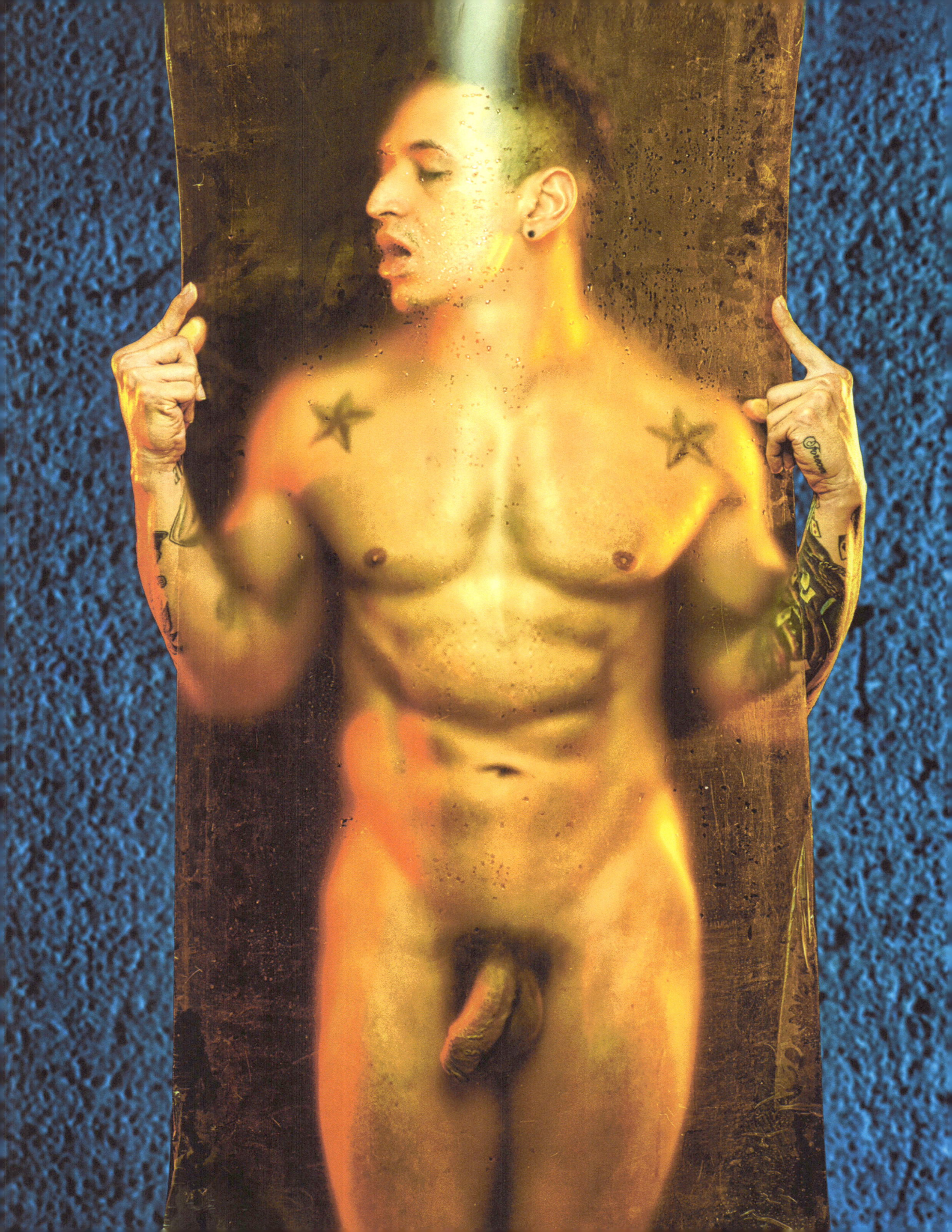

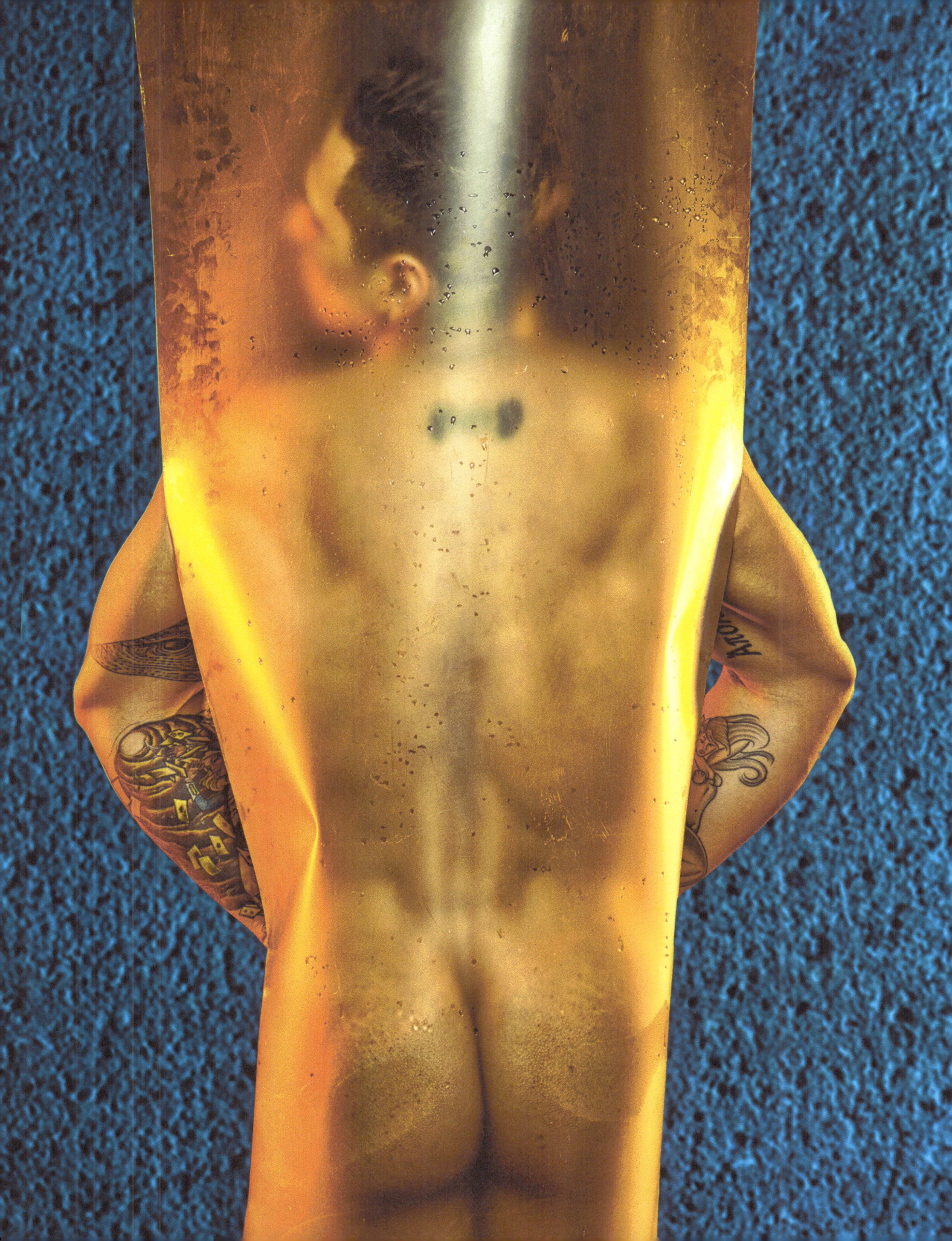

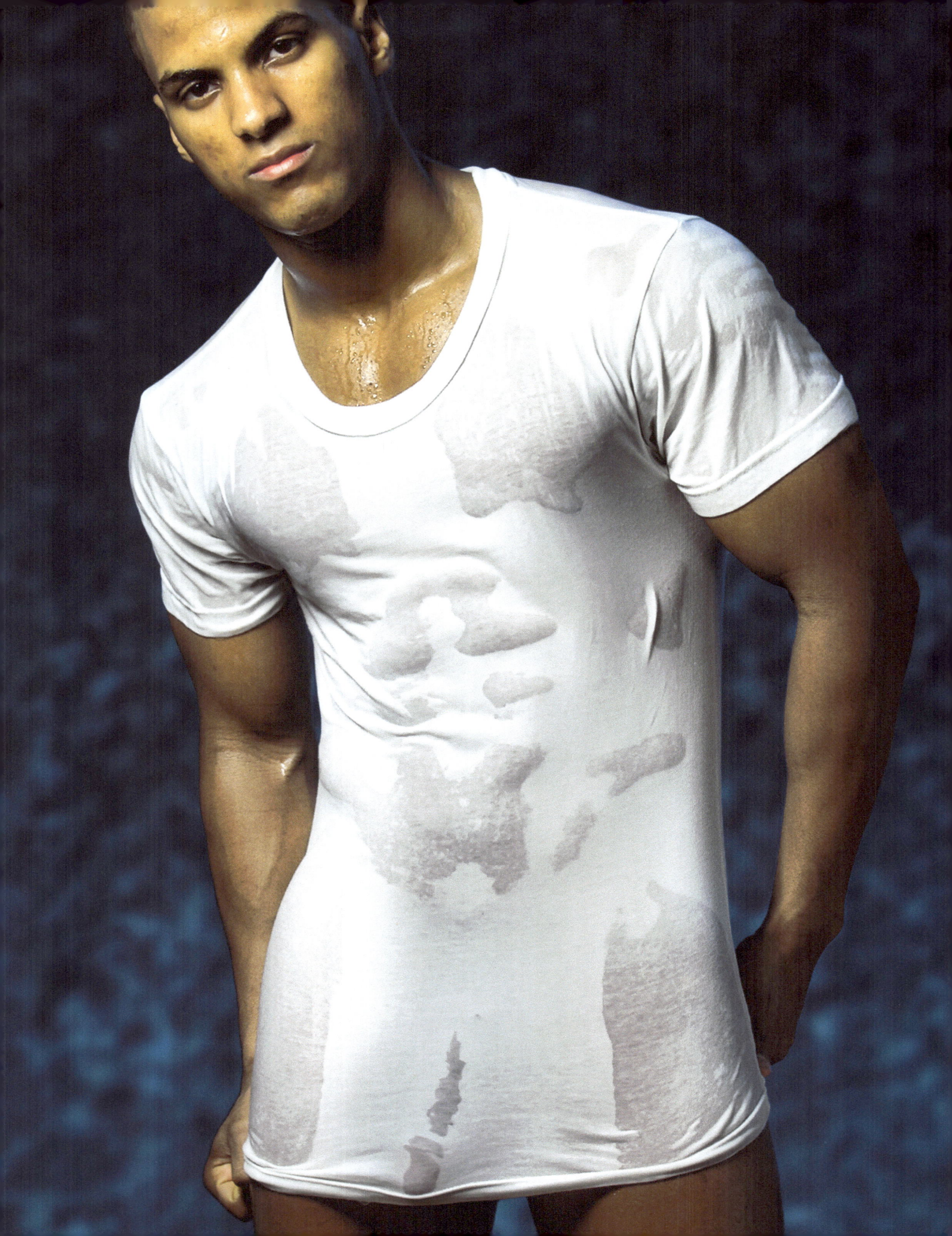

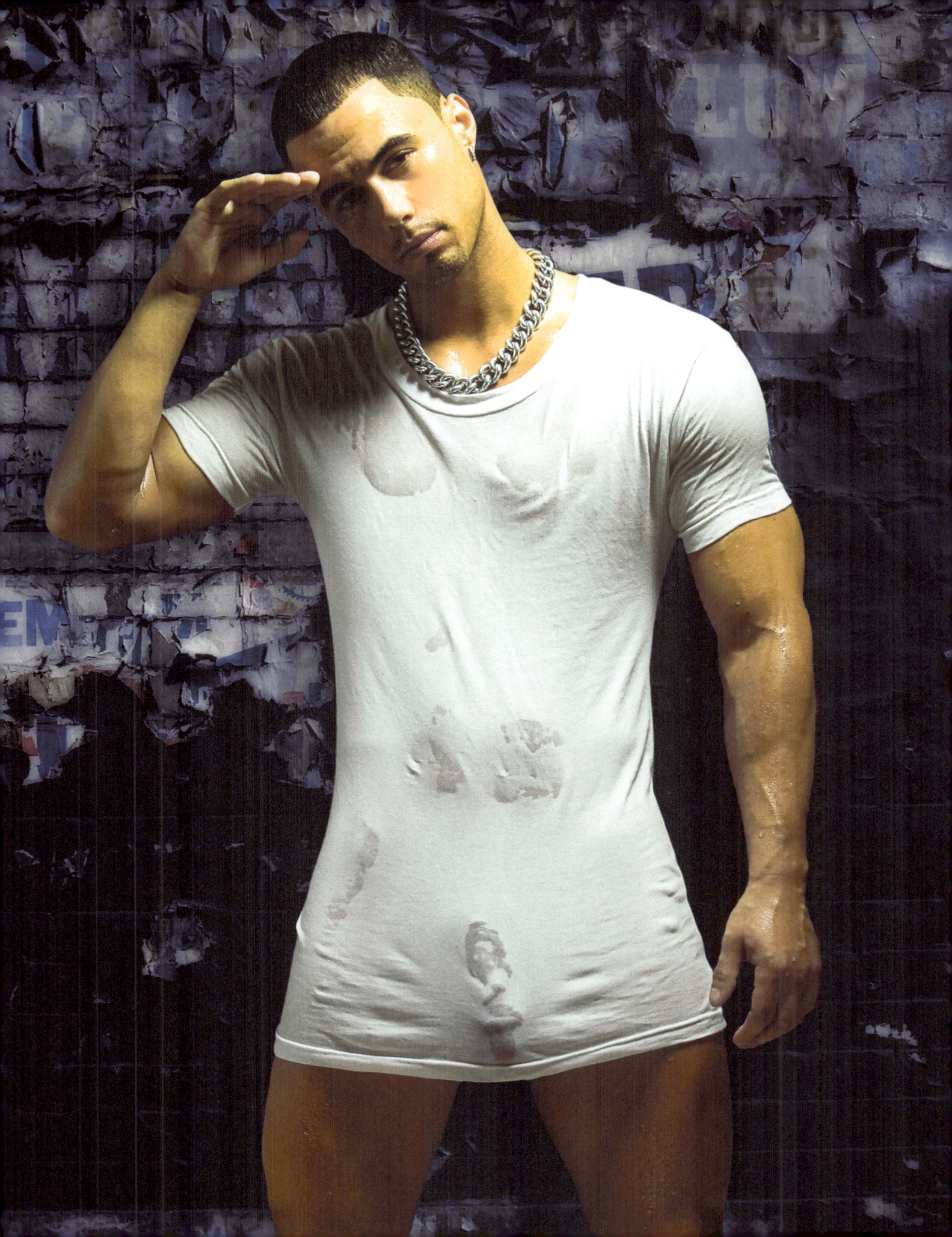

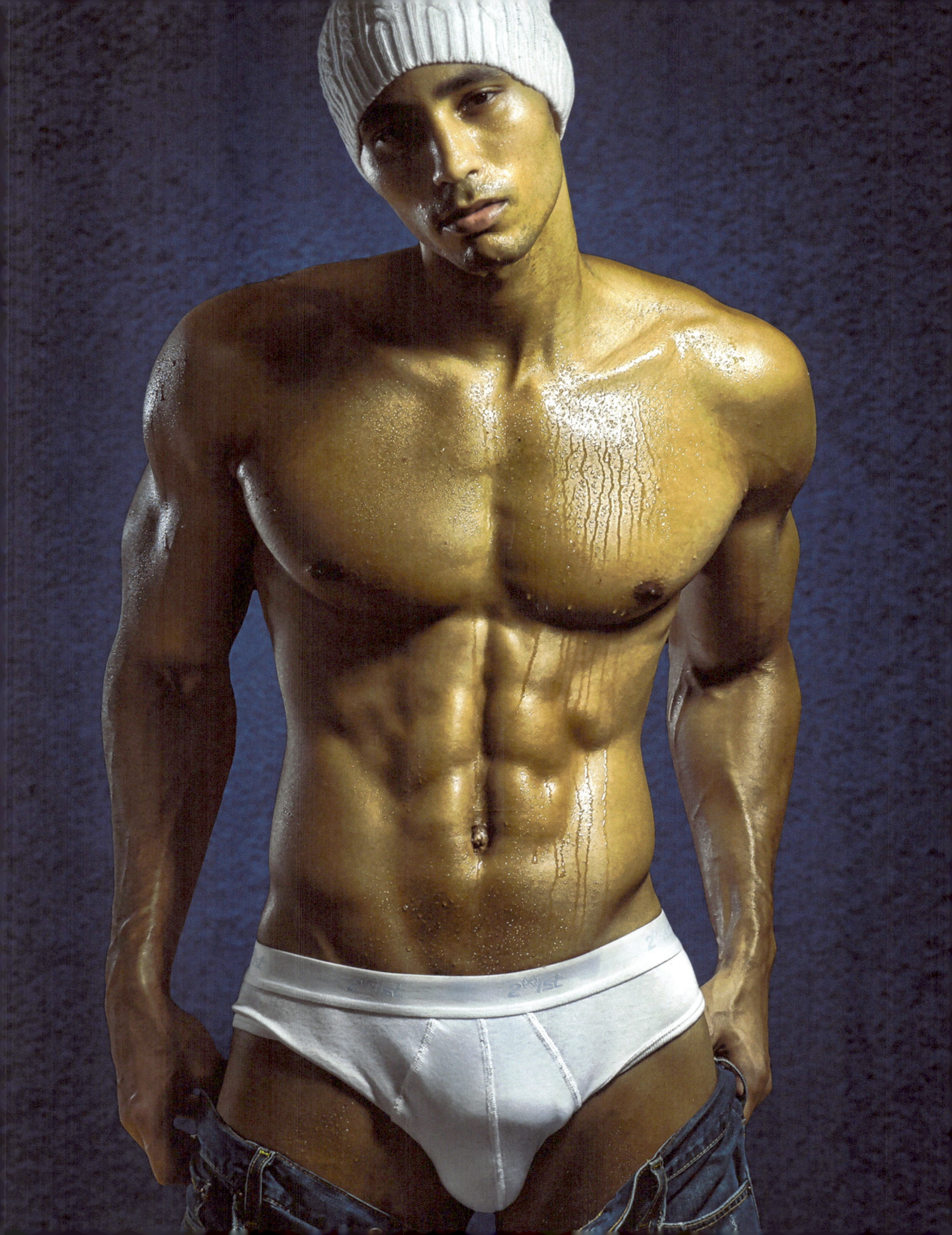

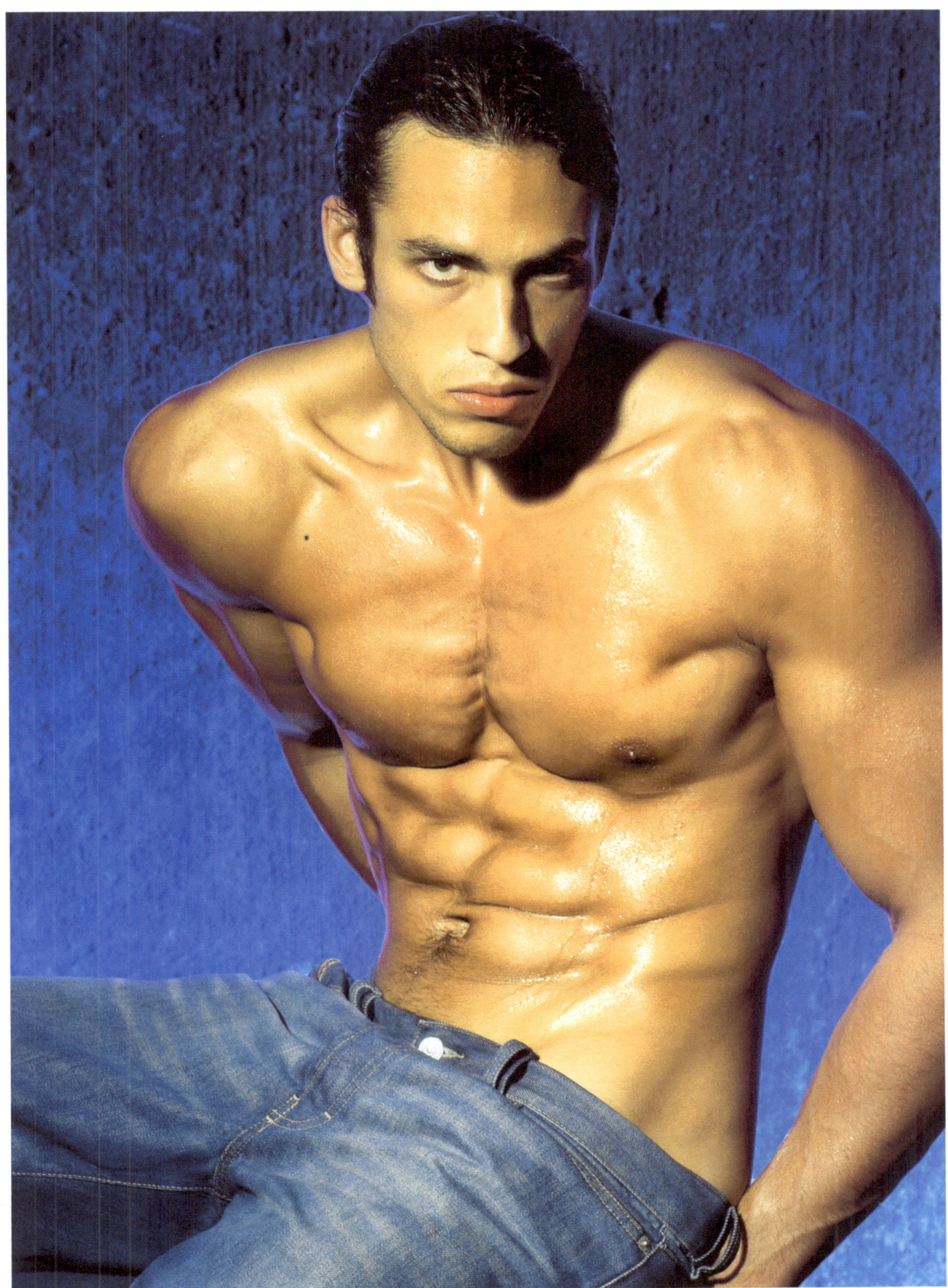

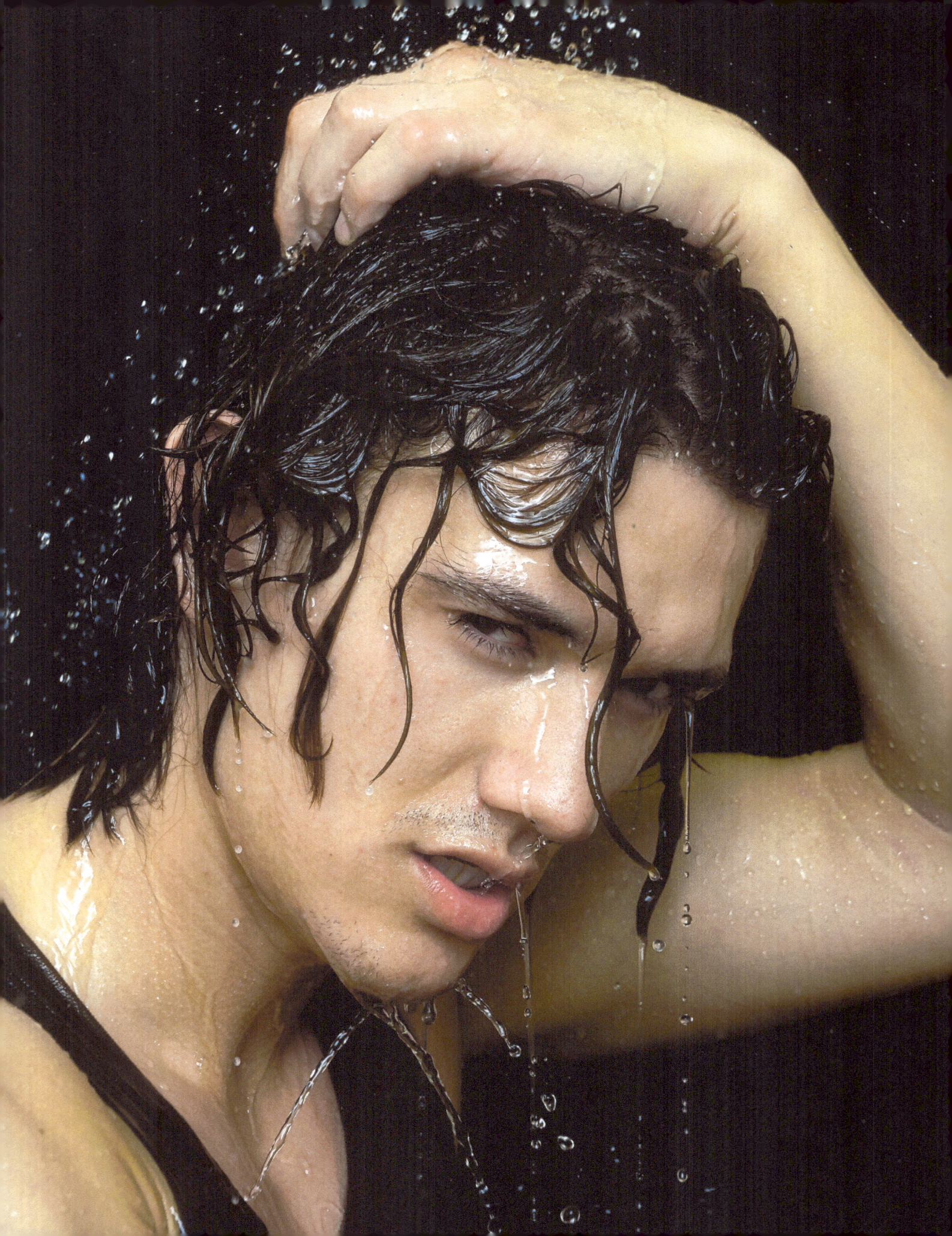

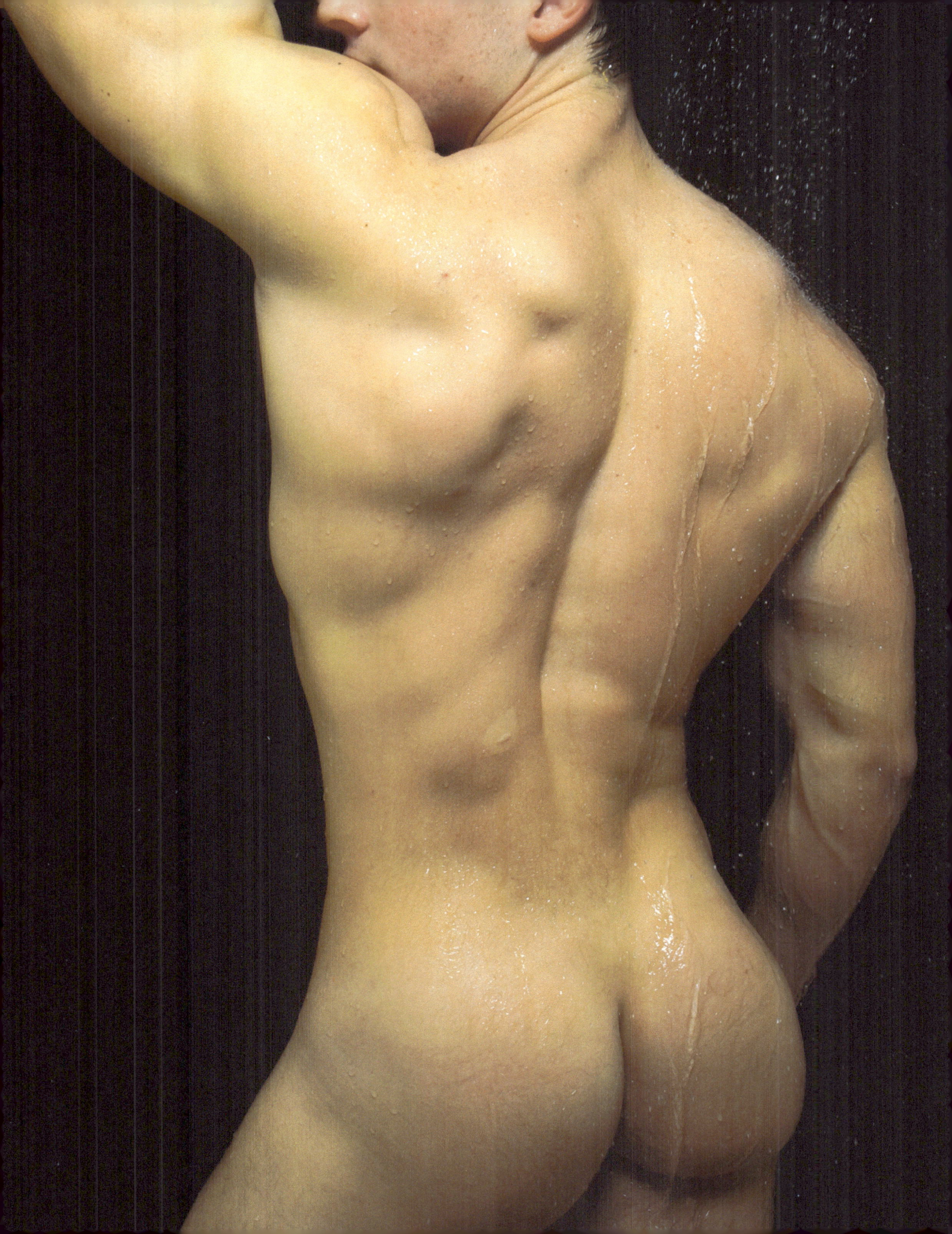

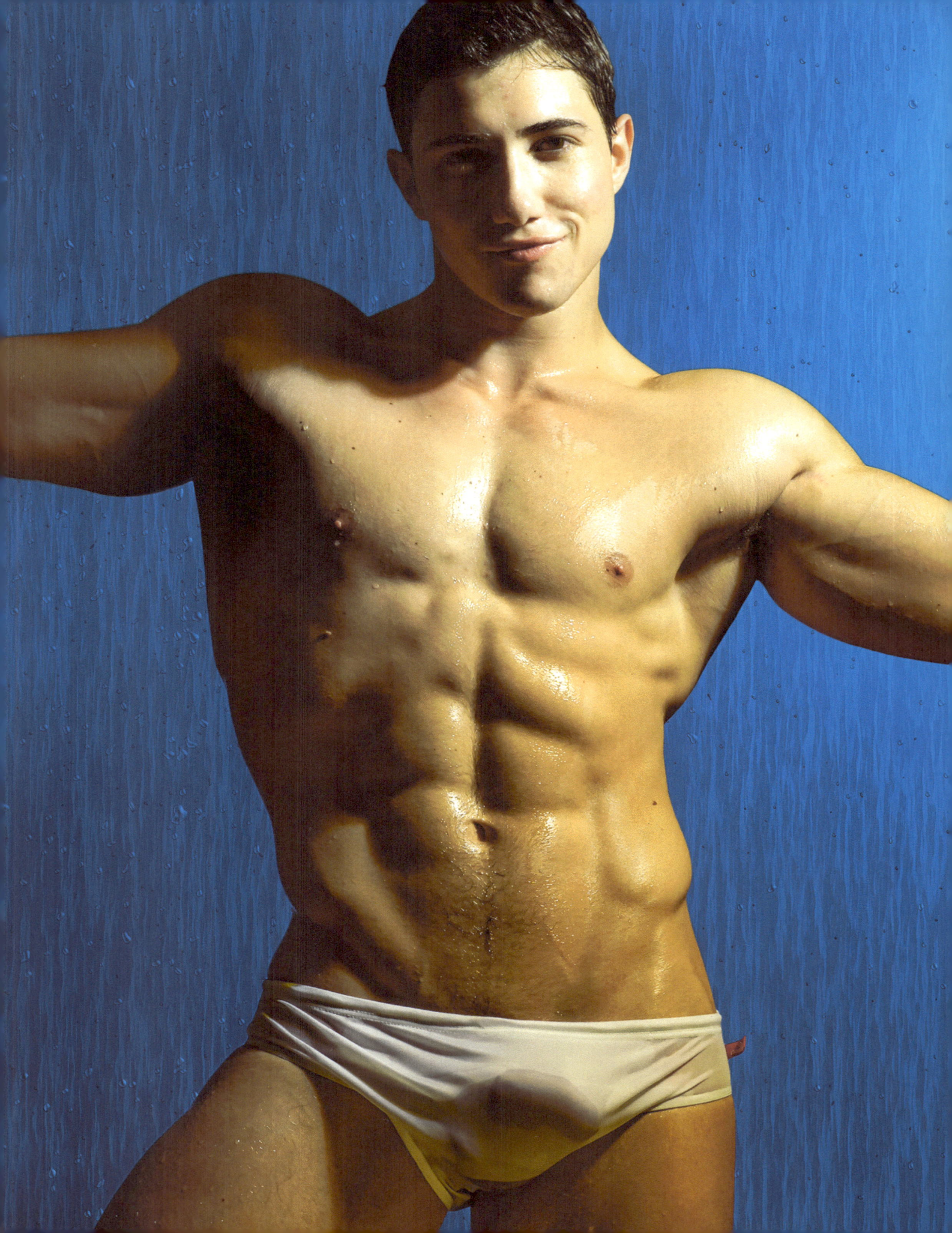

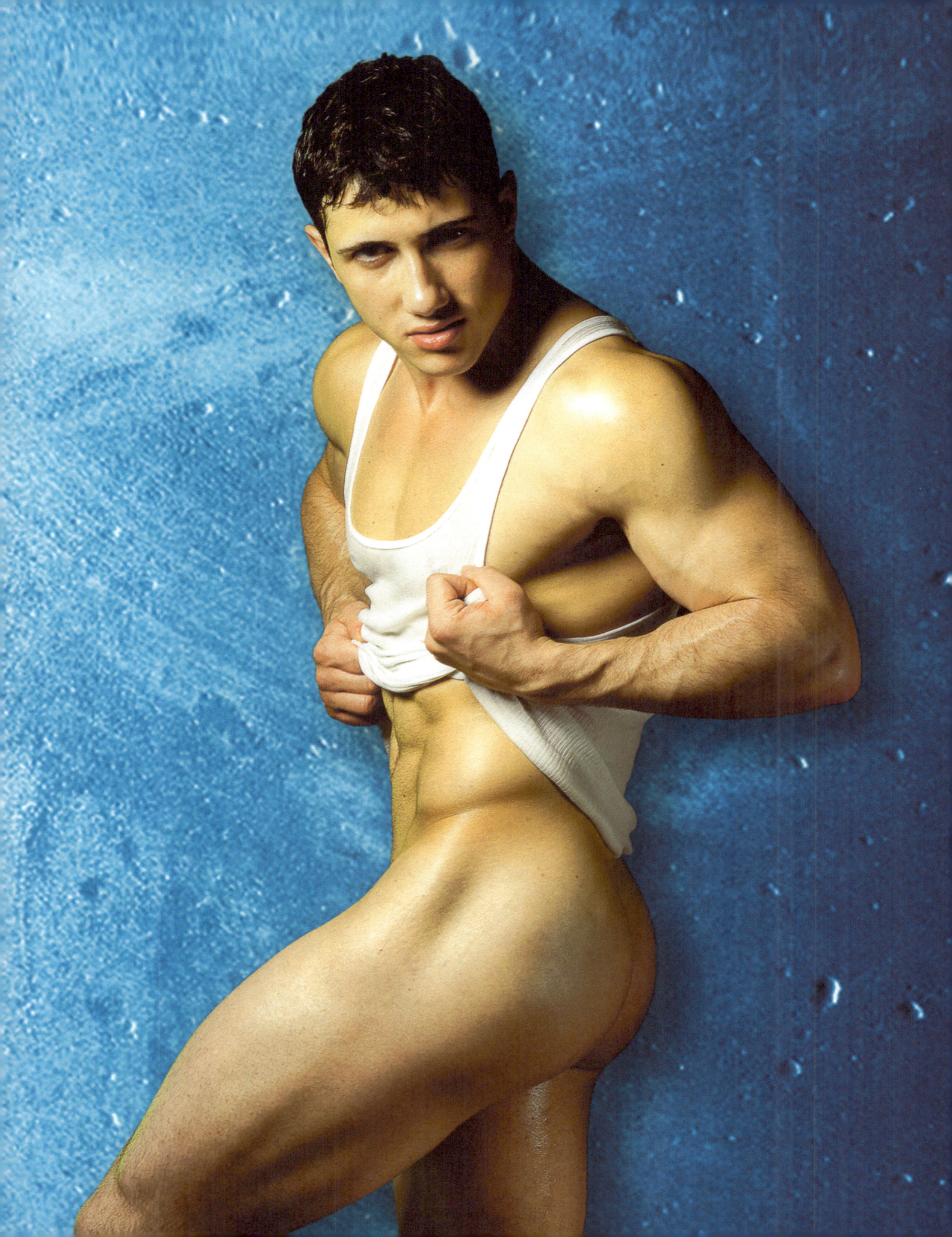

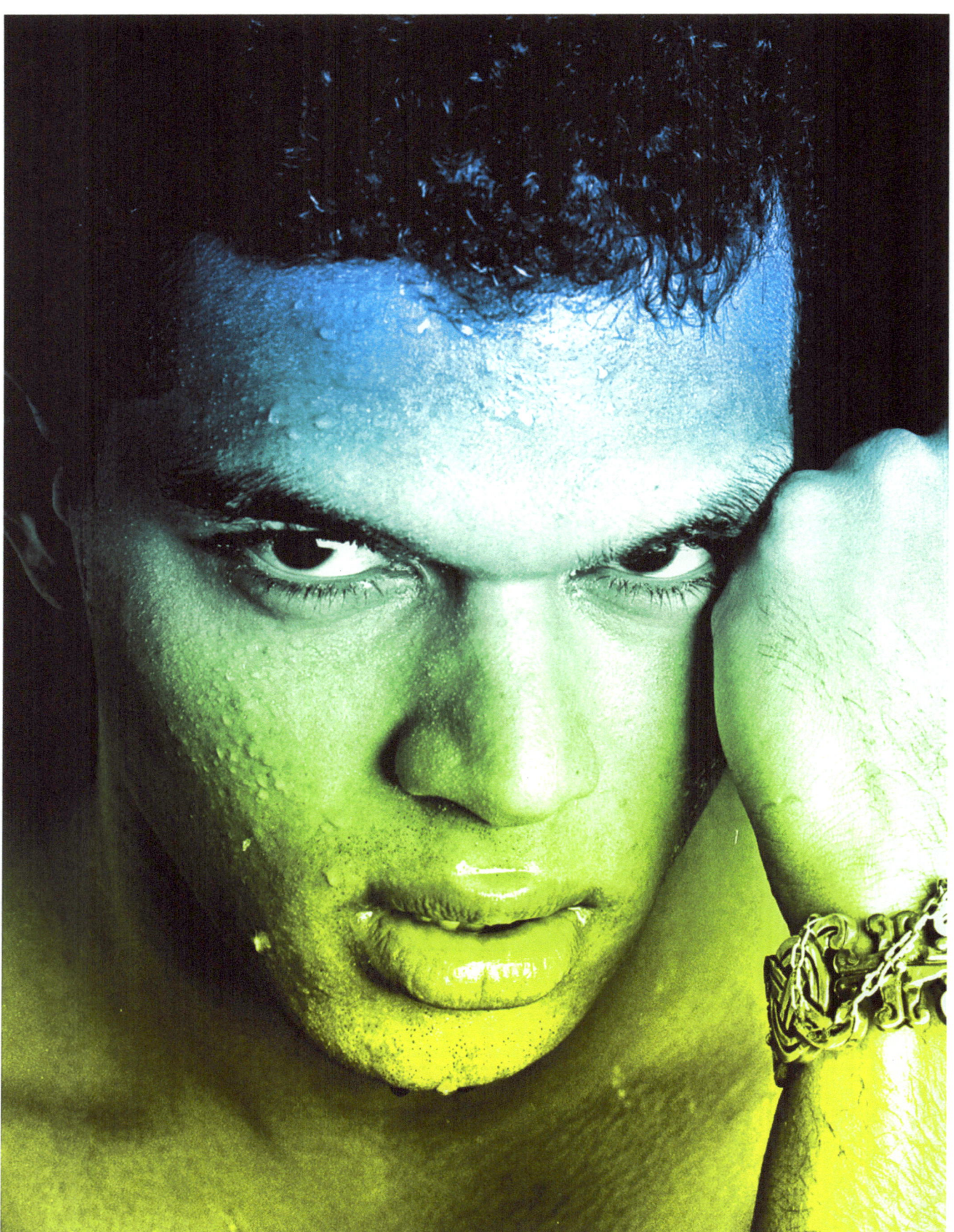

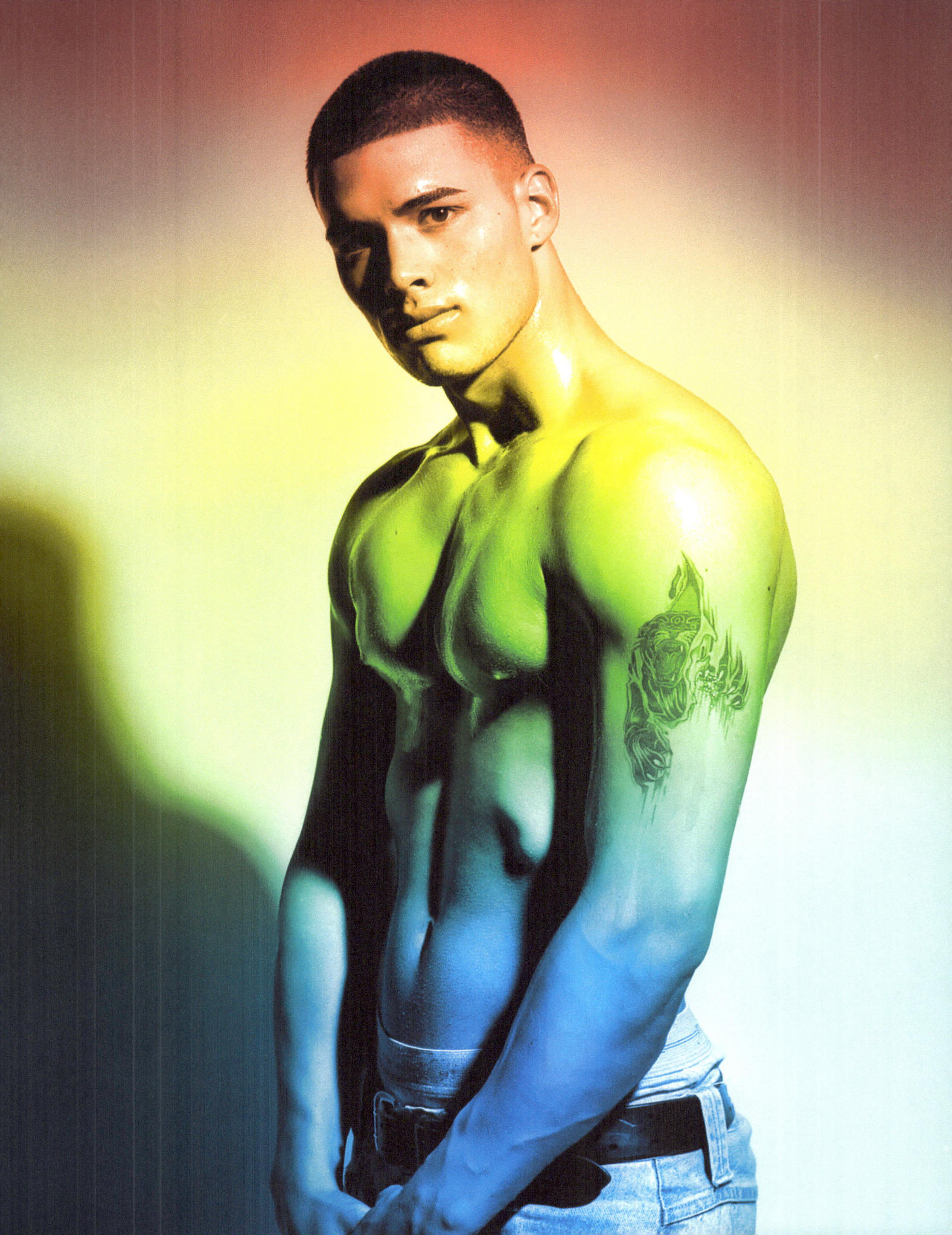

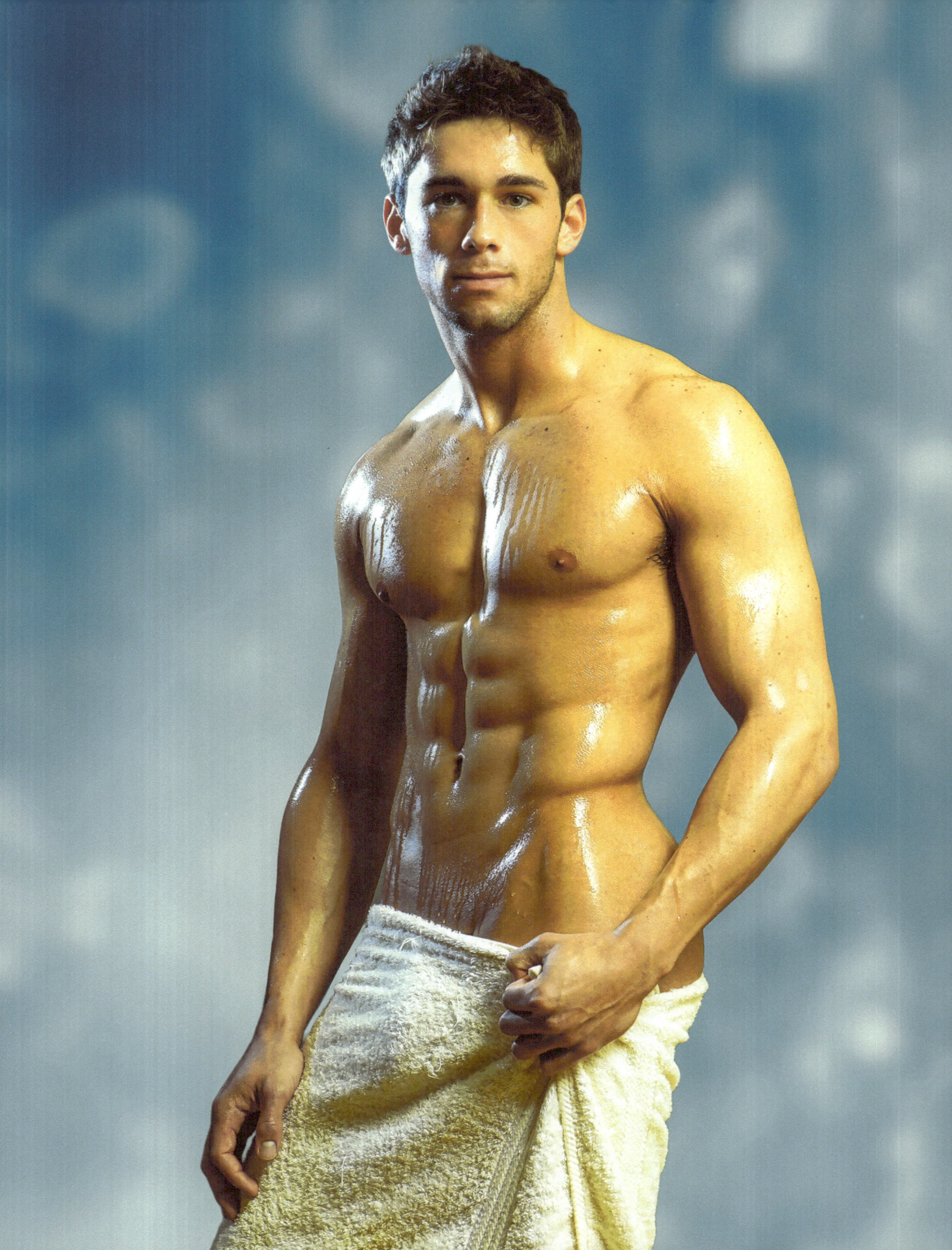

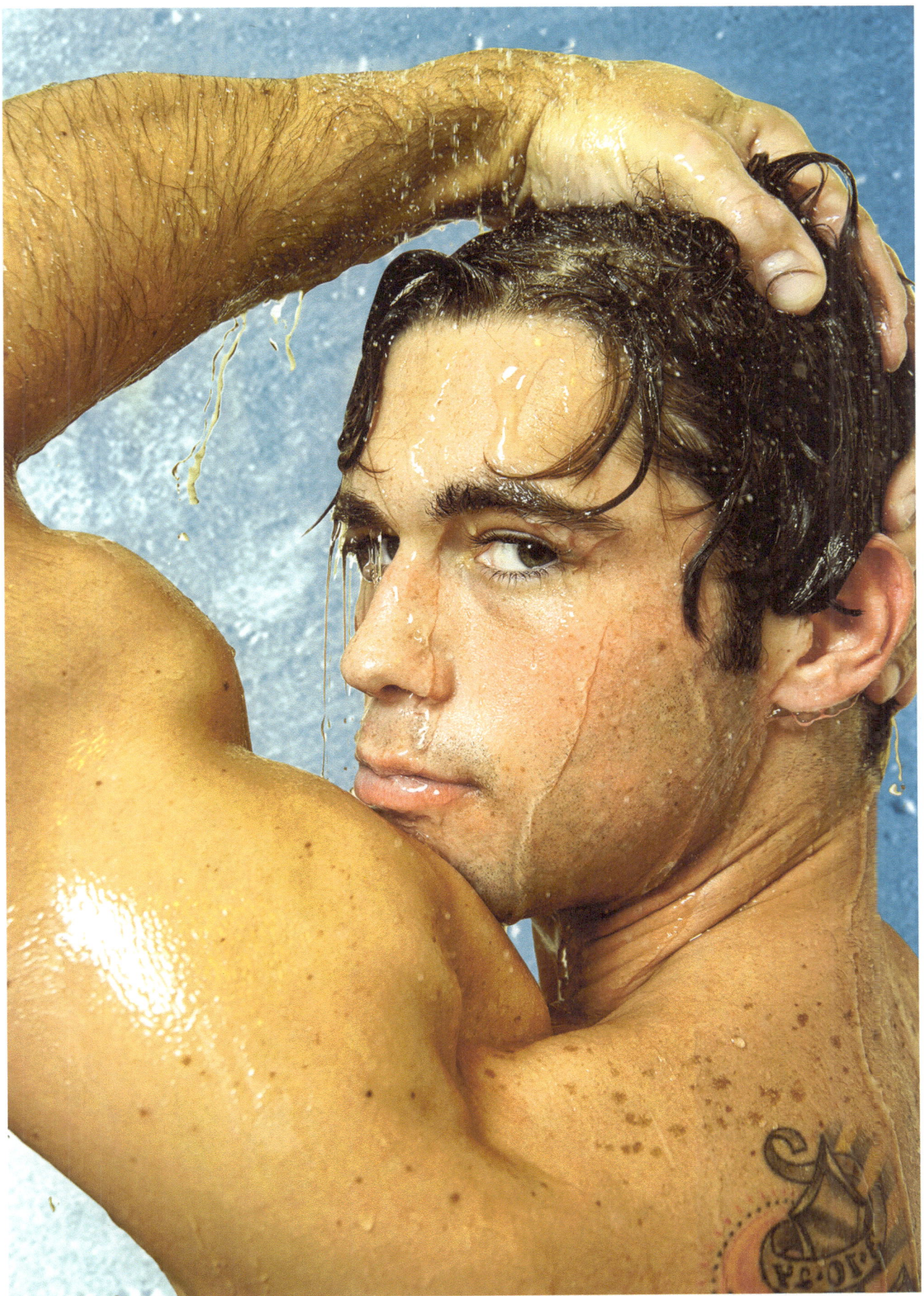

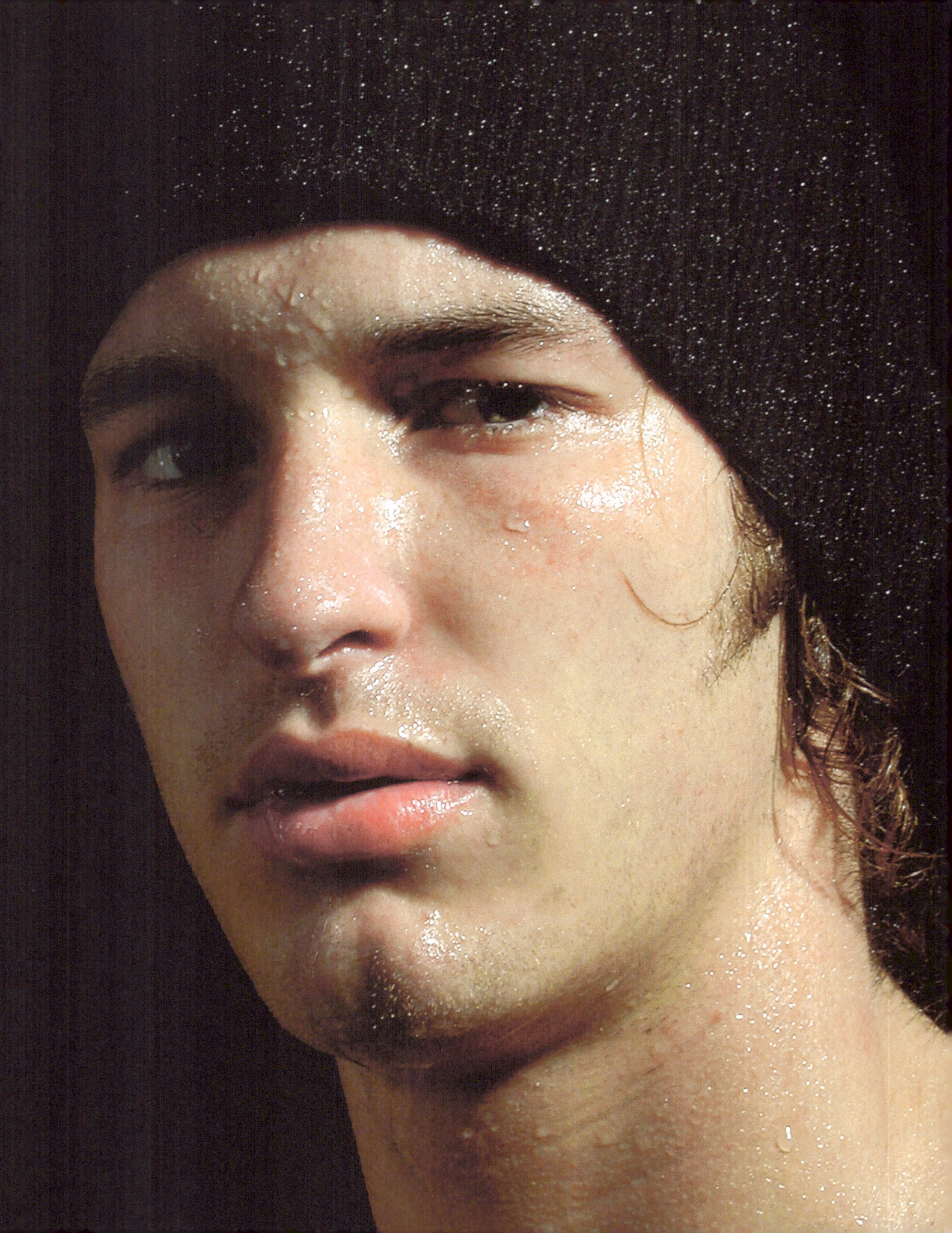

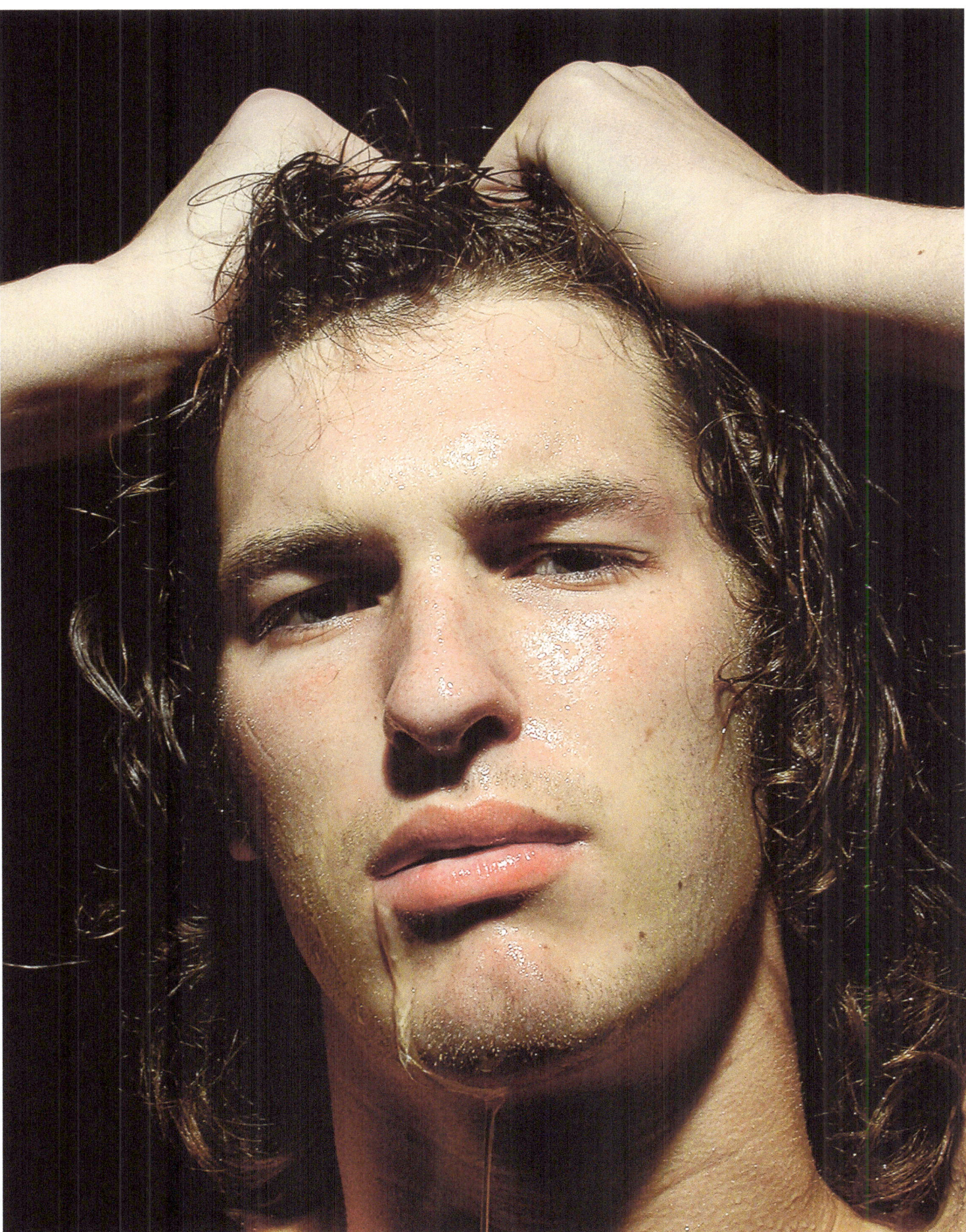

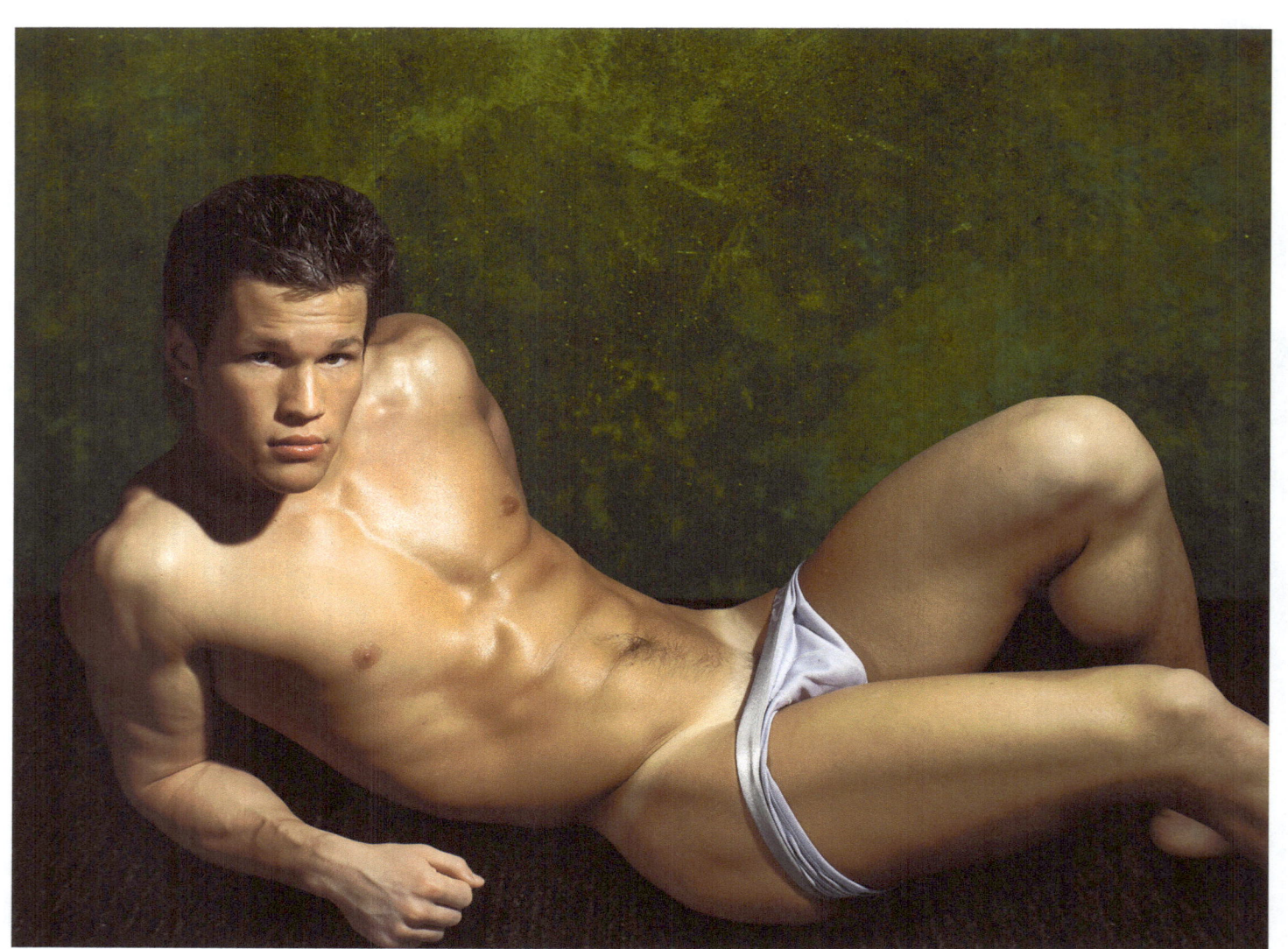

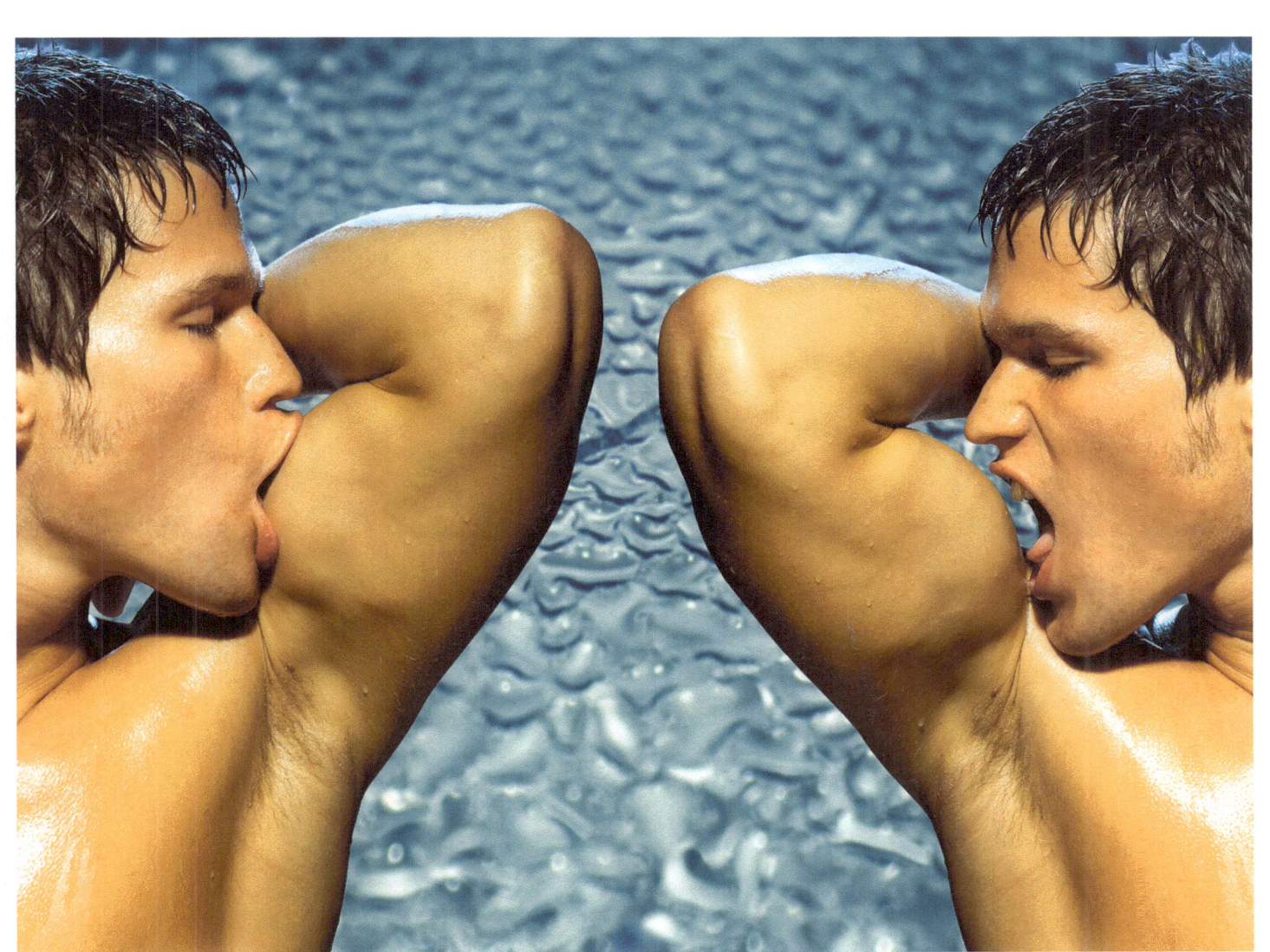

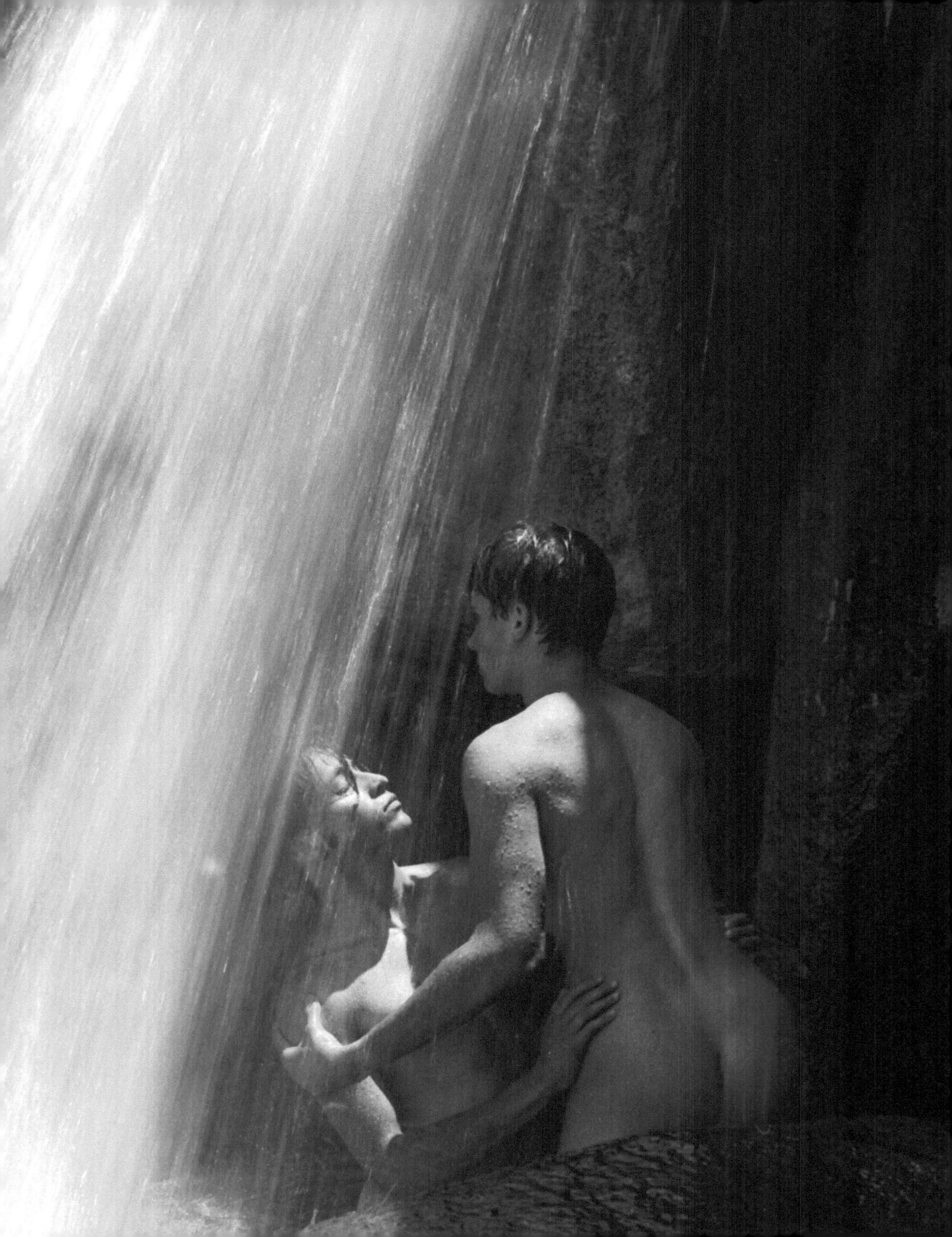

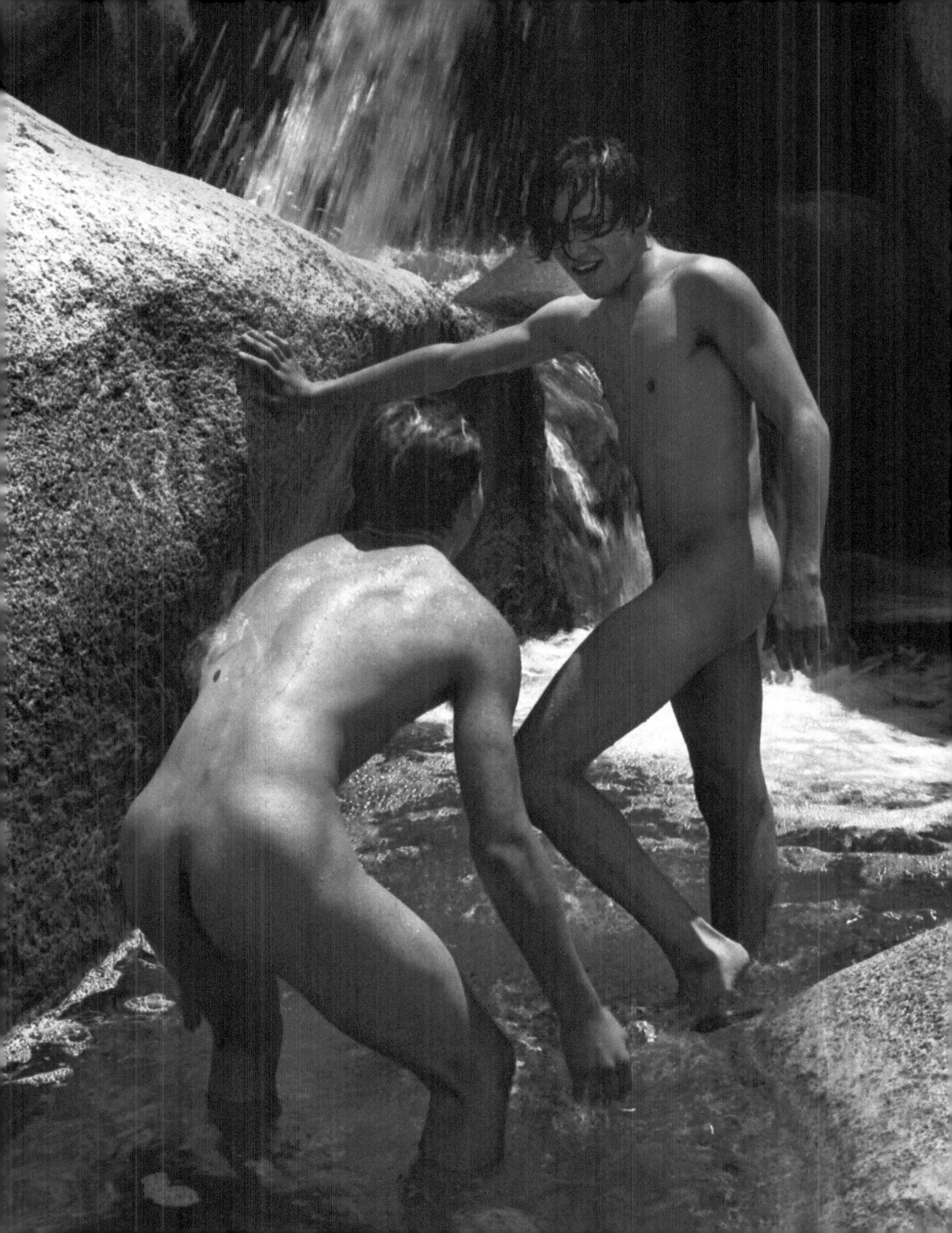

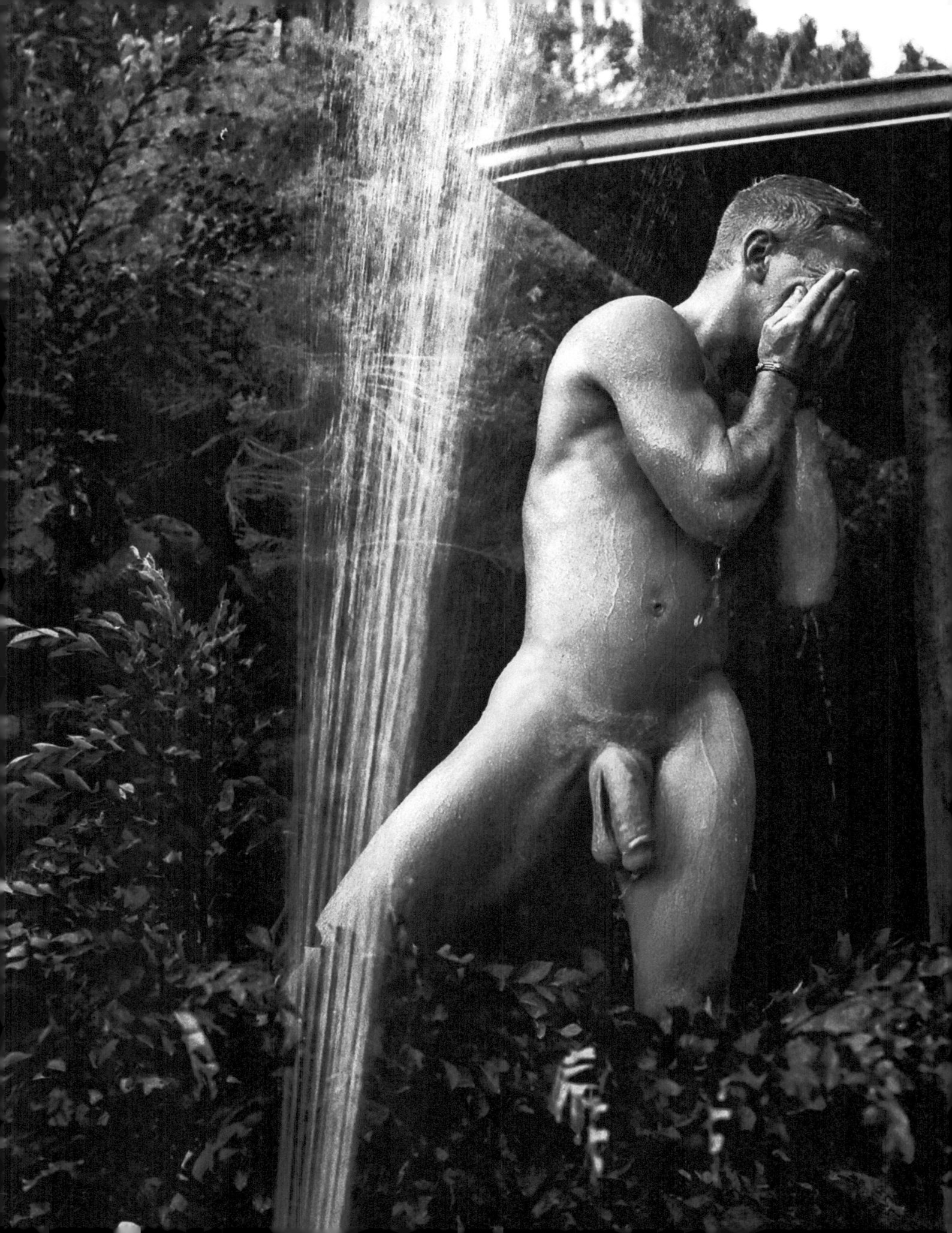

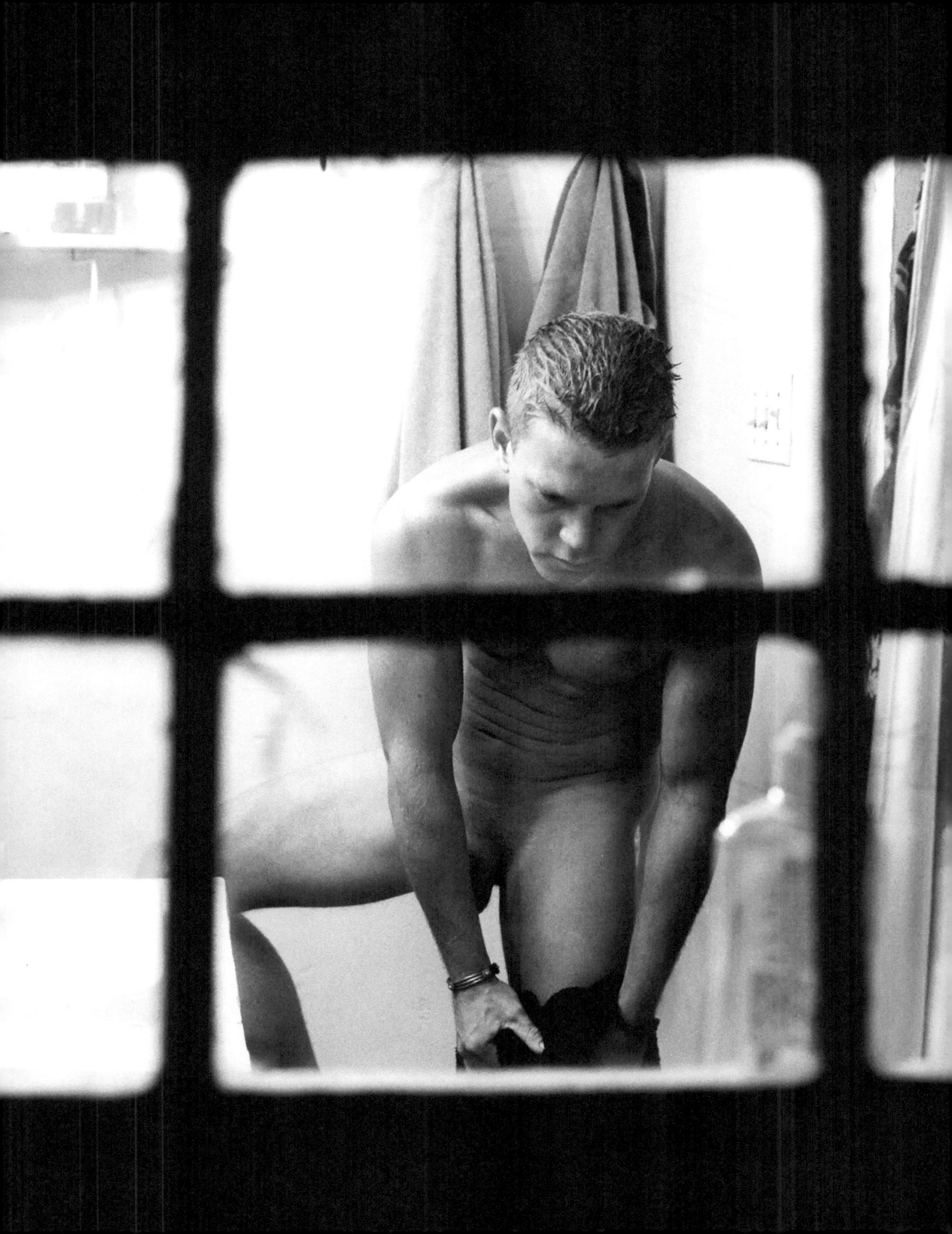

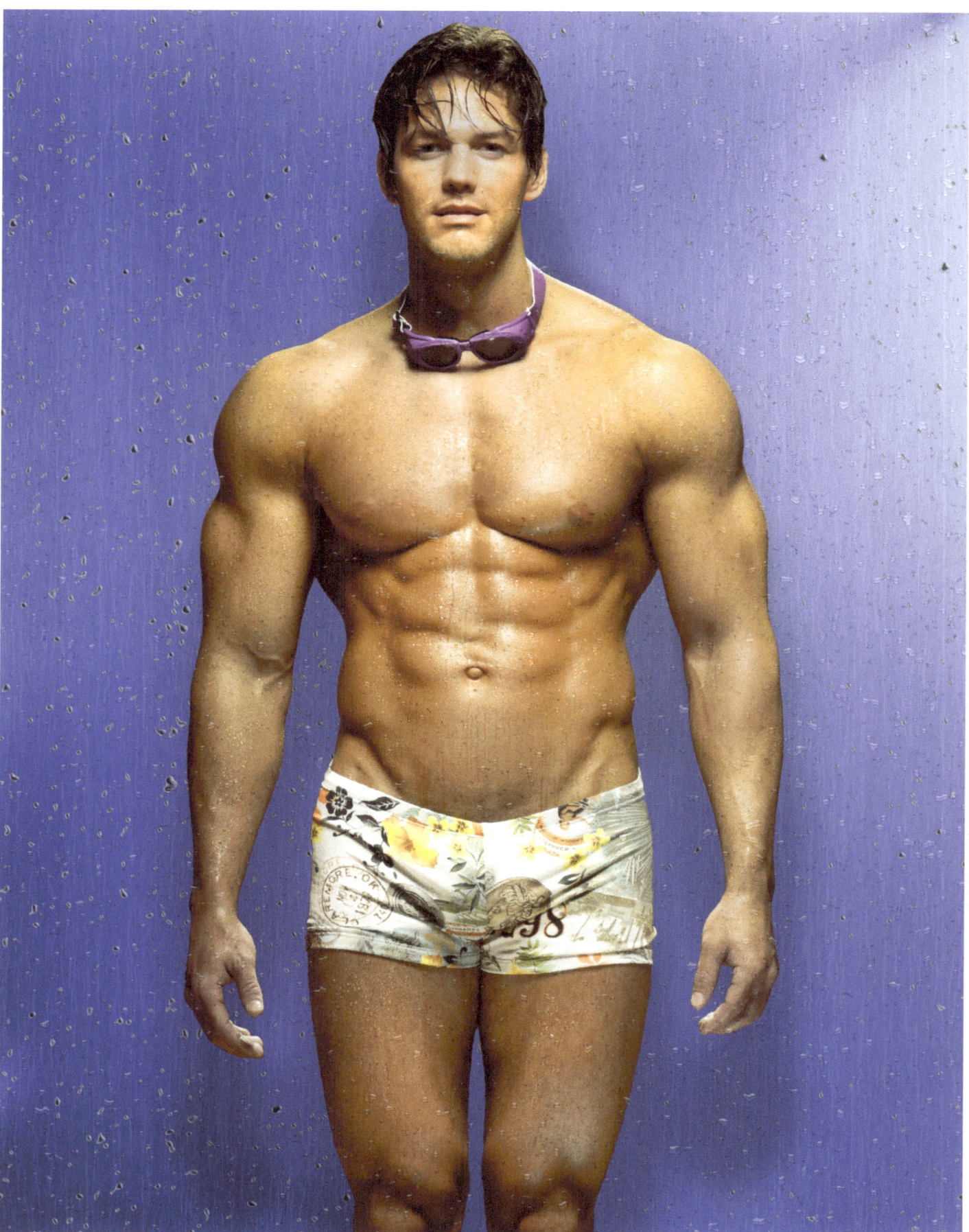

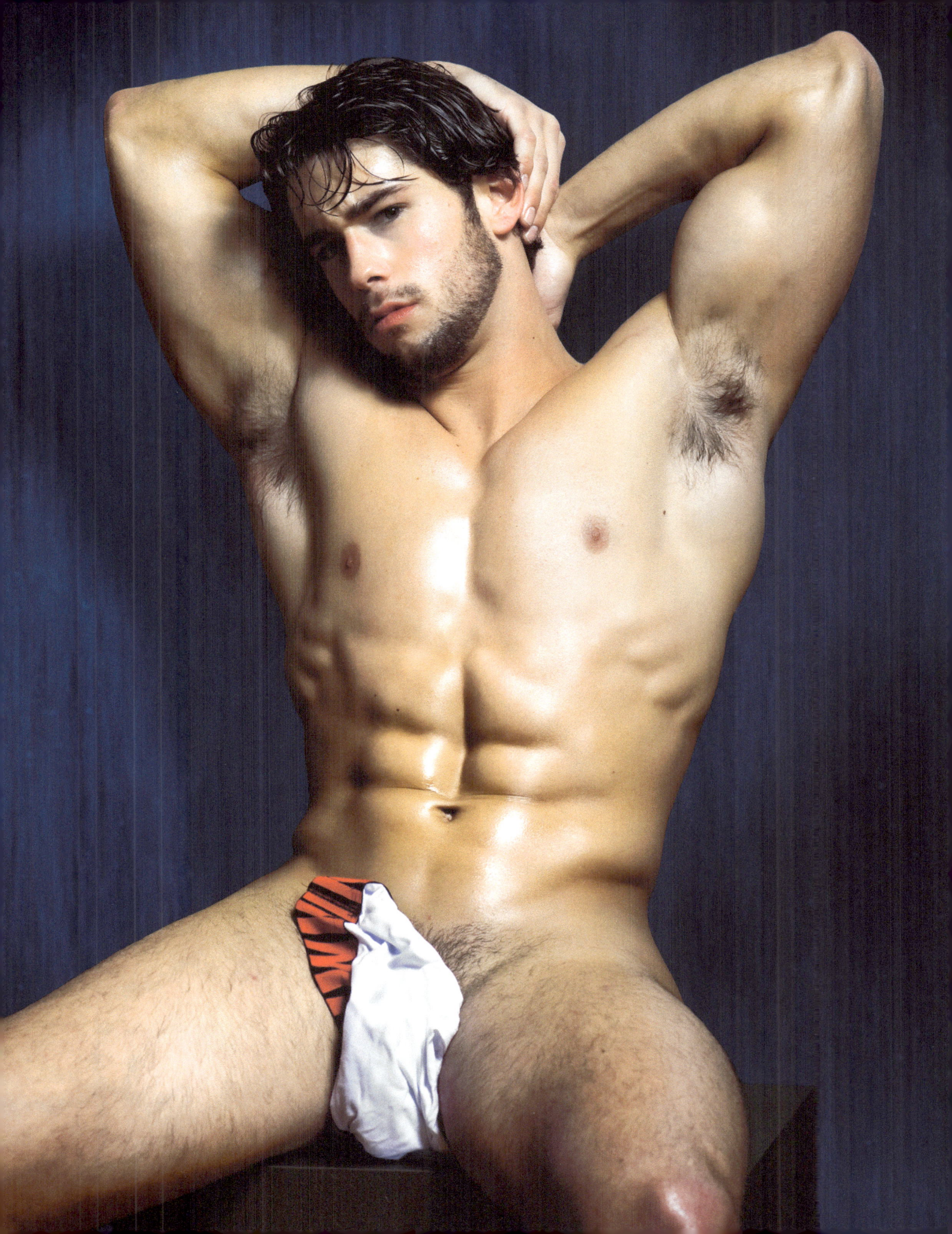

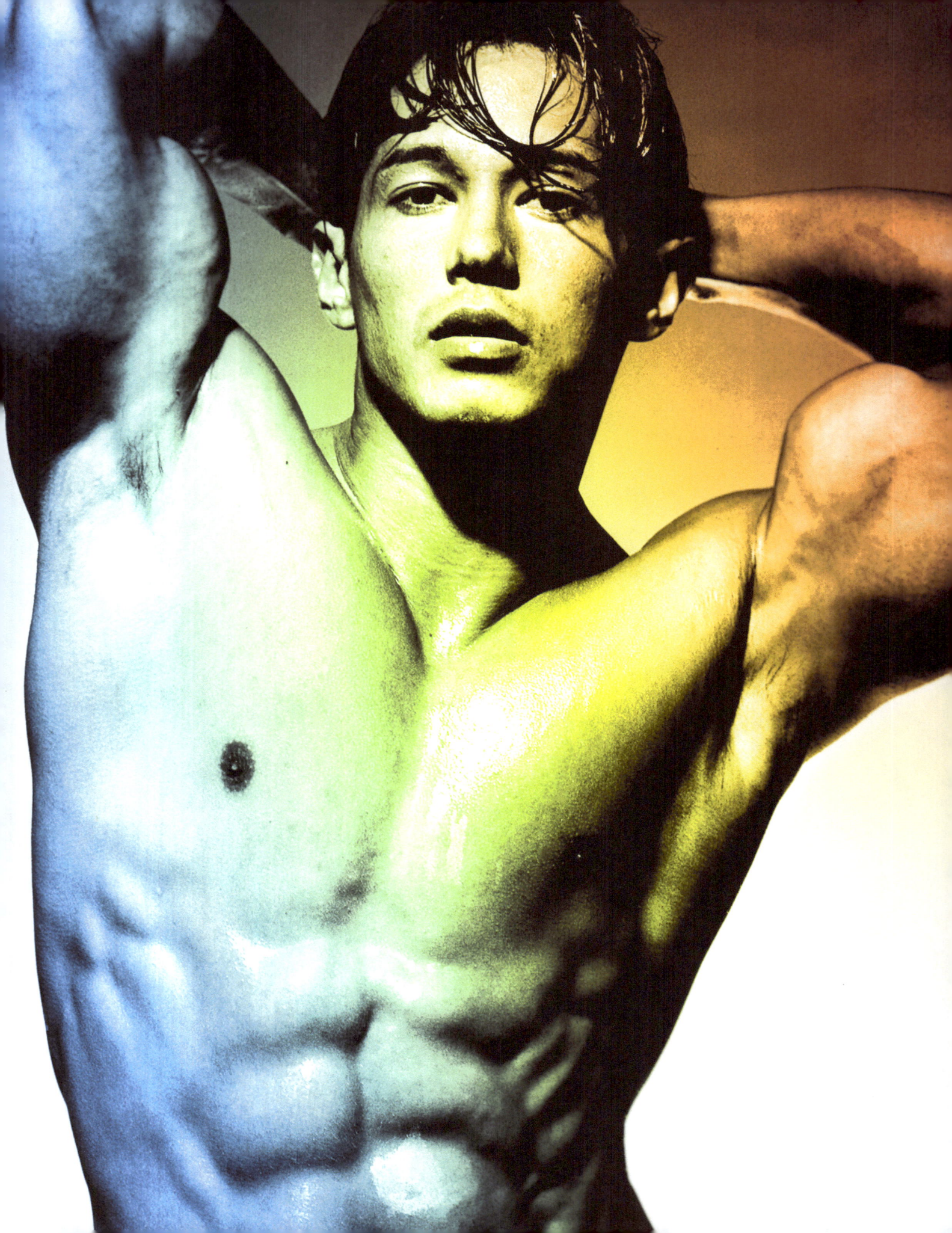

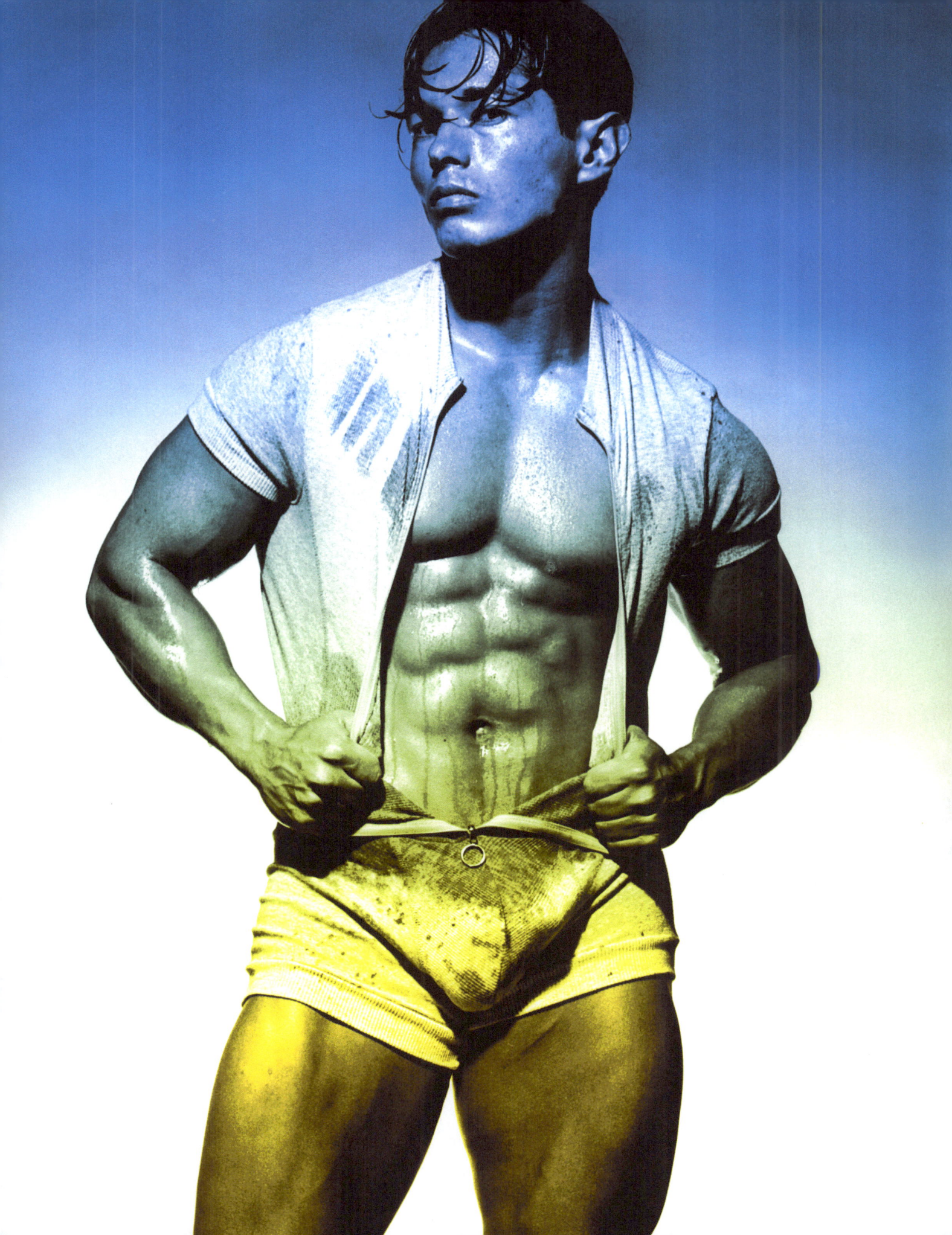

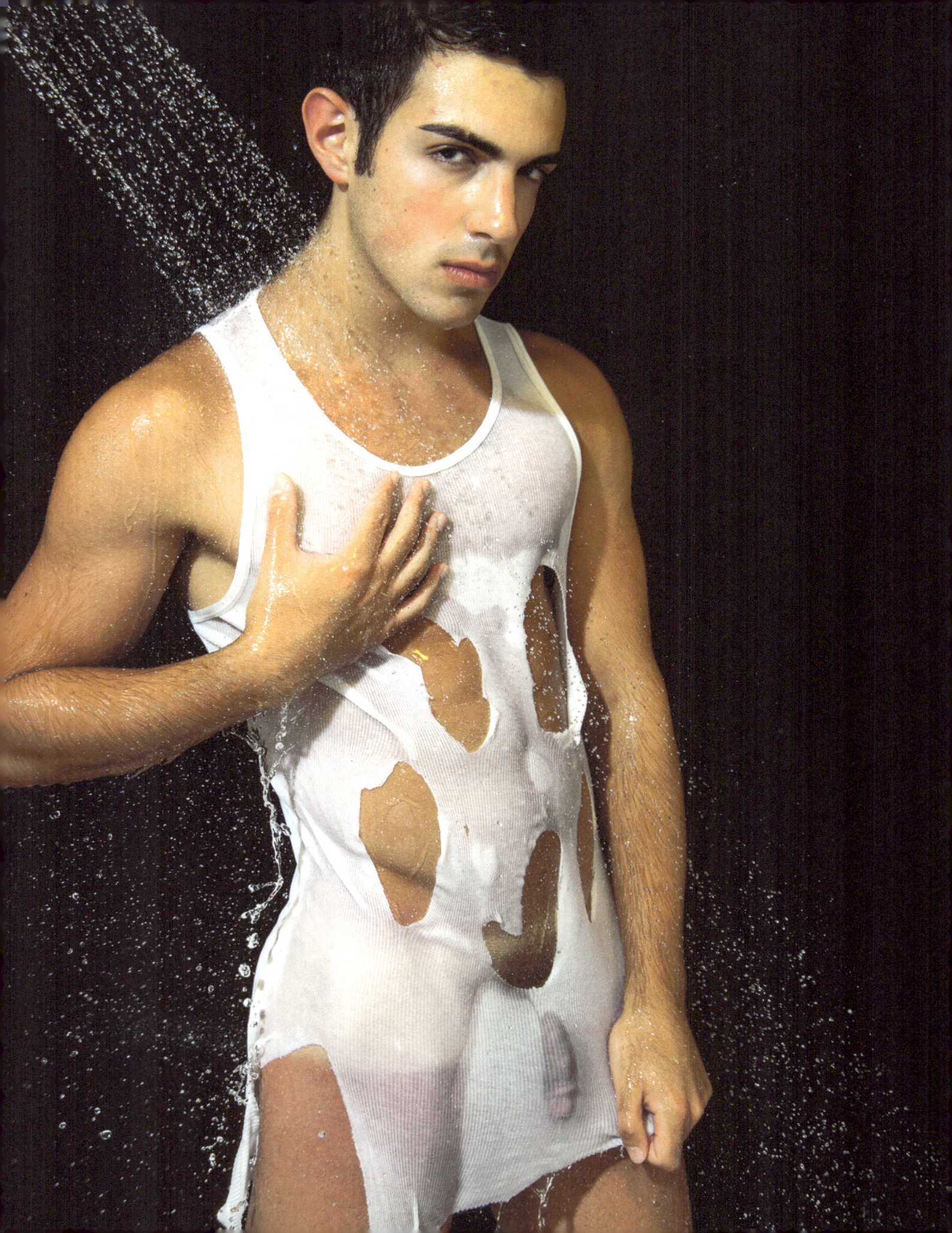

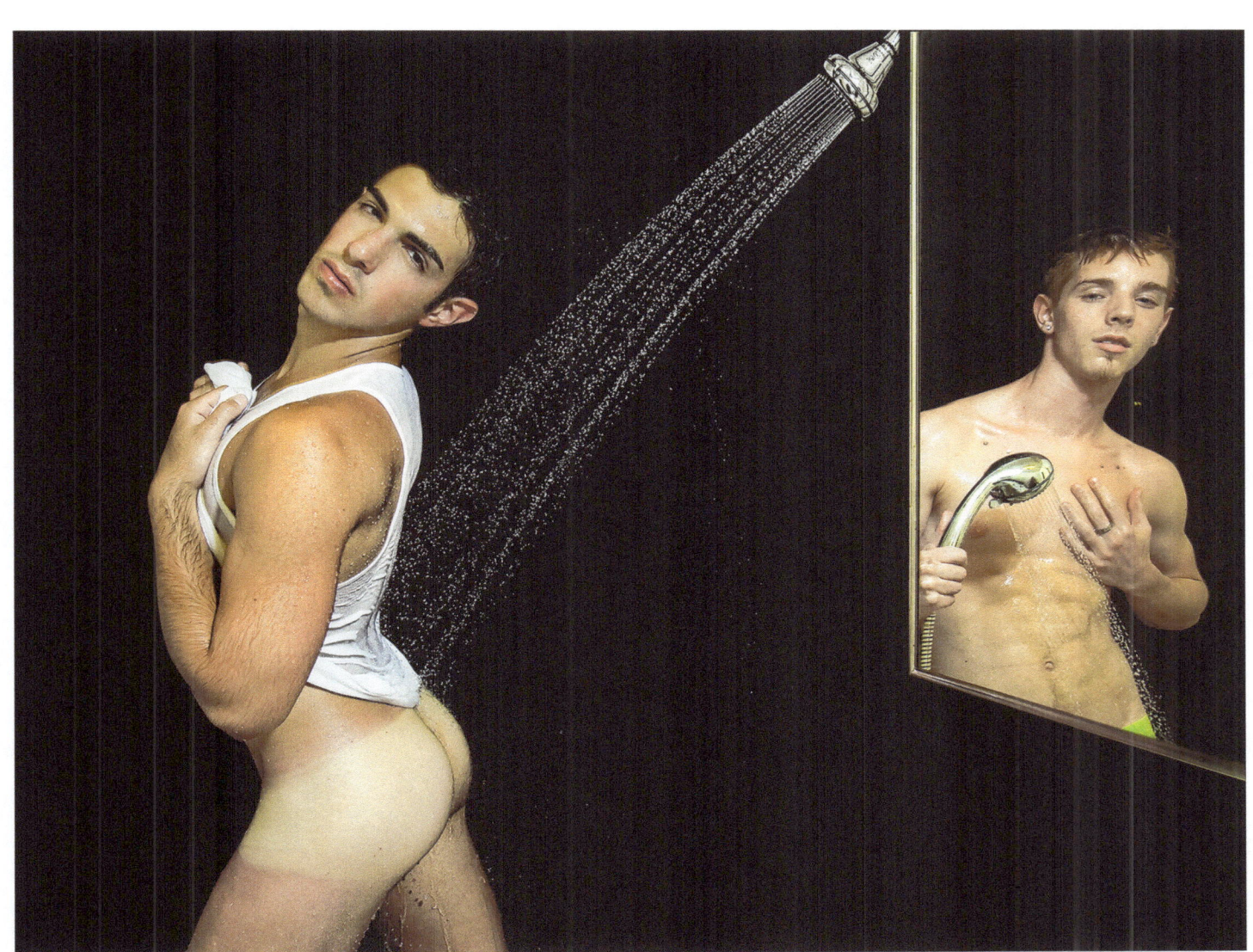

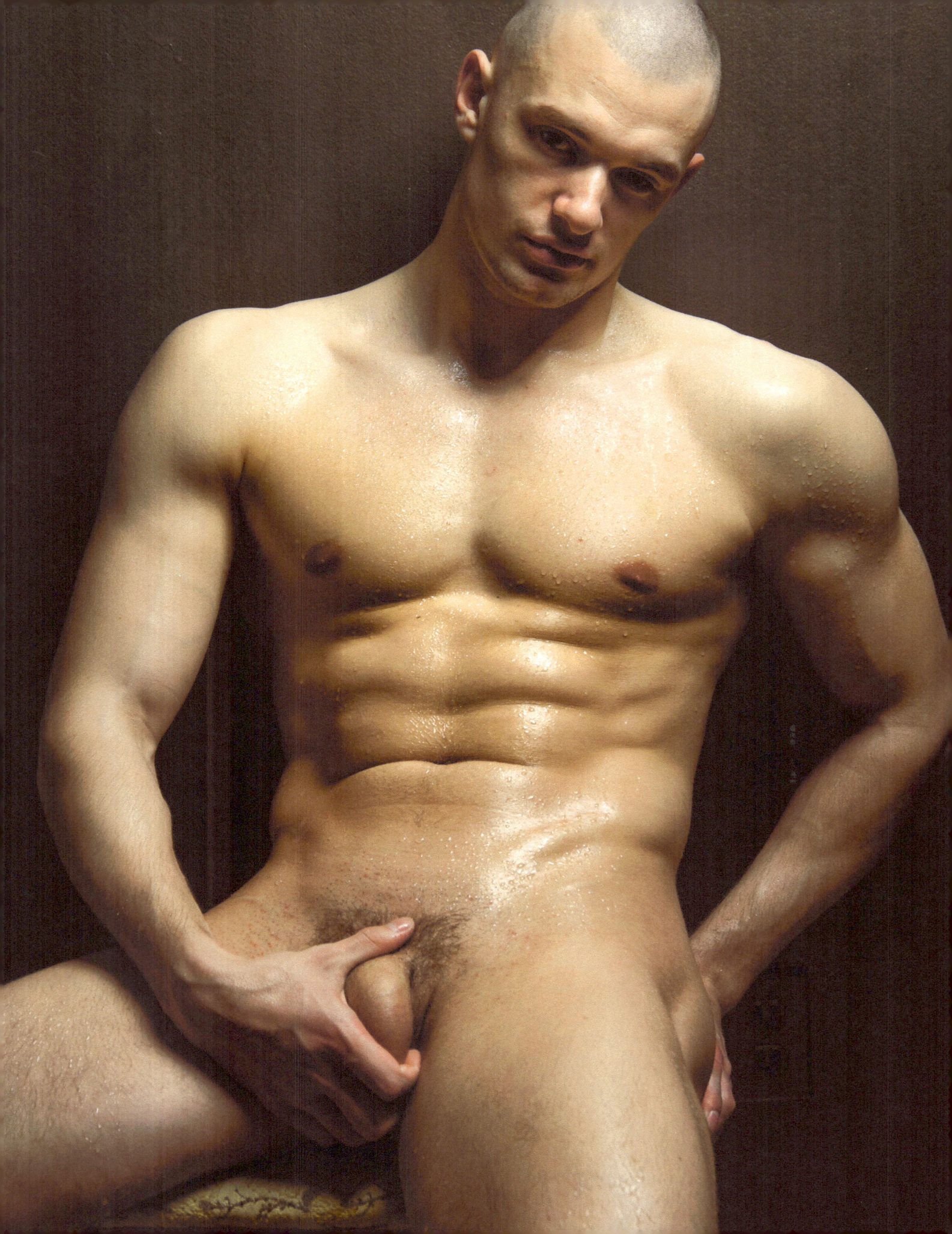

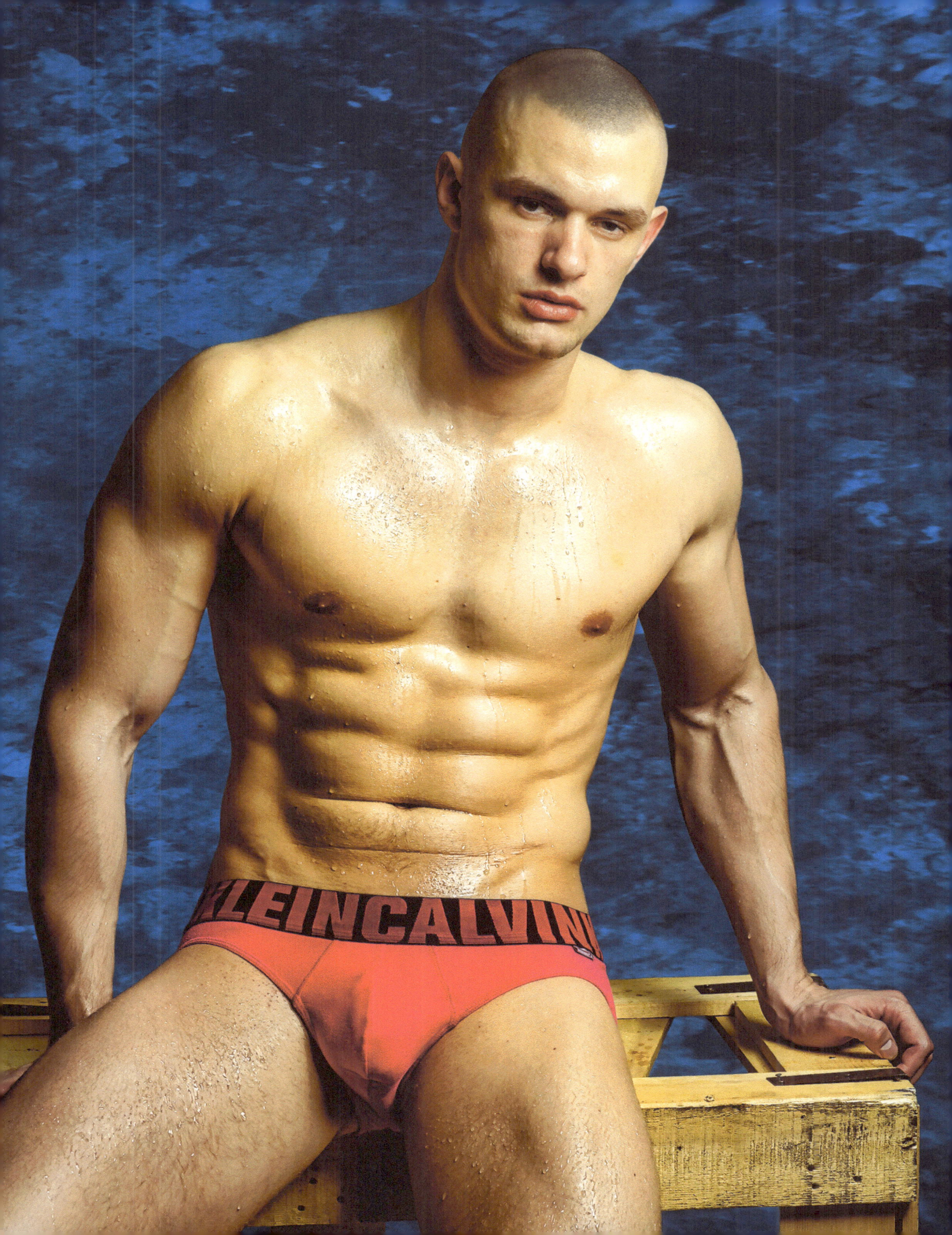

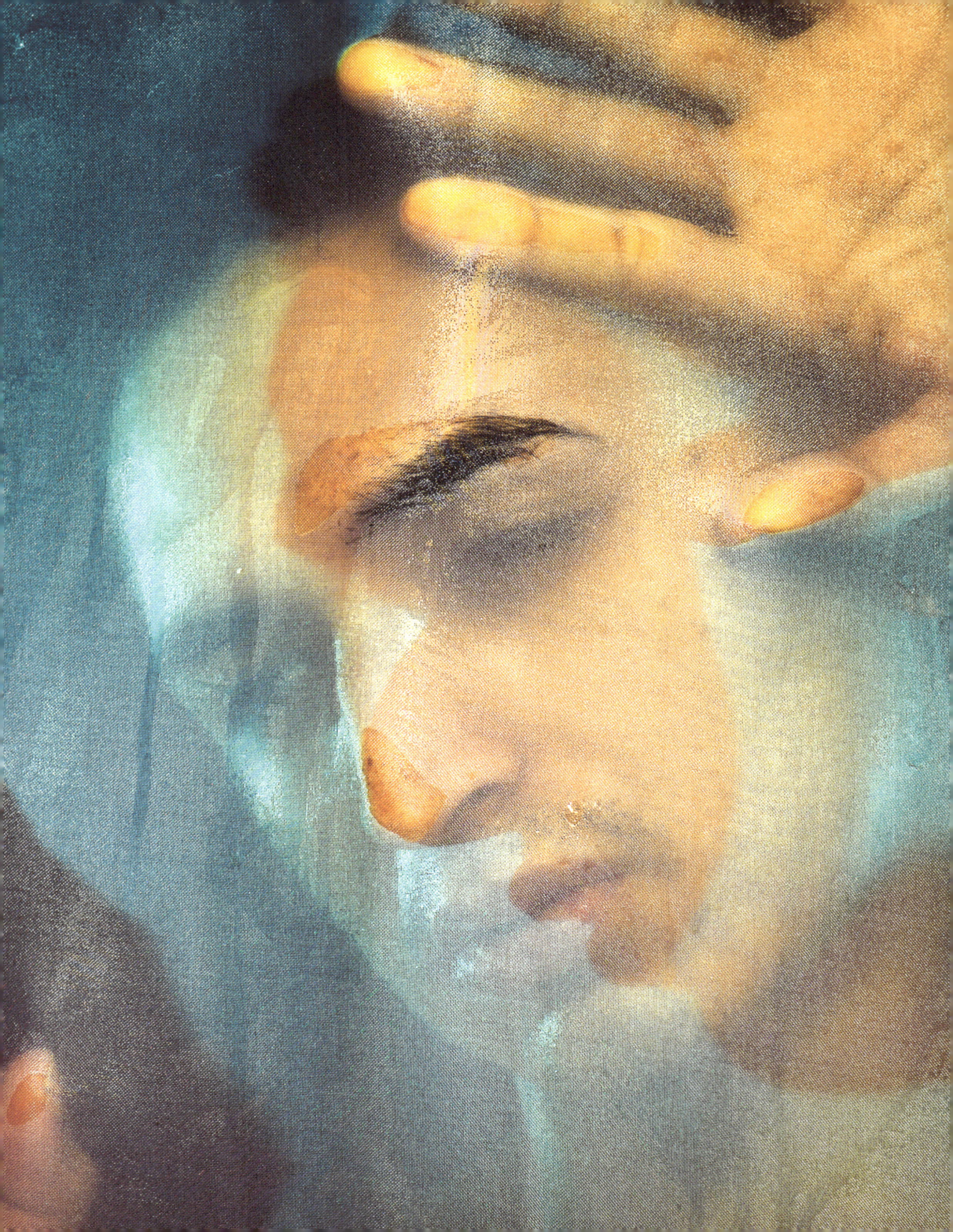

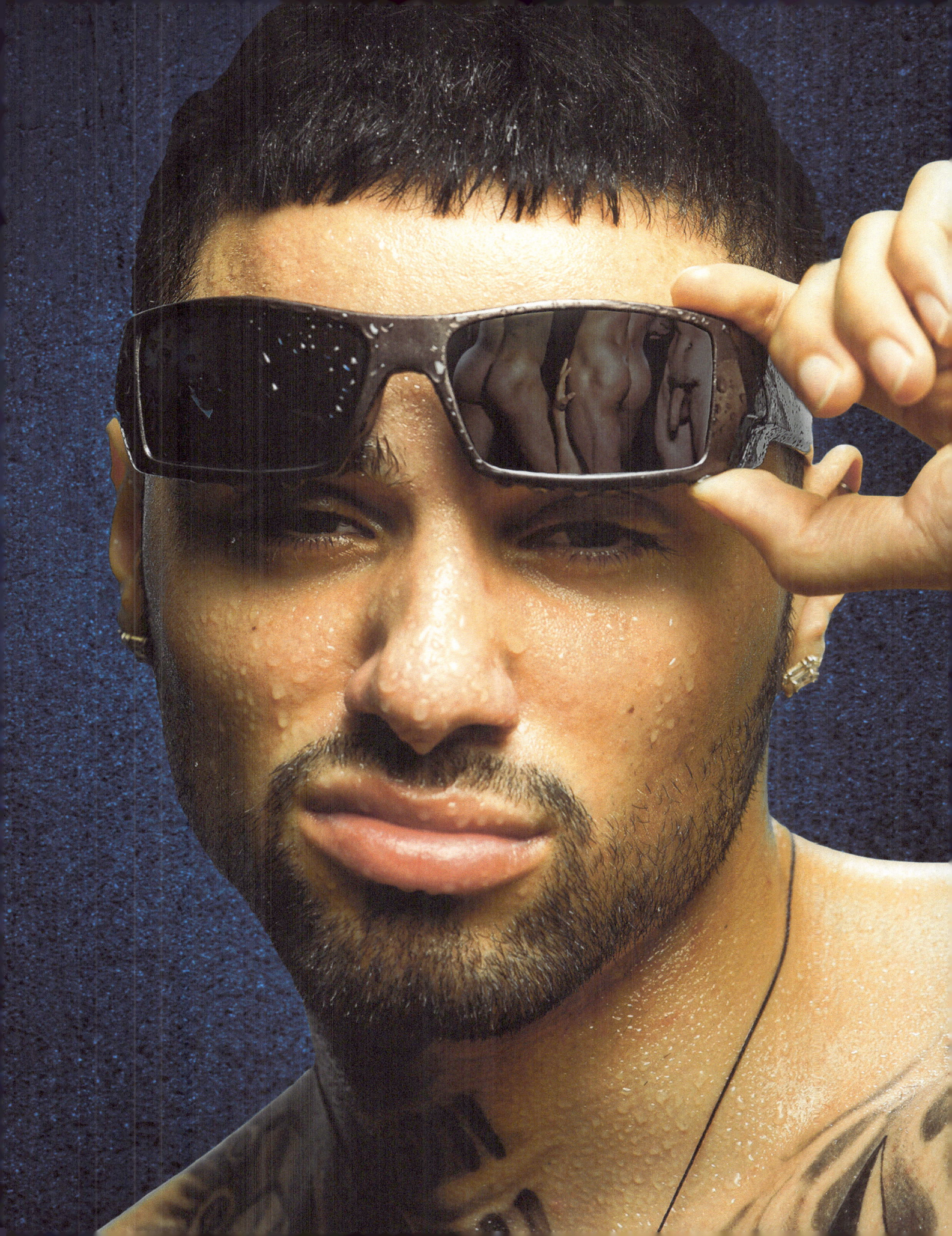

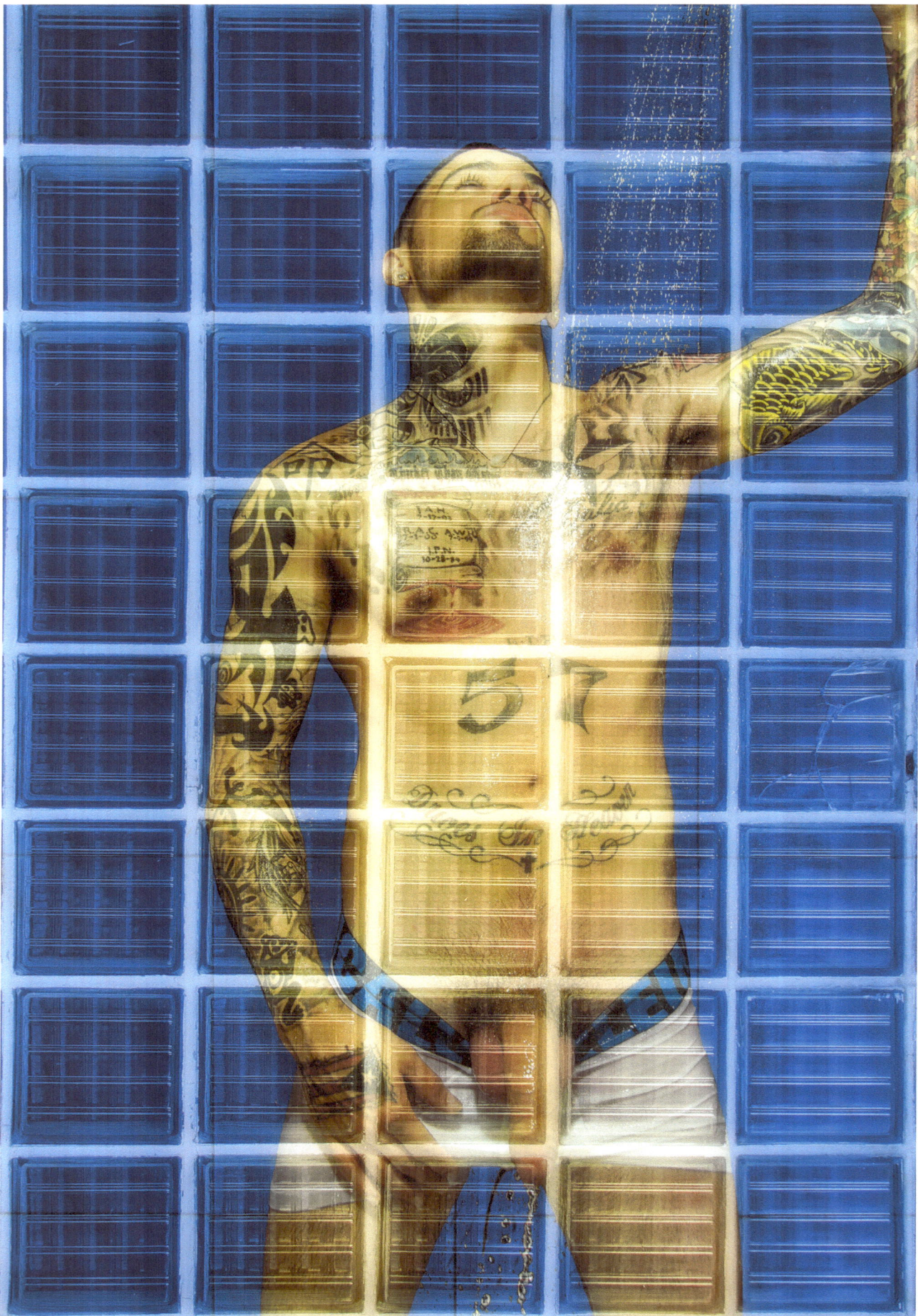

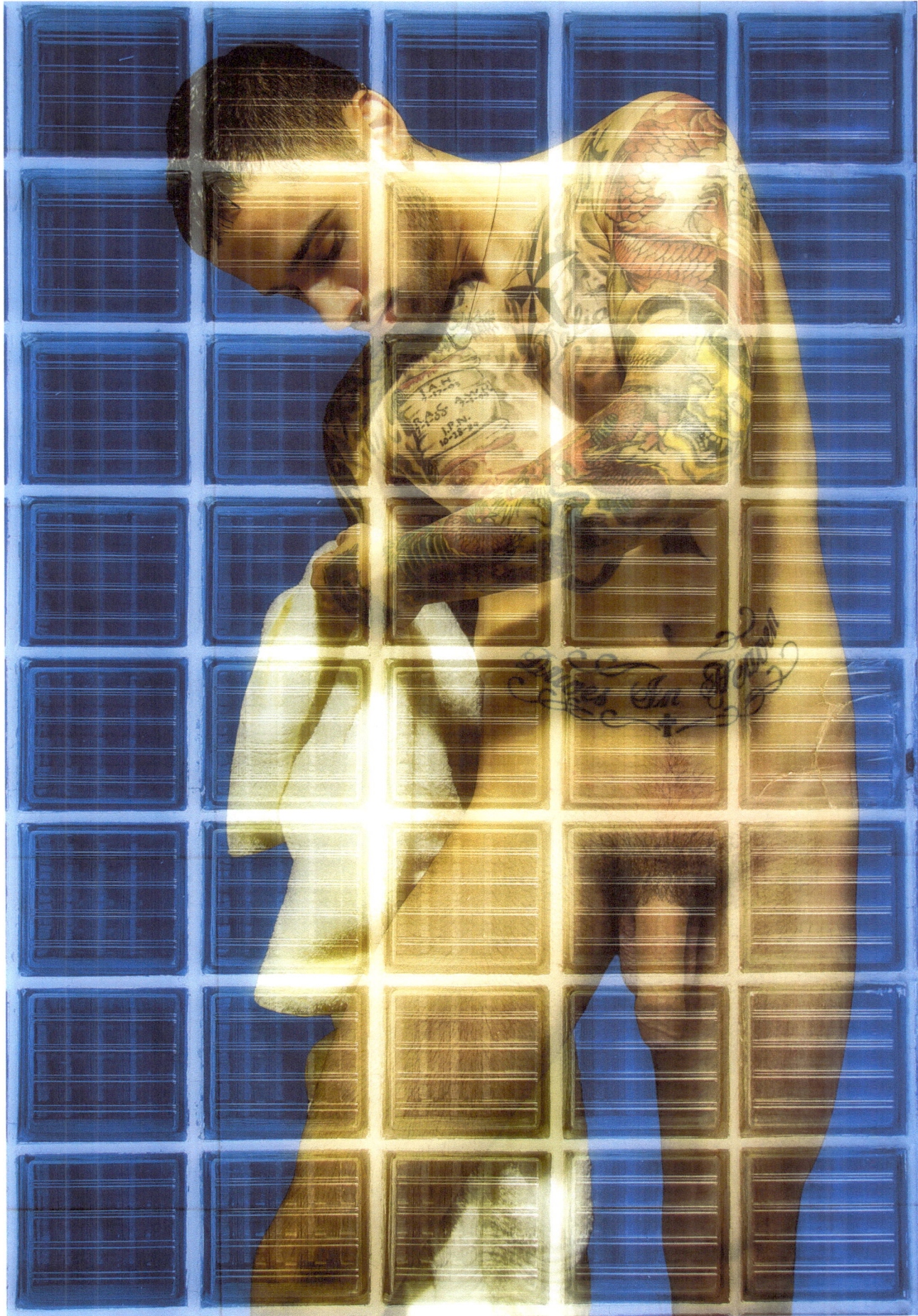

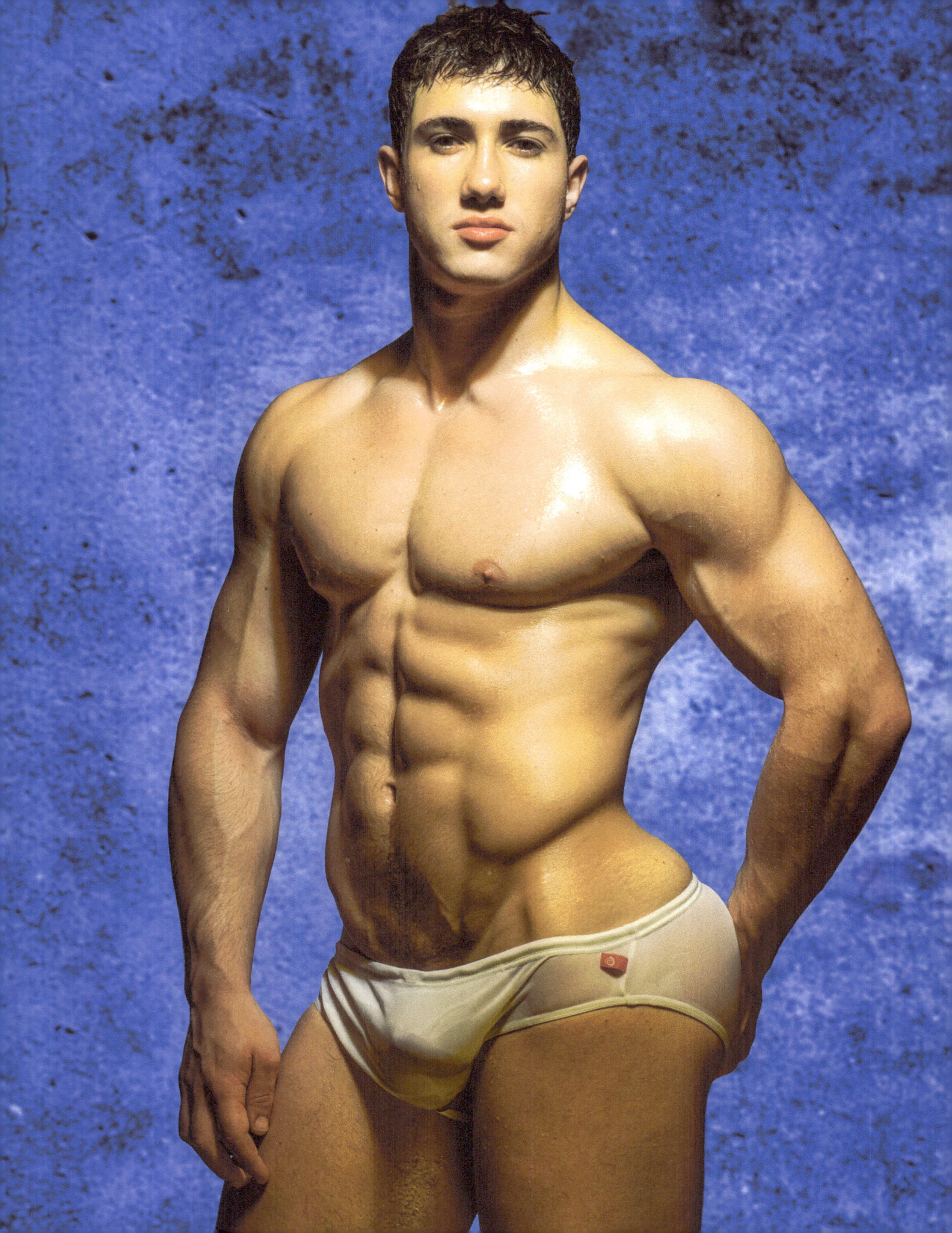

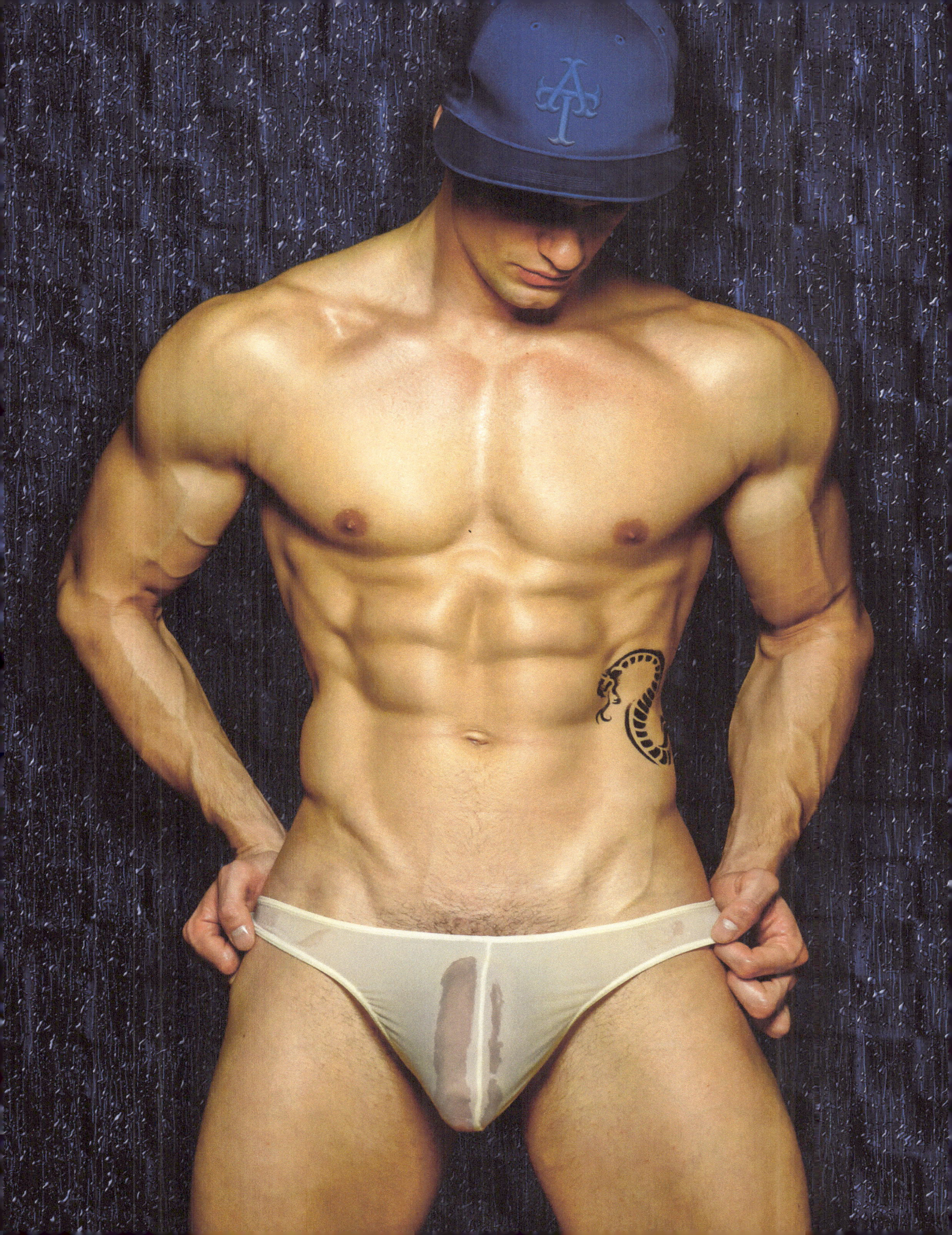

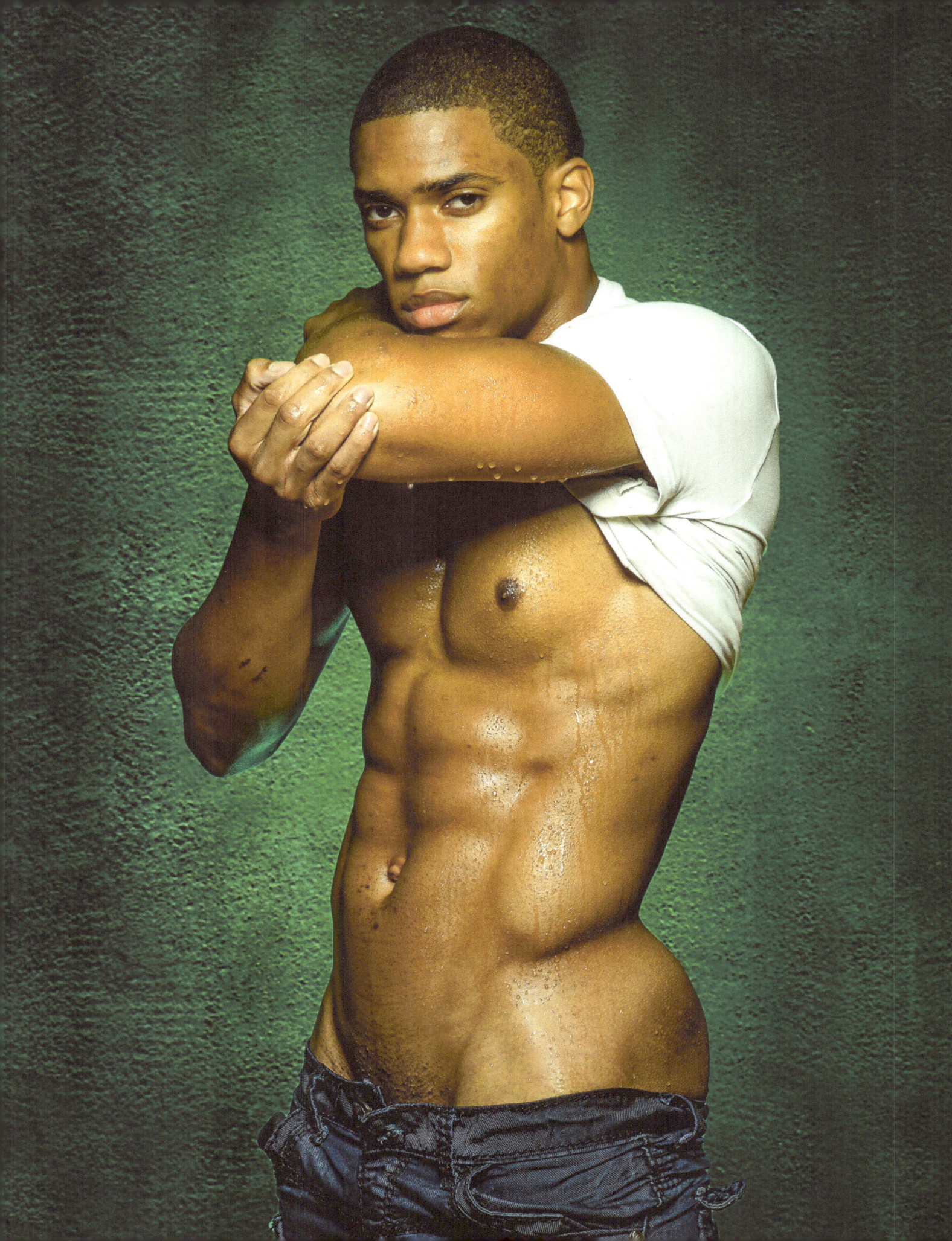

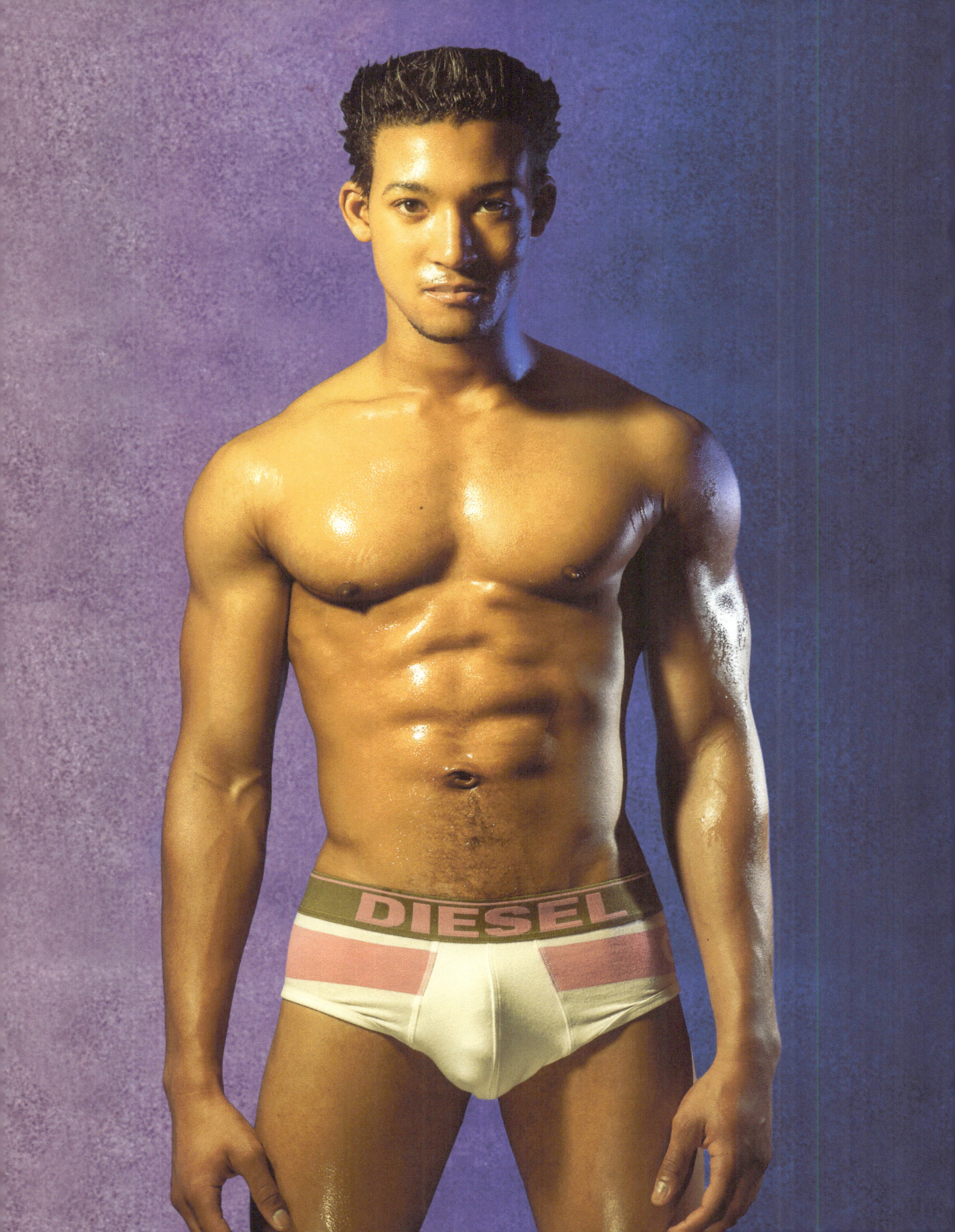

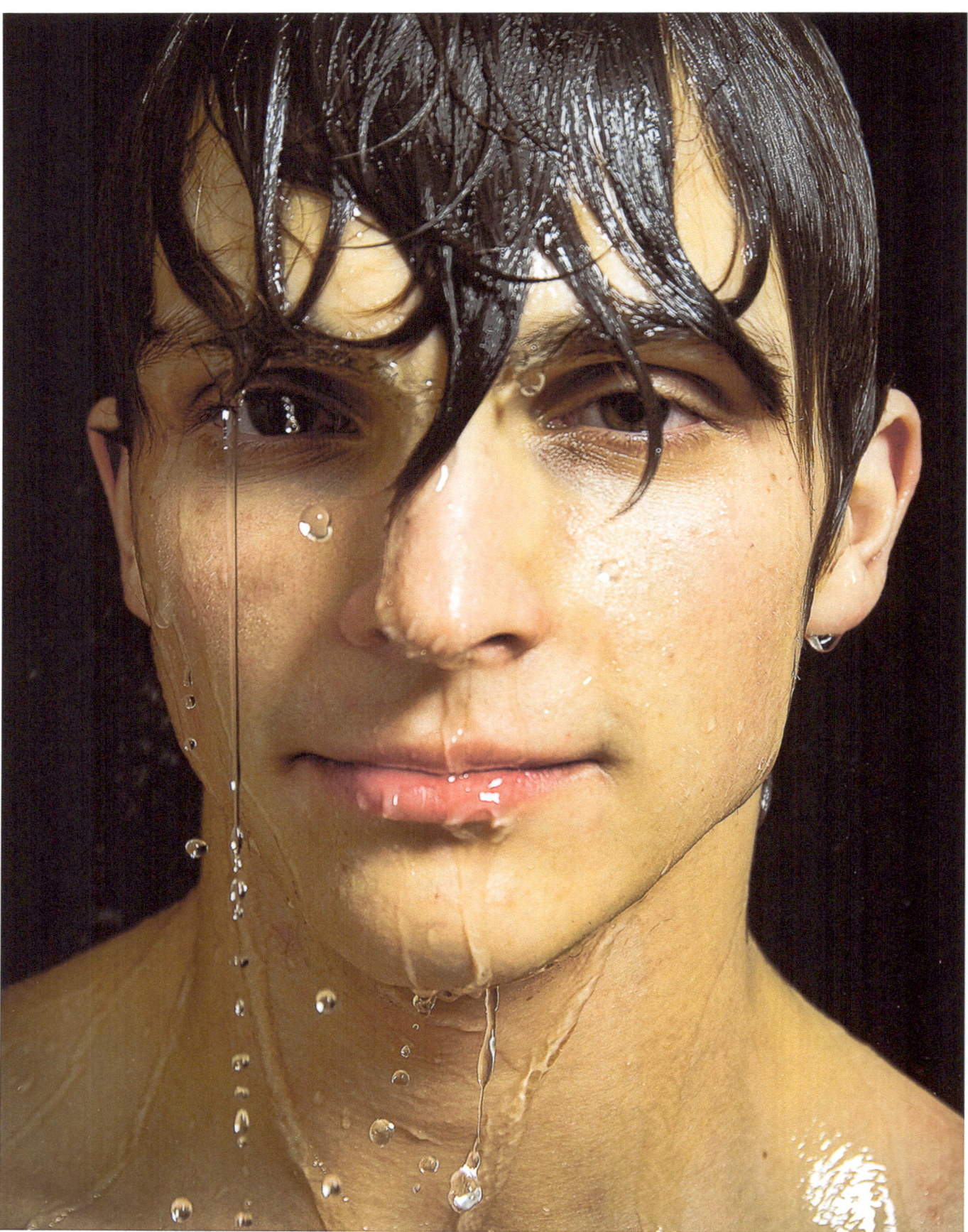

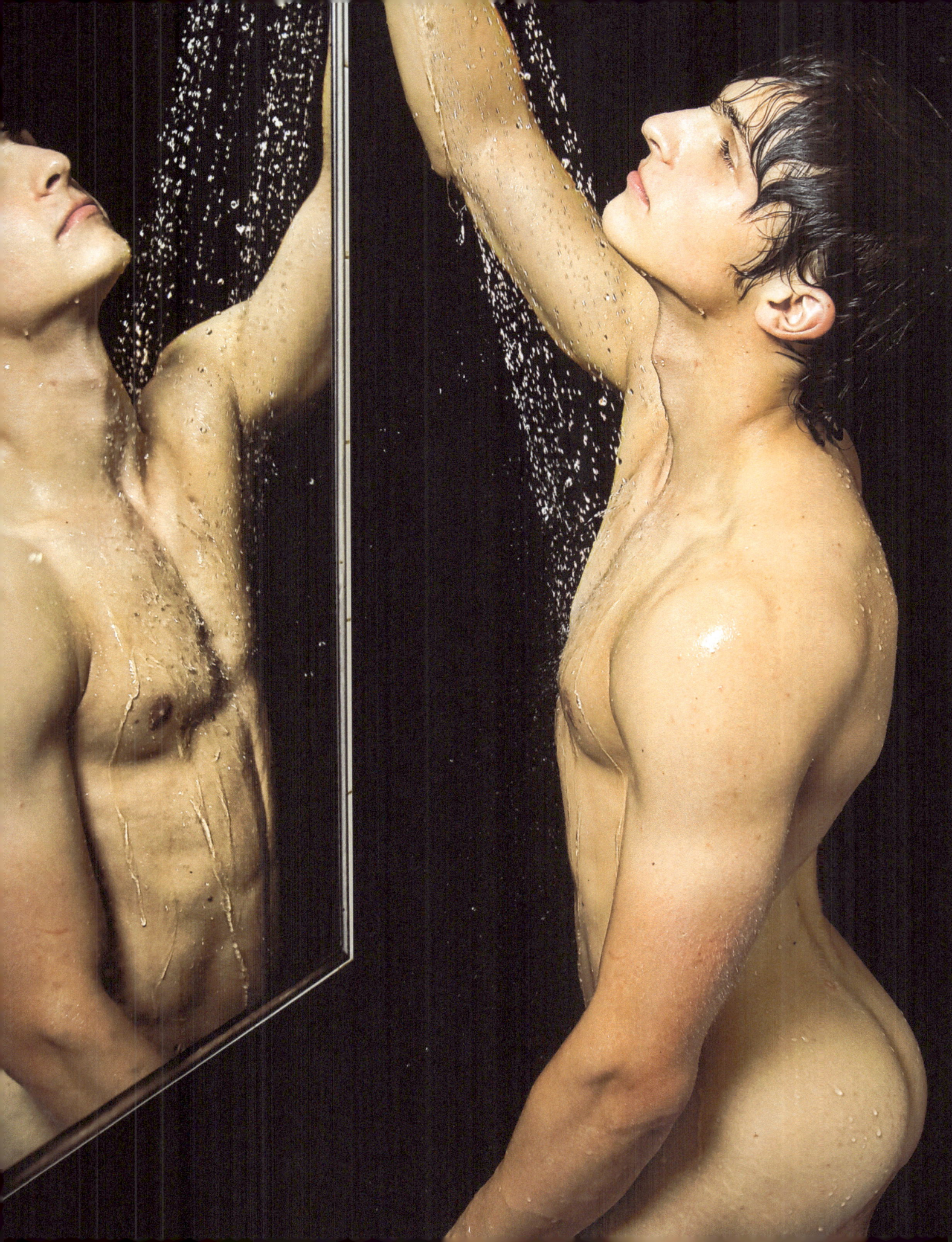

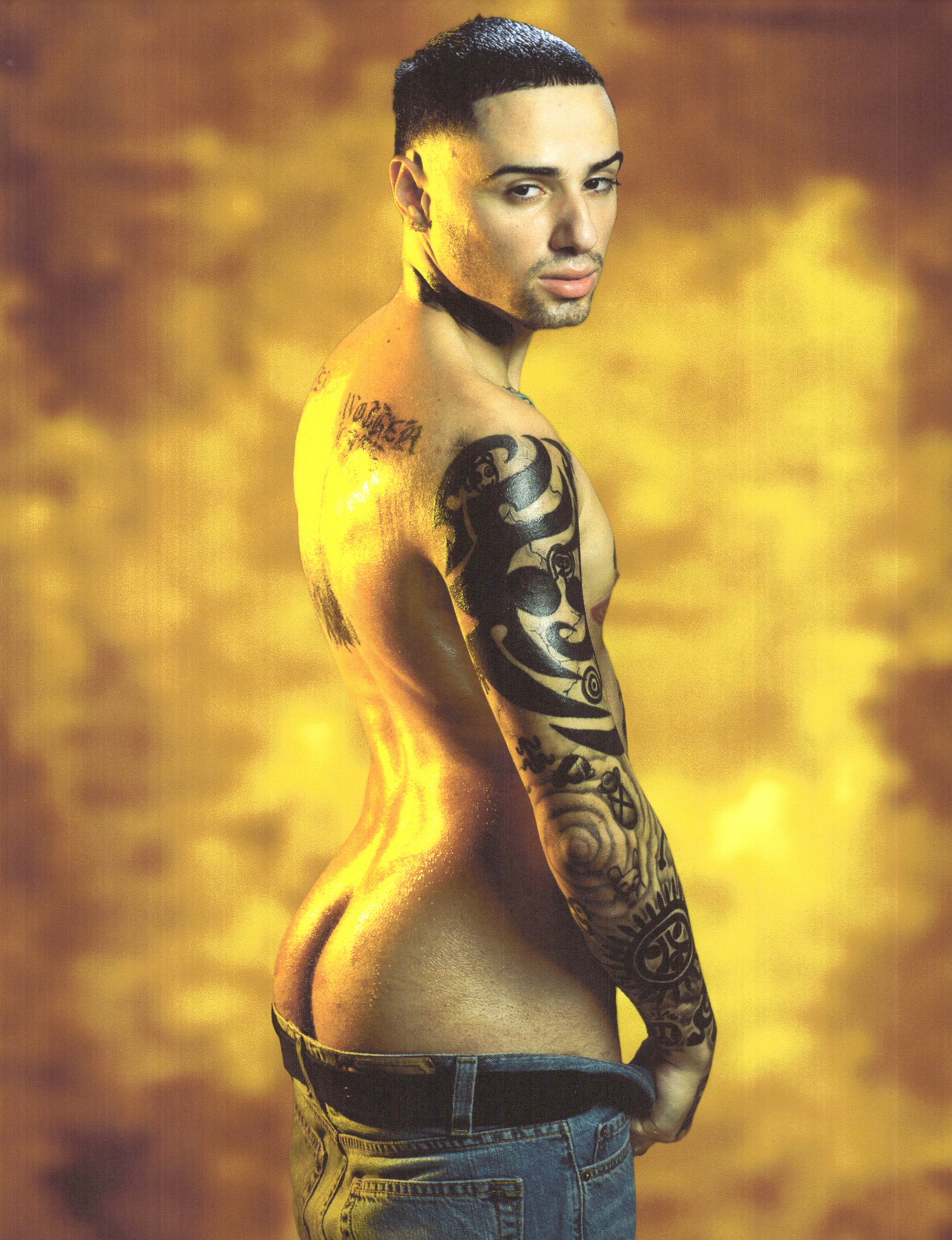

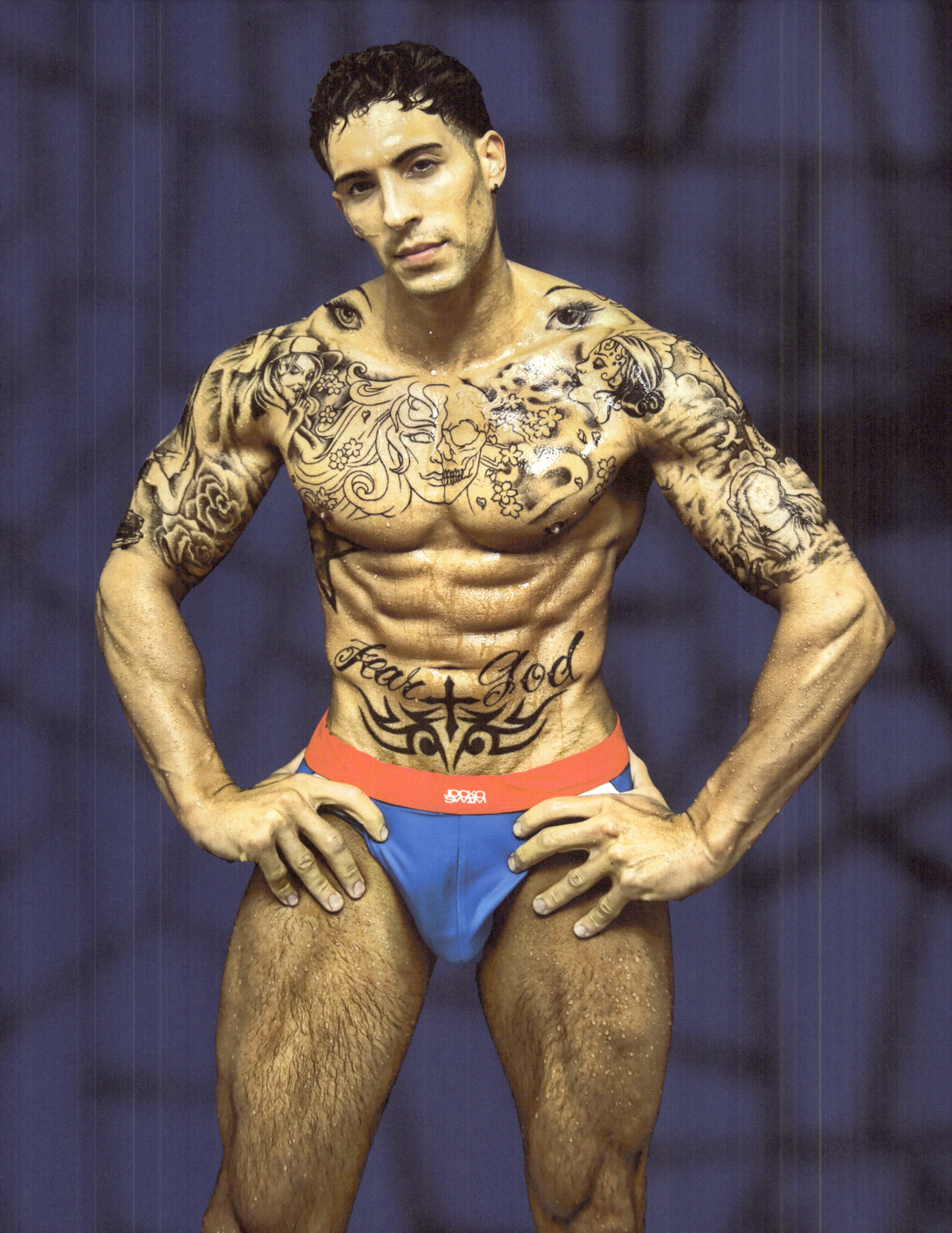

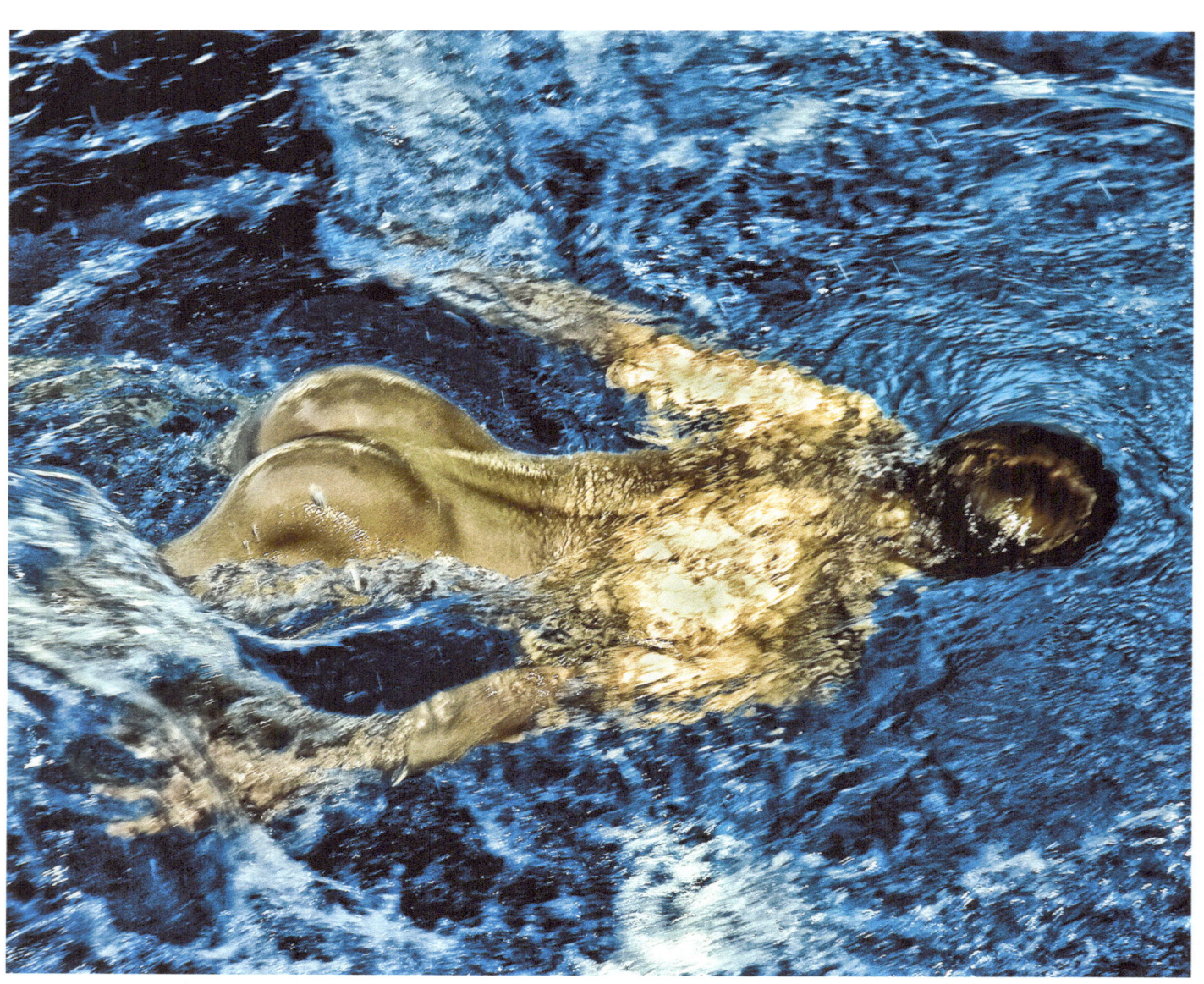

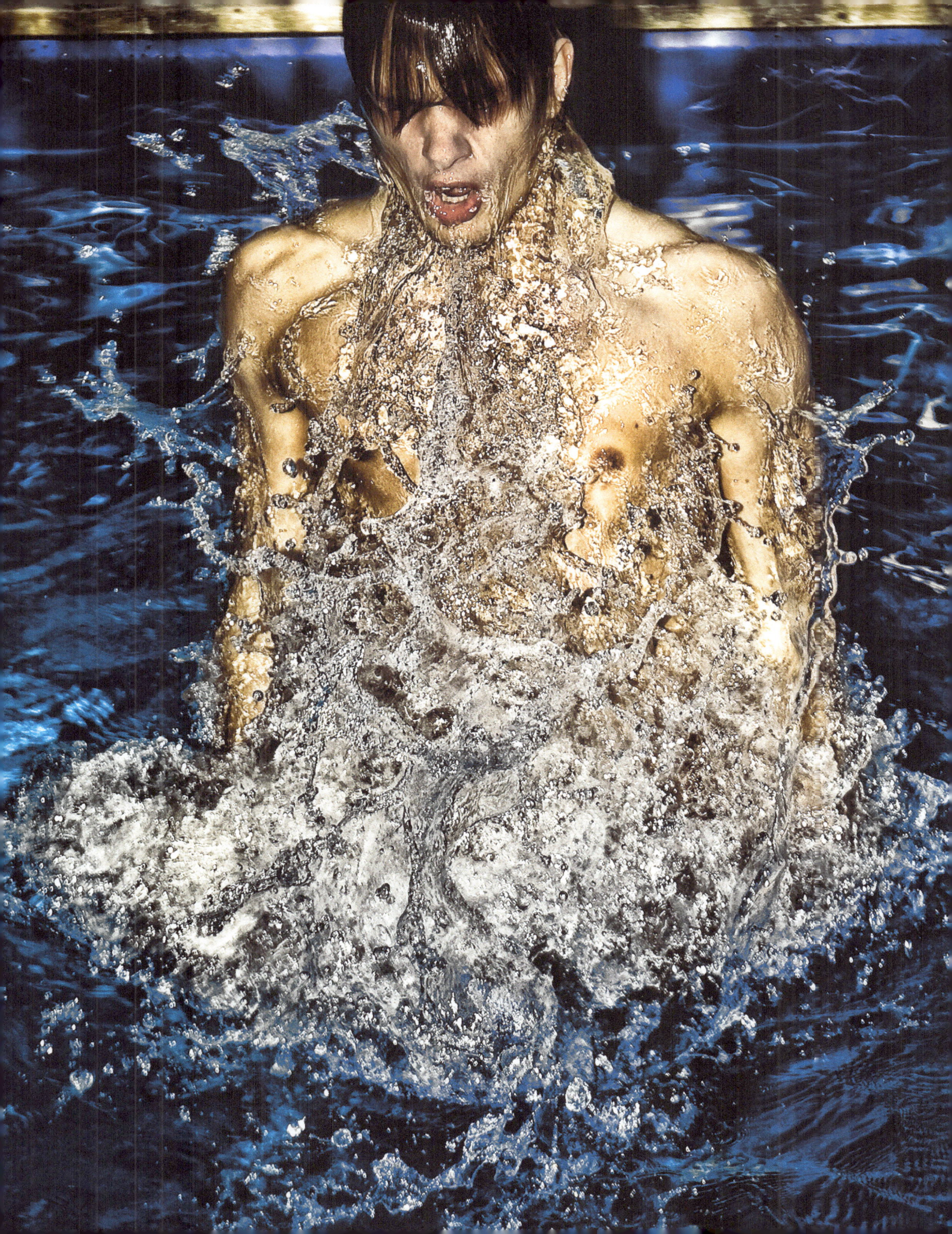

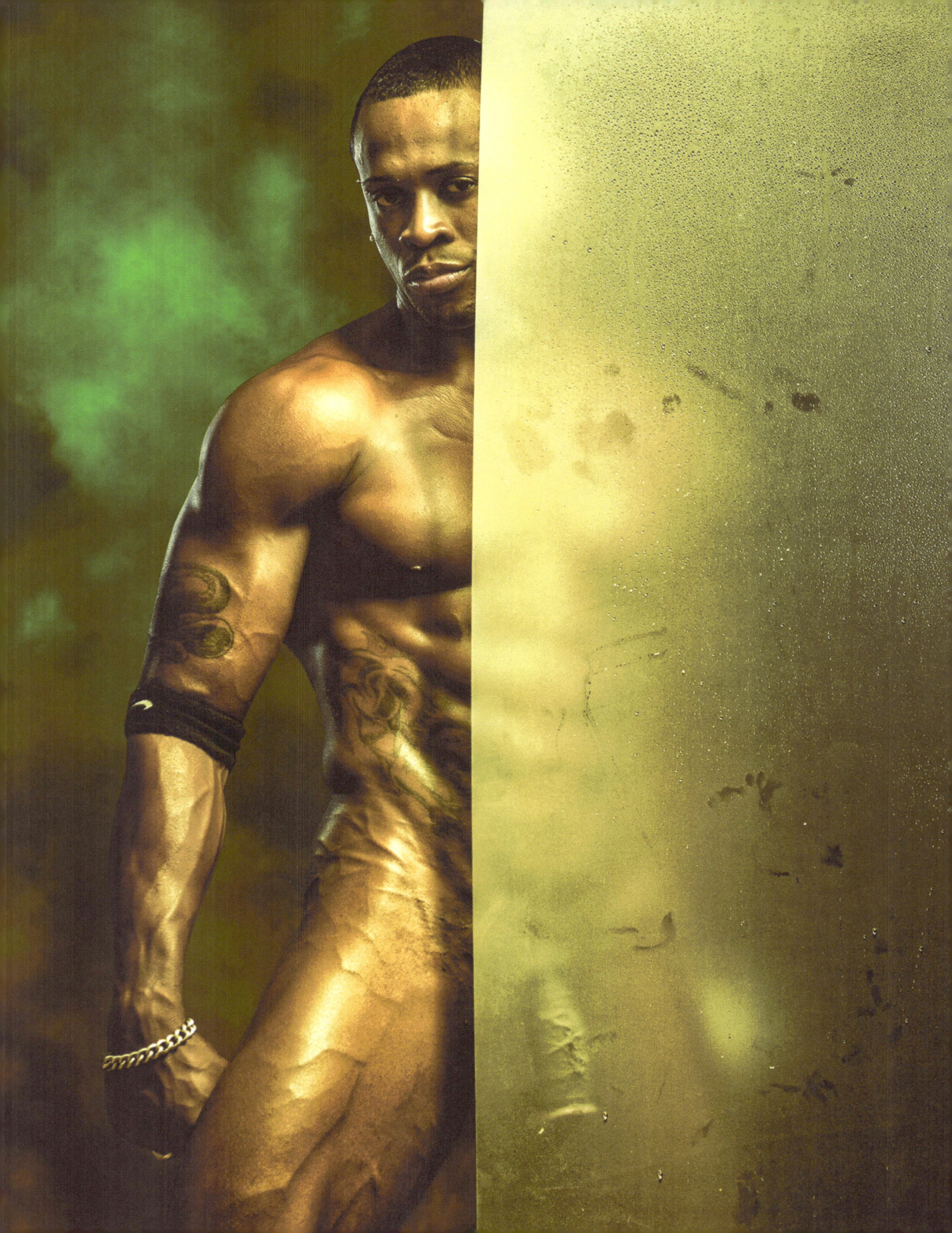

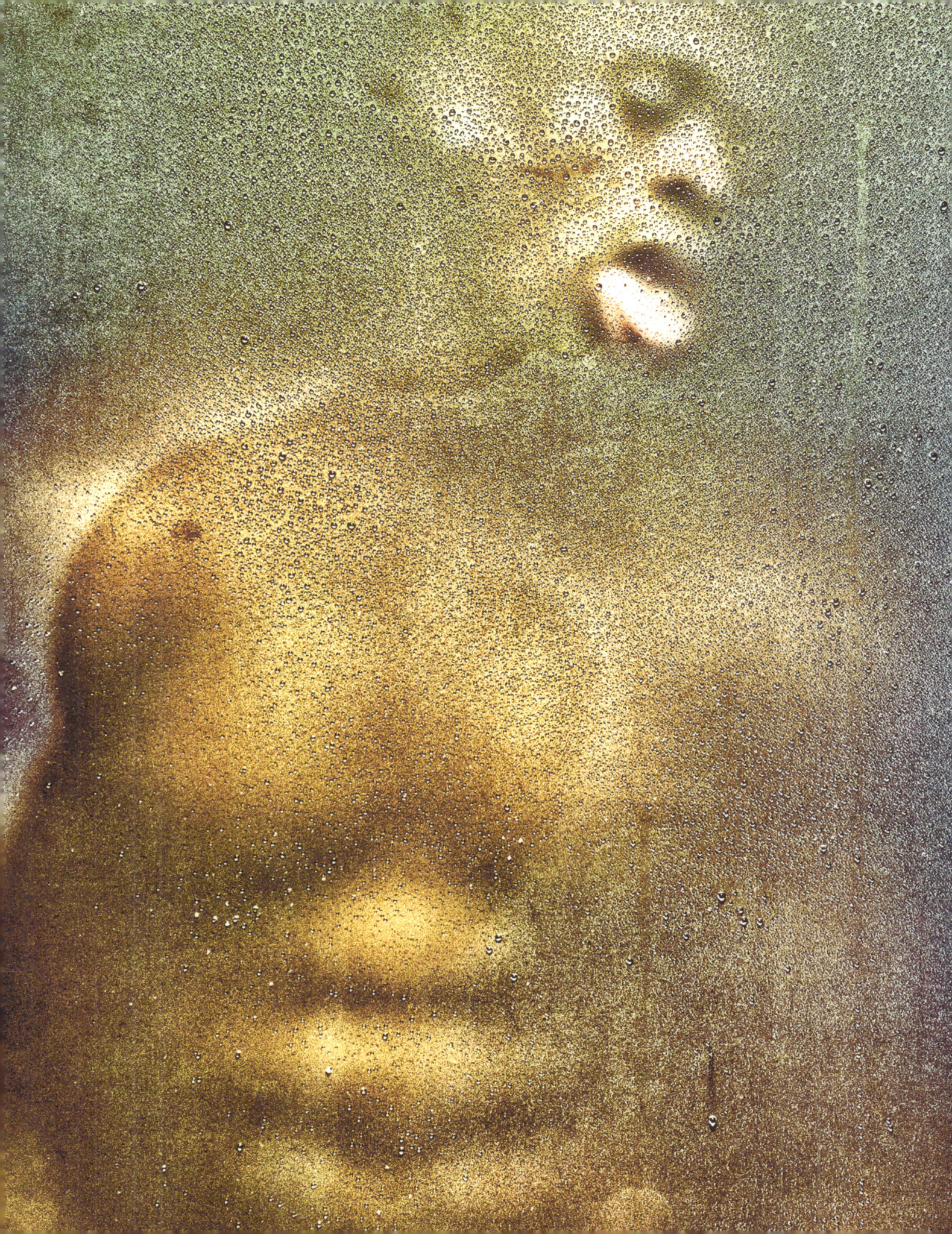

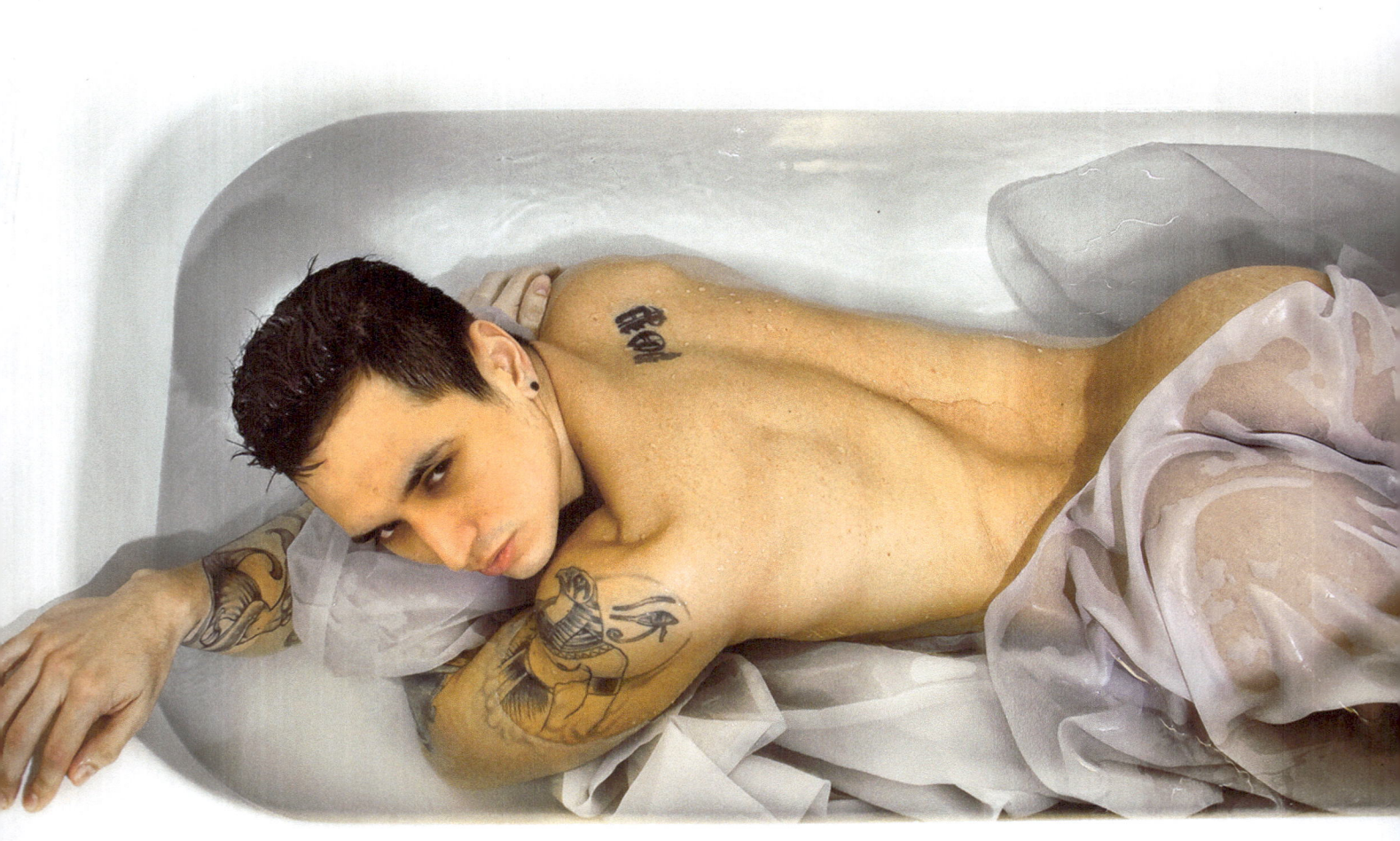

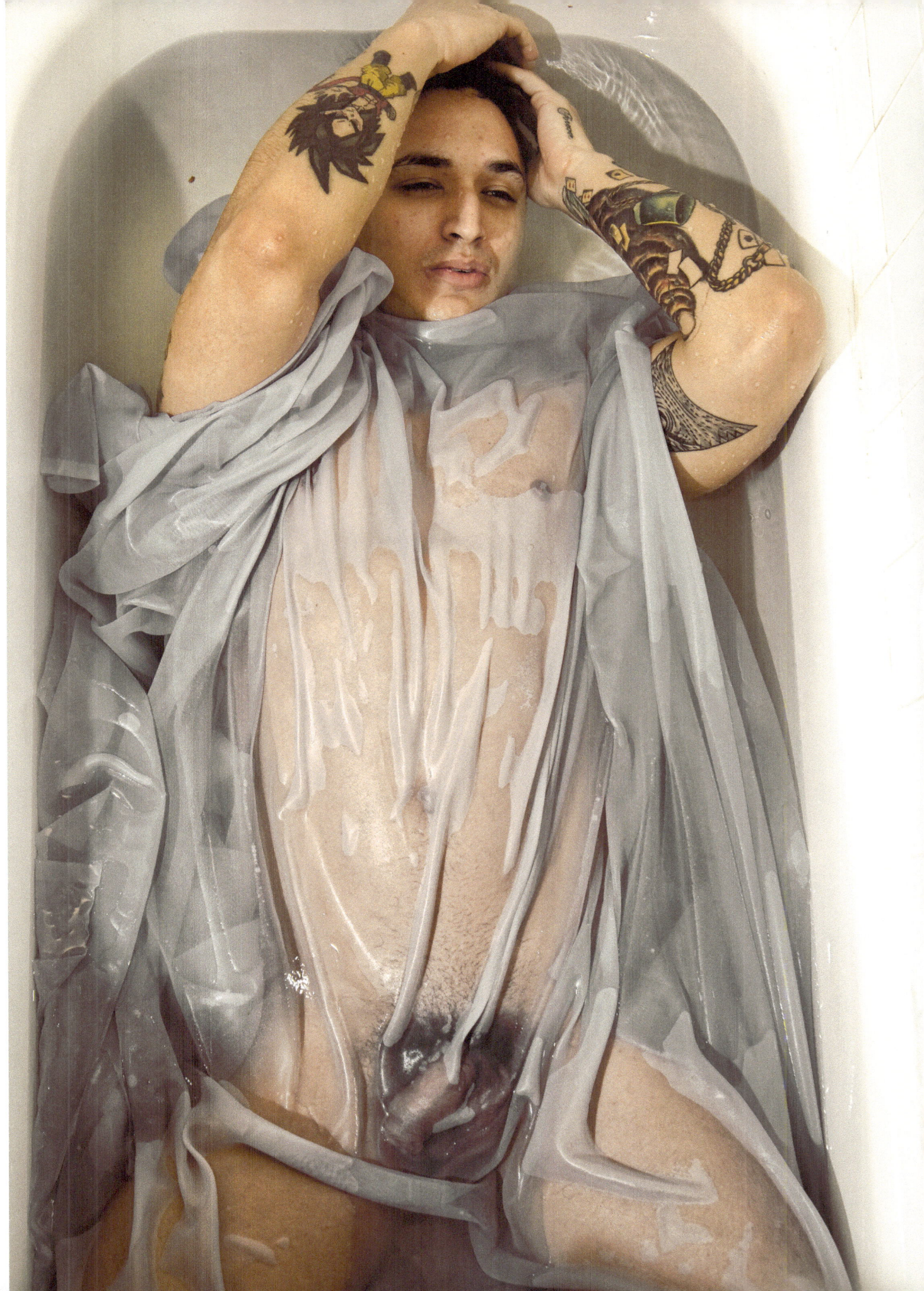

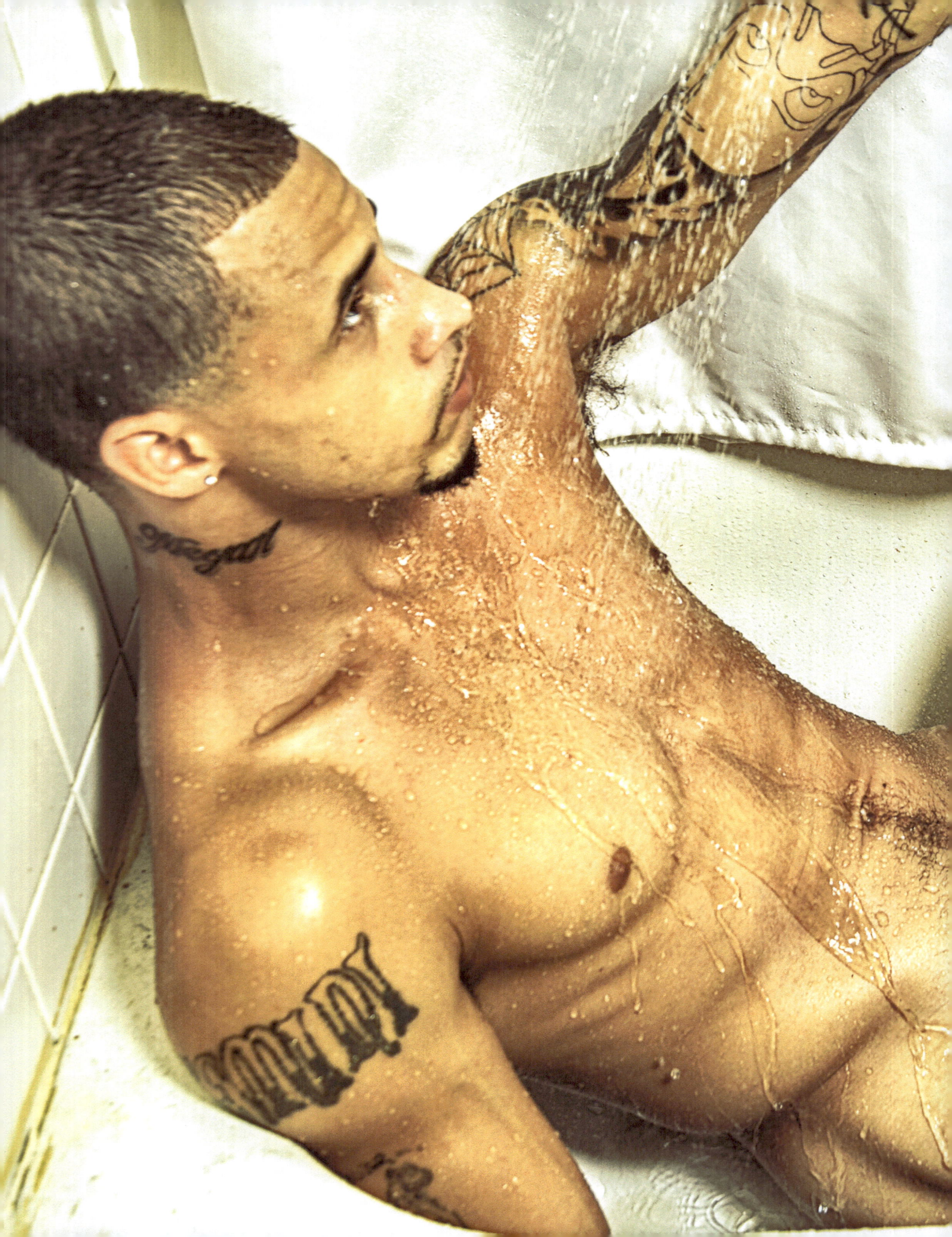

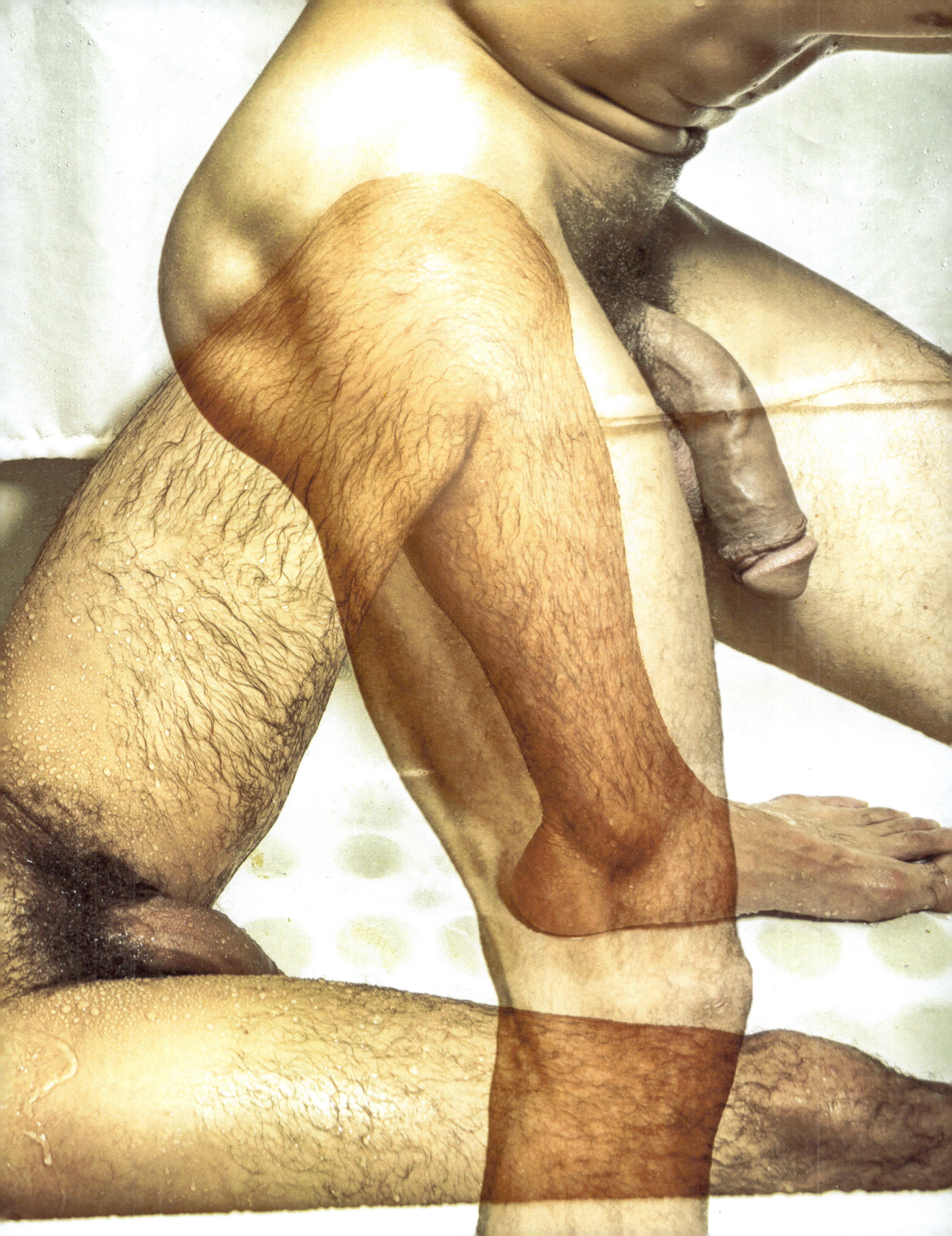

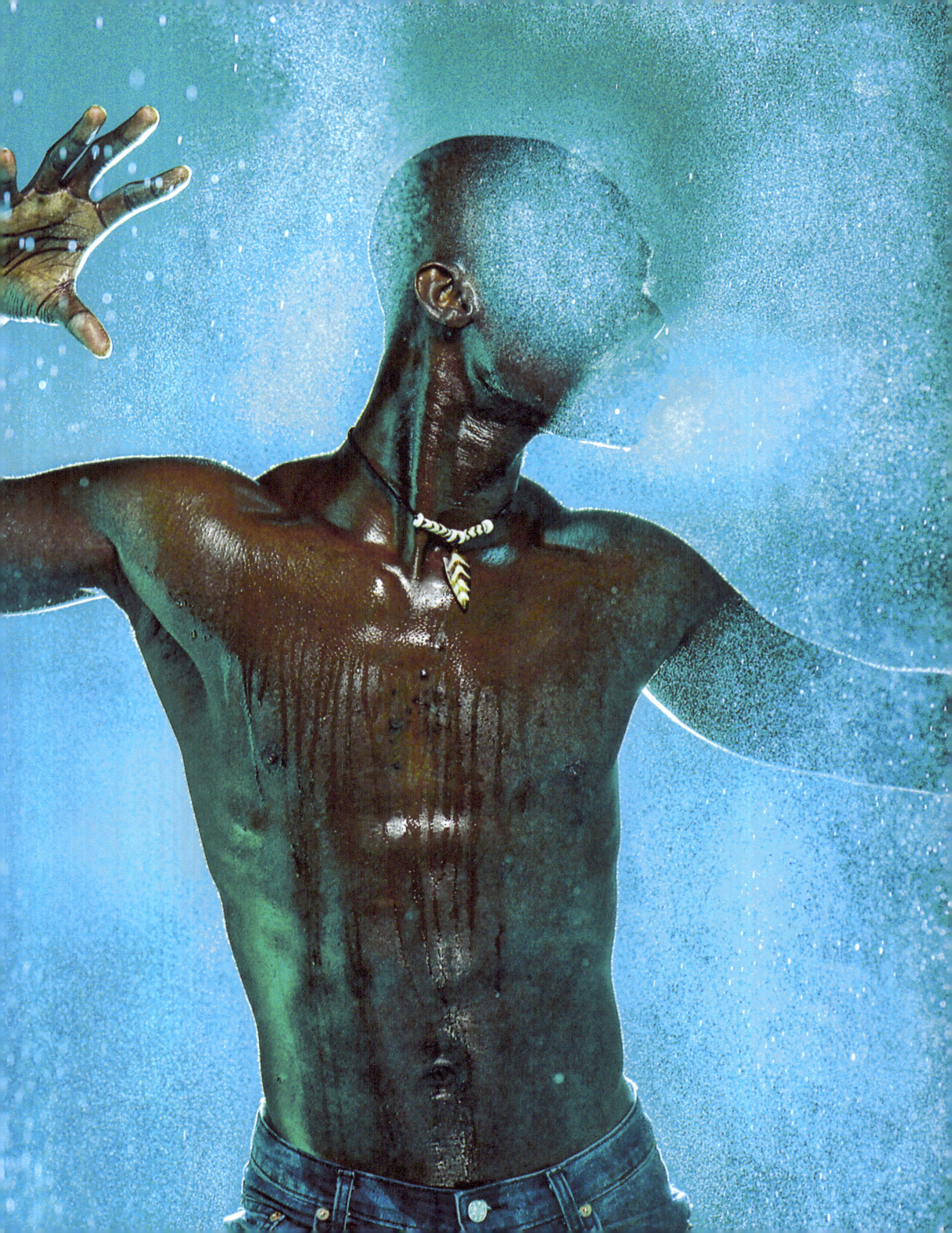

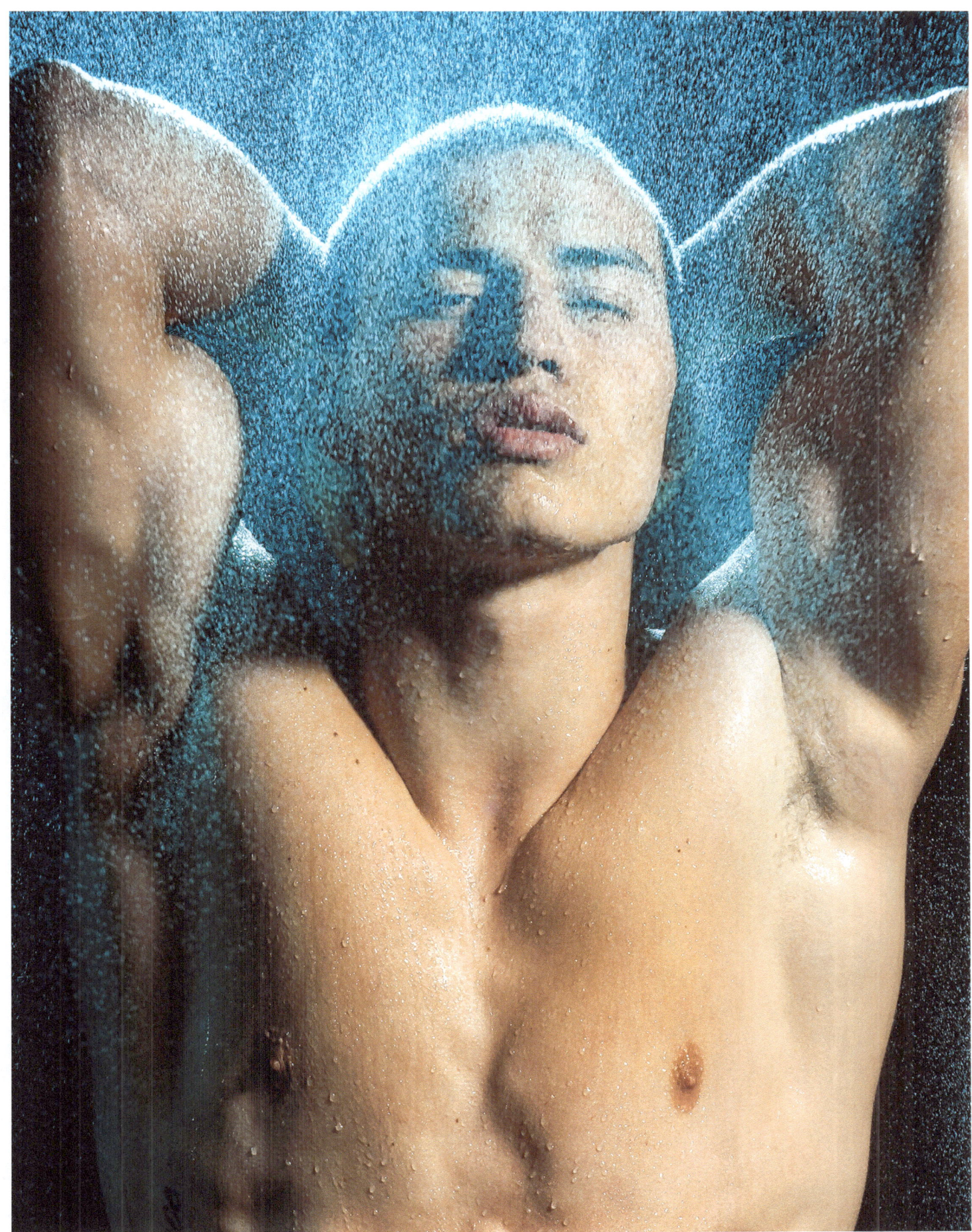

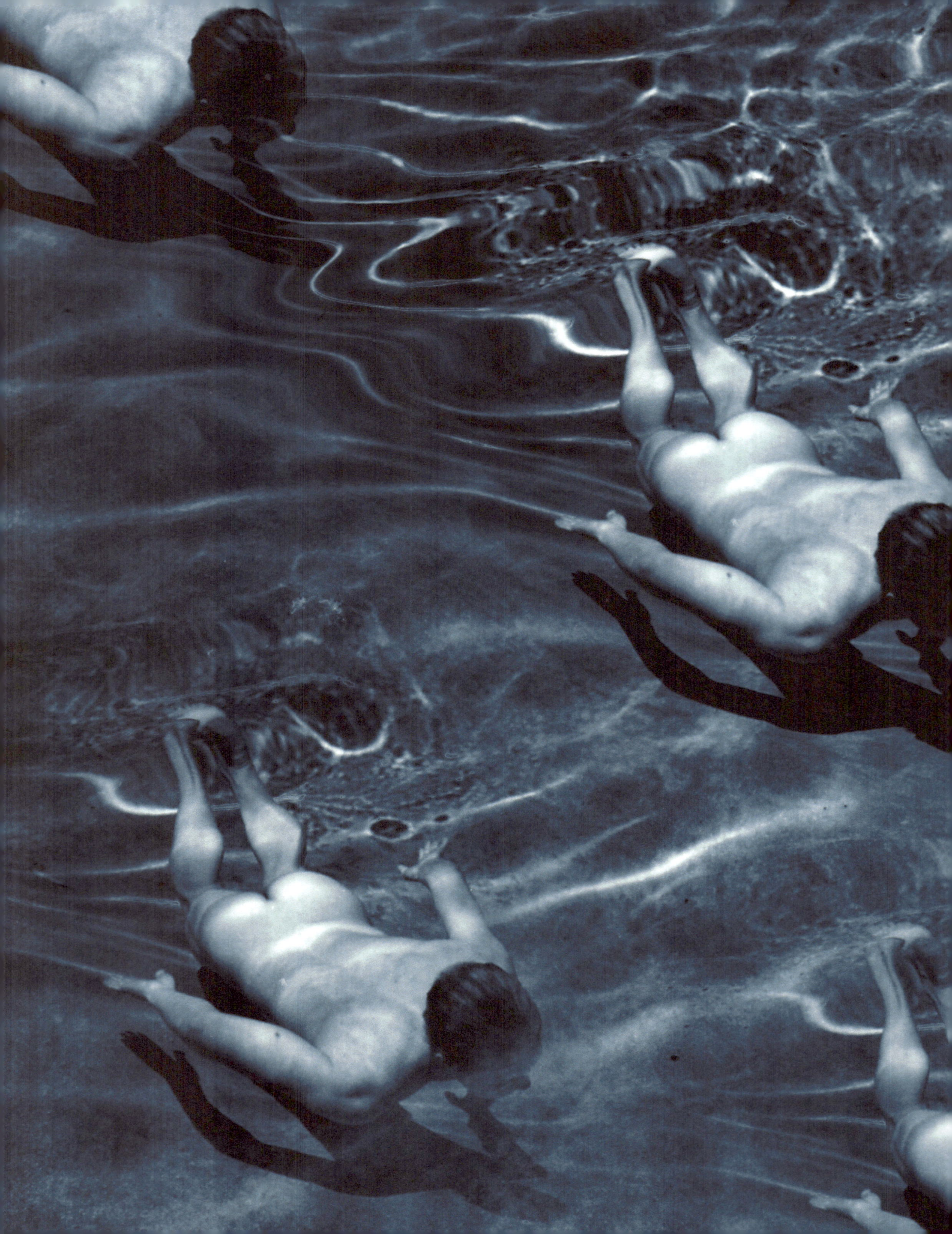

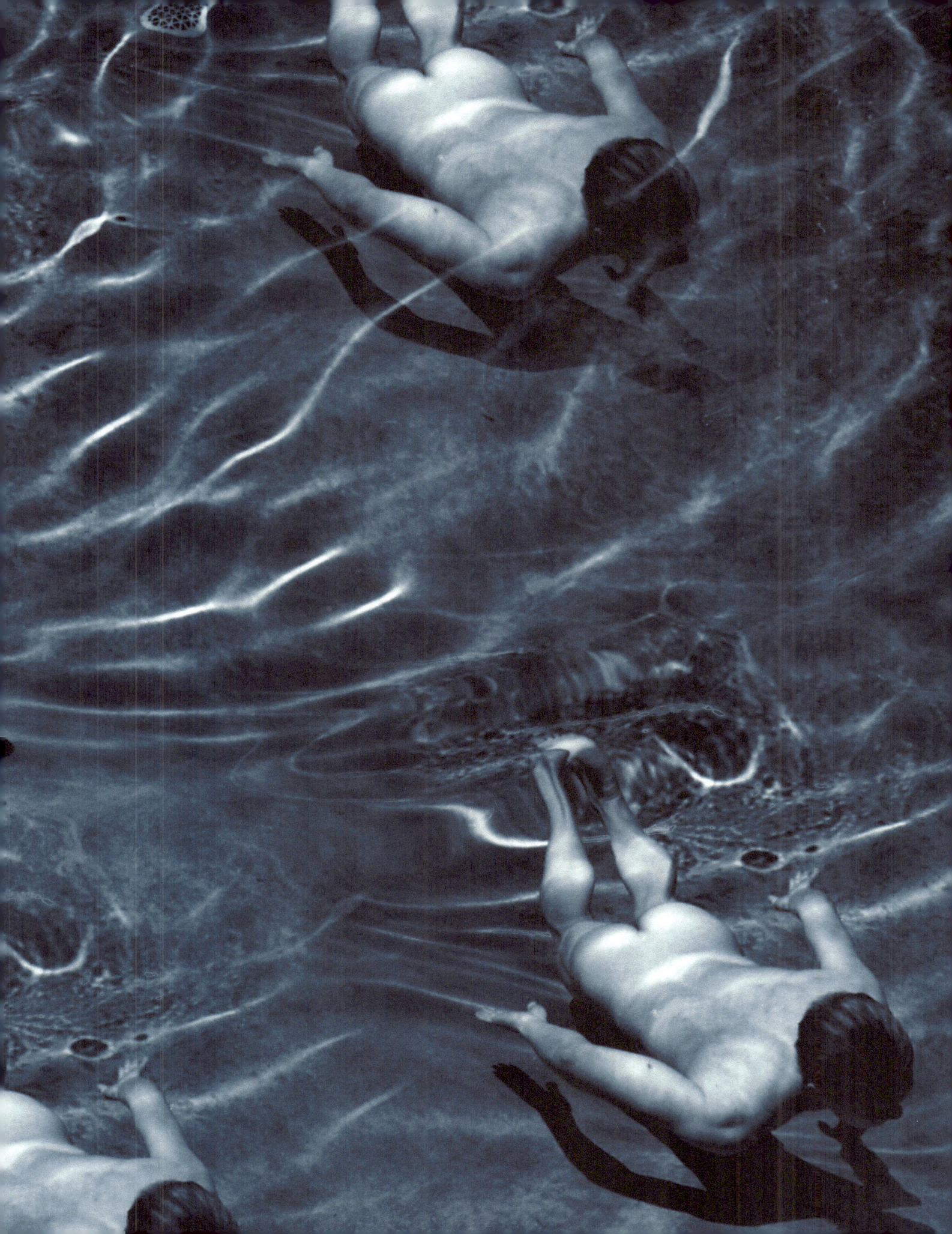

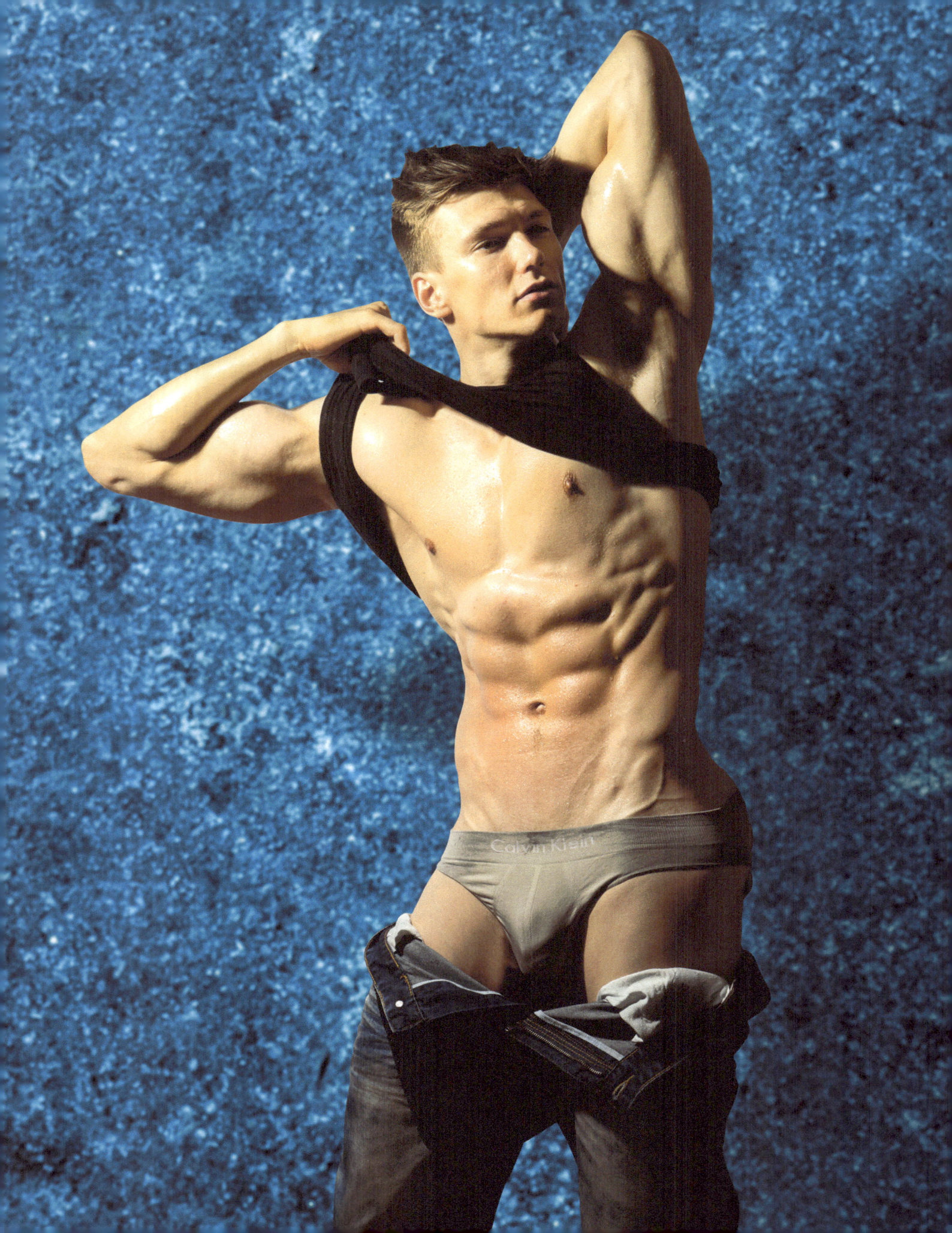

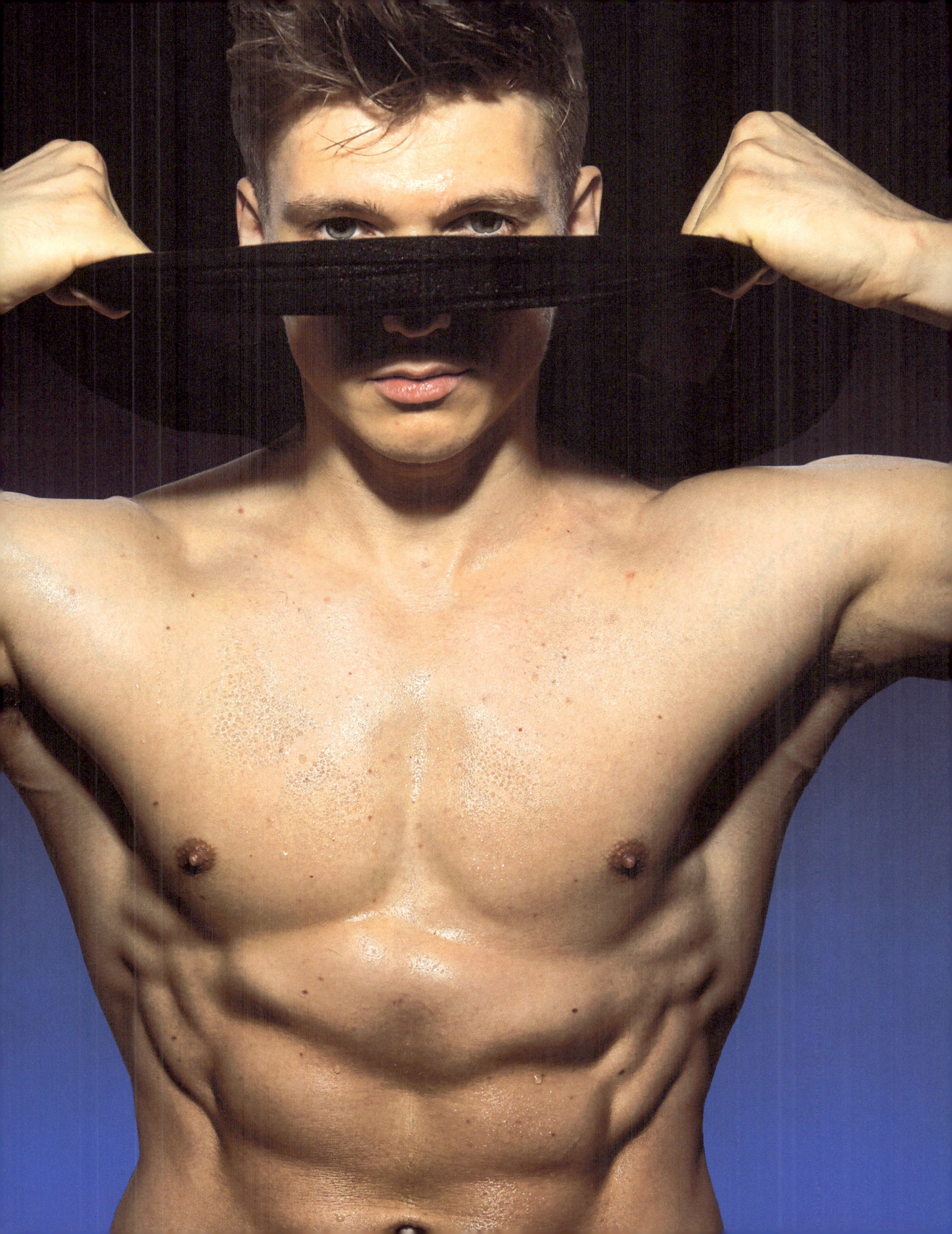

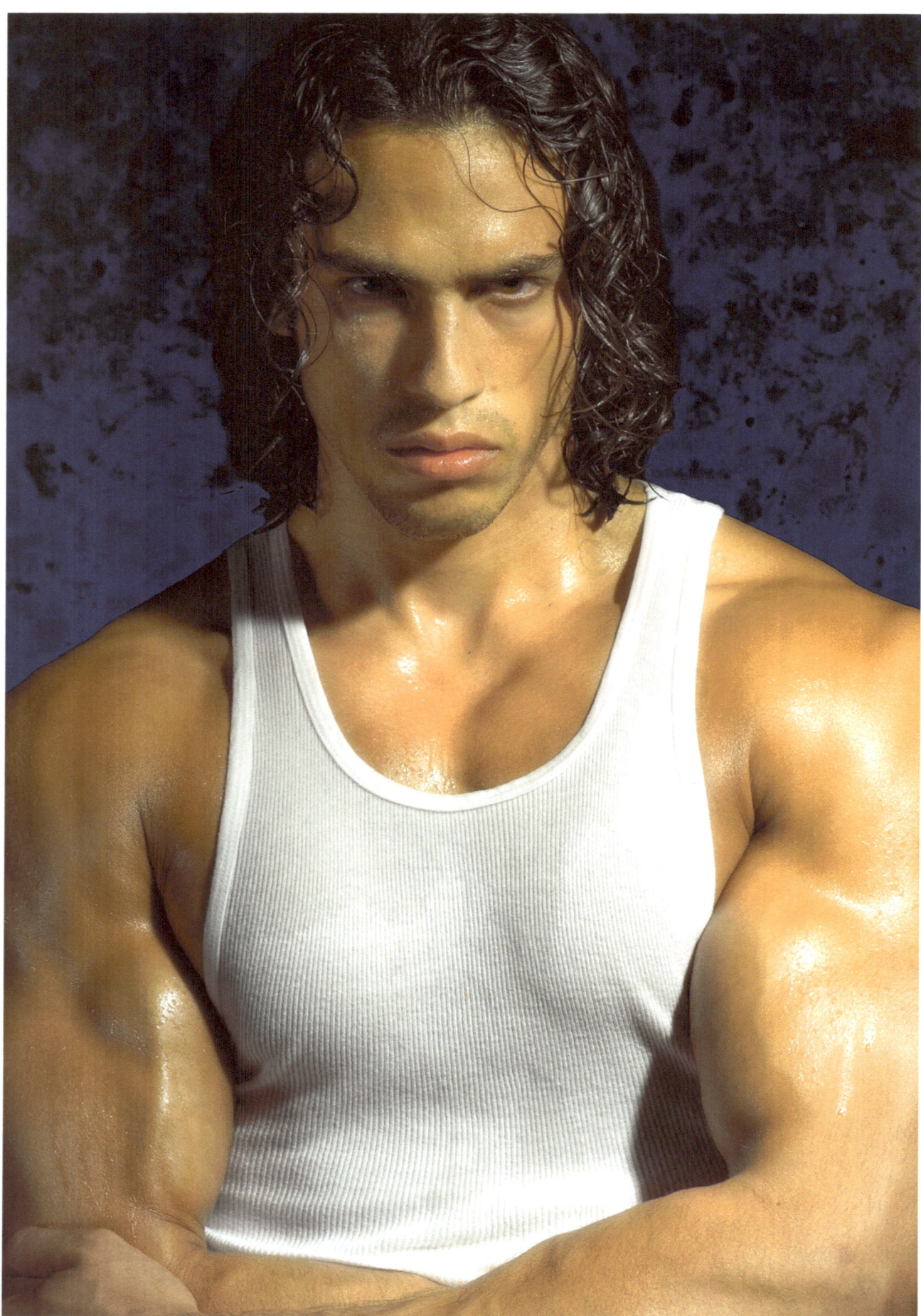

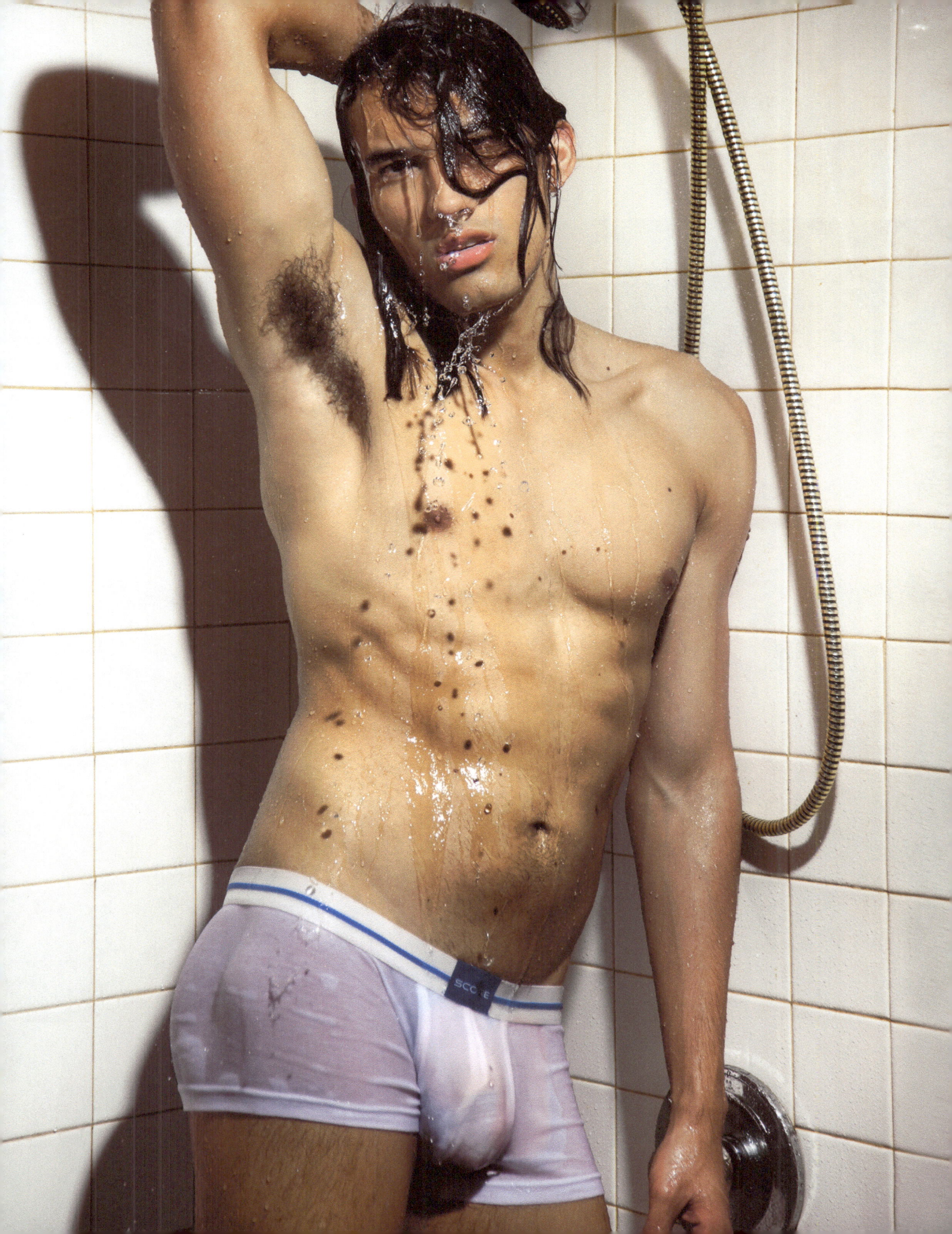

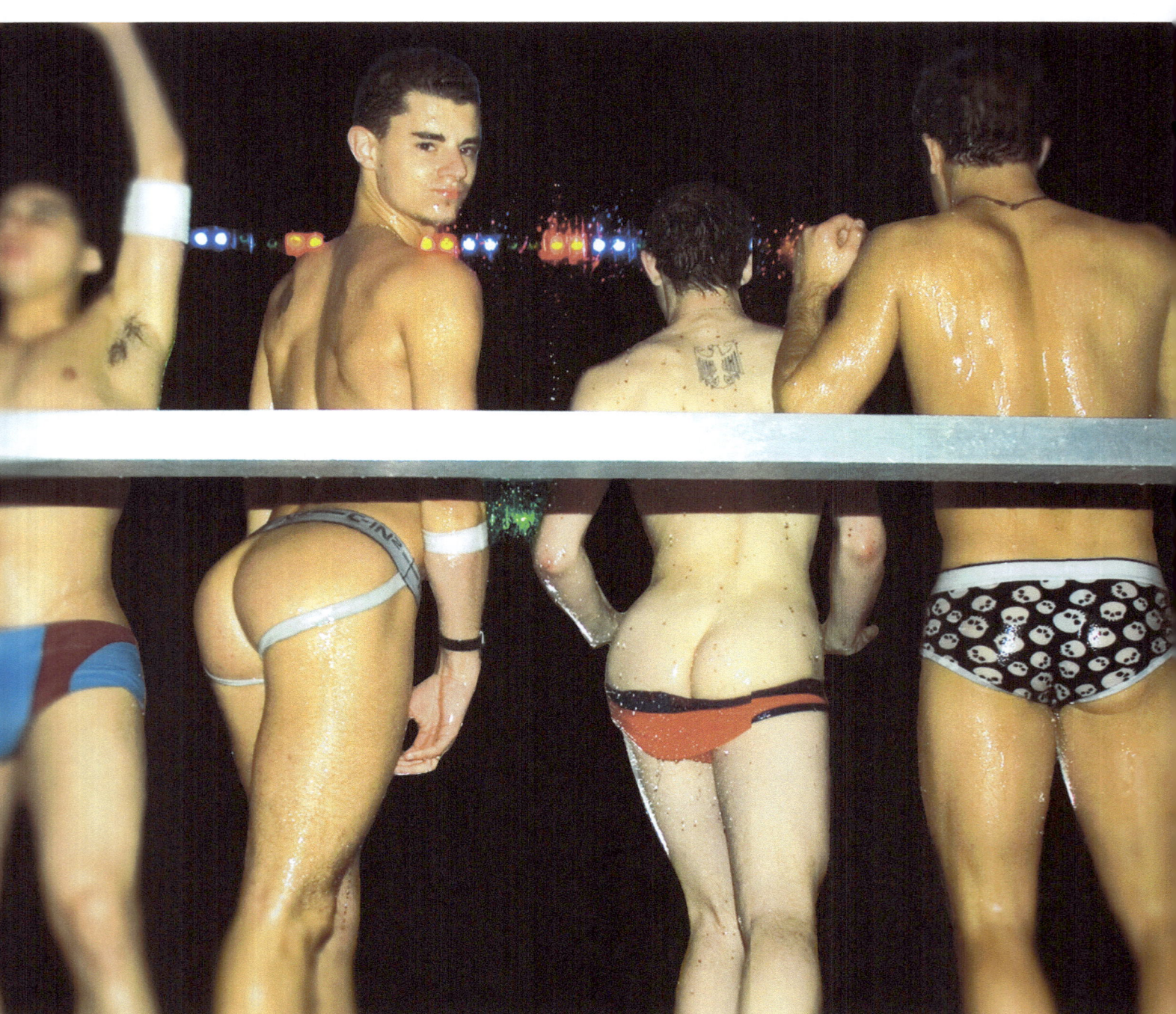

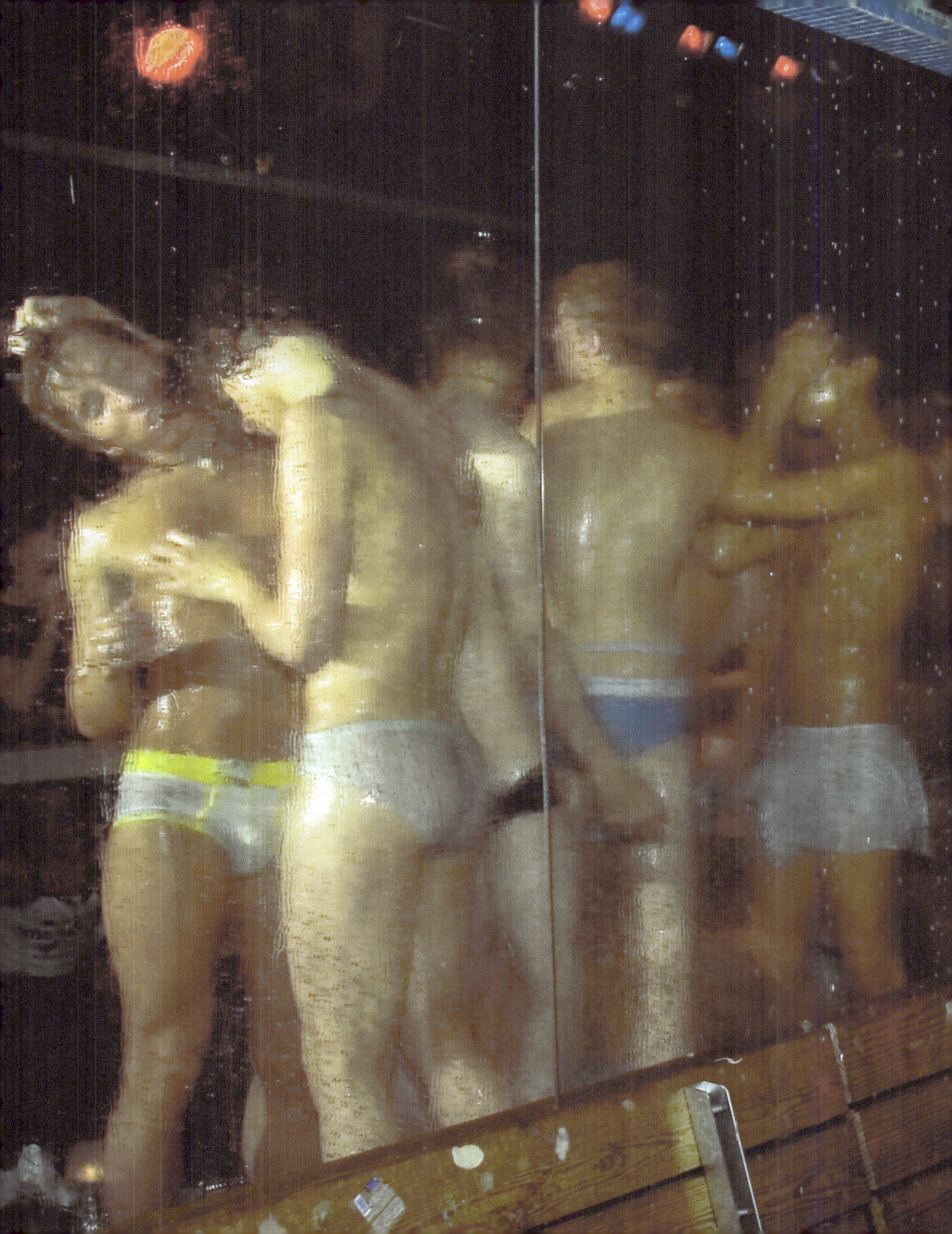

acknowledgments

Very special thanks to Arthur Lambert, Rick Harper
George Sanborn, and Richard D. Piper for their help
in creating this book. Thanks also to all the Models and
Lucas Entertainment who were involved.

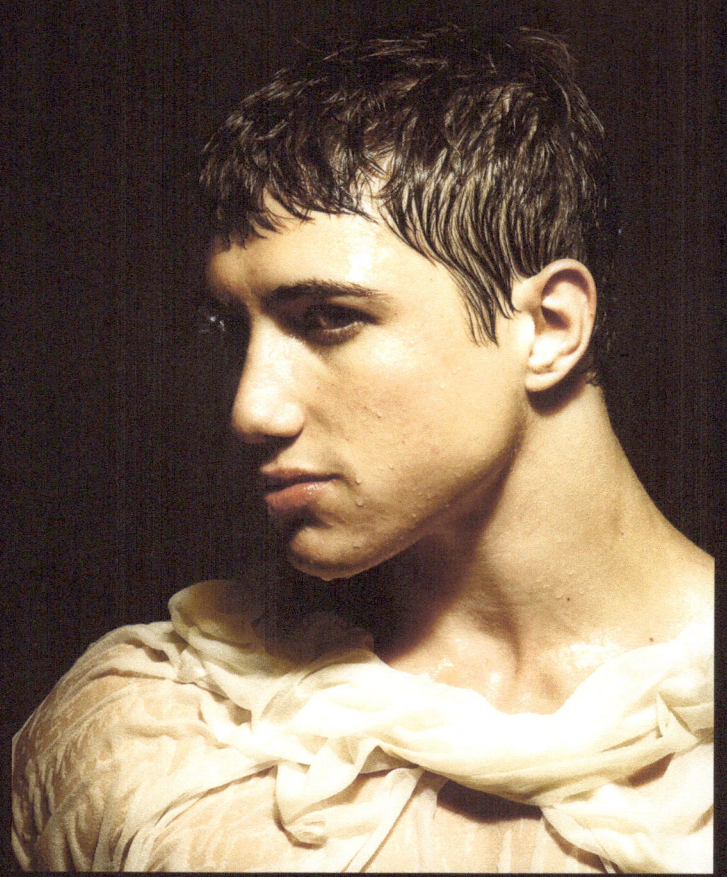

WATER MOVES

Photographed by Hans Fahrmeyer
Foreword by Richard D. Piper

   Hans Fahrmeyer is a recognized photographer of male and female portraits combining both technical skill and artistic expression. He has published three books, created a large portfolio of arresting portraits, and has been widely shown in many international publications.
   Hans was born in Bochum, Germany, where he developed both his professional and artistic skills. After leaving Germany he worked in Paris, Cannes, and London. He immigrated to the U.S. in 1979, establishing a studio in the West Village of New York City concentrating in portraits for private clients, agencies, and the Performing Arts.   He has successfully combined great technical skill in all aspects of photography (black & white, color, and digital) with creative inspiration devoted to presenting the human body as sculpture concentrating on the interplay of content and light and shadow. He has achieved his own unique quality in the creative art form of capturing both male and female models, concentrating primarily in the male. His photographs have been published in international publications including Time, Newsweek, Harper's Bazaar, Vogue, Burda, Madame, Connoisseur, Opera Monthly, and Camera & Darkroom. He has a comprehensive collection of portraits that includes more than 5,000 subjects.

   Published books include: *Between Men, Between Men and Women, and Colours of Men.* Each volume is approximately 140 pages (8.5 x 11), in hard and soft cover, published by Jansen Publishing, Los Angeles, CA. Several thousand copies of these books have been sold to date.

HAMBURG GROUP